BUSTING THE MYTHS OF MARS AND VENUS

Gender: Reality, Myth or Disaster

VERONICA SCHWARZ

DOWN TO EARTH BOOK 1

Disclaimer

All the information, techniques, skills, and concepts contained within this publication are of the nature of general comment only and are not in any way recommended as individual advice. The intent is to offer a variety of information to provide a broader range of choices now and into the future, recognising that we all have widely diverse circumstances and viewpoints.

The author and publishers do not assume any responsibilities whatsoever under any condition or circumstances. It is recommended that the reader obtain their own independent advice.

Dedication

I acknowledge my debt to the many women, and the men who supported them throughout history and still today, who fought and wrote and spoke out and suffered in a struggle to raise women to their rightful place as partners not property.

I thank my late mother, Doris Catherine Anderson who, although not a feminist, gave me the freedom to choose my beliefs and my life.

I thank my late ex-husband, Ian Patrick Mullins, for his support and participation in my growing awareness of our prisons of gender, and for helping to raise our beautiful free-spirited daughter, Kristel Maroszek..

And I thank my many wonderful friends who supported and encouraged me over many years of my journey on the feminist path, through my publication of *The Dawn* for ten years, for their advice, positive criticism, and their love. In particular, I am deeply grateful to my friend, Edna Russell, who worked through the penultimate draft with me.

Finally, I dedicate this book to all the girls and boys now living and still to be born. I wish you a future where you can truly be yourselves, proclaiming your individuality and developing your marvellous potential, talent, and love, out of the cage of conformity or down from the pedestal of gender roles.

Graphics

Foreword

Equality between women and men is still a thing of the future. In most cultures and societies, it has not been a reality for five to ten thousand years.

Women's secondary status is designed and maintained through the illusion of the feminine gender stereotype as well as its many supporting myths. In other words, it's rigged. Cultures mould us from birth so that we behave, dress, and think "appropriately" for our culture, our social class, our age, and our sex We learn to conform and perform. Most of us, male and female, are unconsciously subjected to the dehumanising processes of gender stereotyped cookie-cutting where we are supposed to all come out just the same. Cookies with pink or blue icing.

My aim and hope is to provide women and girls with some information and tools to help them see through the gendered socialisation process, the gaslighting and the beliefs about themselves, to help them grow stronger, more confident, independent equal partners with men, to step out of the cage or off the pedestal of gender expectations to become more truly themselves. While the book is primarily about women, it demon-

strates that men and boys live within a prison of gender also.
The hope is that we will recognise the constraints and excesses
of "masculinity" that are thrust upon most of our little boys and
change our child-raising practices for both sexes.

The solutions I have found for myself, or even the many I
suggest in this book, are not necessarily right for you. The major
aim is to ensure we know we have a choice.

The ideas in this book also apply to many other forms of stereotyping, prejudice, and inequality. However, the insidious nature
of Sexism is its universal application, its "naturalness", its
normalization, and its subsequent invisibility. Many women
themselves do not recognise or believe that Sexism exists. The
nature of the problem is made more complex by the intimate
relationship between males and females. Men are our fathers,
grandfathers, brothers, sons, lovers, friends, and partners. We
identify with their needs as easily as we identify with our own,
sometimes more so.

My goal is to help to right some gross injustices, to eliminate
the violence, cruelty, the wanton waste of talent and economic
opportunity, and to recognise the common humanity of males
and females in particular, and all other marginalised groups
regardless of race, religion, or skin colour.

I acknowledge my debt to the many women and the men who
supported them throughout history and still today, who fought
and wrote and spoke out and suffered in a struggle to raise
women to their rightful place as partners not property. I
mention many of them in this book. The book has taken ten
years of research across many fields of knowledge – at times
exhilarating, at times deeply depressing. It involved re-thinking,
restructuring, and constant updating as more information
became available.

This book is not perfect, but I hope that readers will see my intentions within it and use them as a stepping stone to their own greater understanding of how we came to be the way we are, and how we can change ourselves to make our world a better, fairer place.

Veronica Schwarz

veronicaschwarz.com 2021

It Starts with You
(MAID OR MADE)

From Birth to Booties

YOU PROBABLY DON'T REMEMBER the day you launched your unique self onto this planet. It's also unlikely you remember the first words you heard upon arrival. For most humans, it was a version of 'It's a girl!' or 'It's a boy', In the local language, of course. There are babies who don't fit into either category, but more on that later.

Depending on the society you were born into and in what circumstances, if you are female, your arrival caused anything from joy to disappointment, delight to despair.

And there you were, hopefully with you and your mother safe and sound. So, what happened next?

They cleaned you up a bit and dressed you. They "oohed" and "aahed" over you, and your mum got to hold you for a while, and everyone else had a turn too.

You maybe got a bit of peace when they stopped clucking over you. Not so long ago, if you were born in a hospital, one of the staff members would whisk you away. In that case, they may have put you in a crib, in a bright white room with a lot of other babies. There you could lie and sleep or cry depending on how you felt about it all.

Then the kid next to you pipes up, "Are you a girl or a boy?'

'I dunno,' you mutter sleepily.

'I'm a boy,' your neighbour confides.

'How do you tell?' you ask with interest.

He pulls back his blanket and points downward.

'Look,' he says, and pauses for effect, 'Blue booties.'

You soon discover pink is your code colour. Floods of it. It's a code to help the adults.

Other than checking out your "booties", there's not much difference between males and females at this stage, so – in Western Culture - we use colour codes like pink and blue. Then everyone can relax. Everything's normal. Ambiguity is uncomfortable and even frightening. We accept and perpetuate things which are familiar. We often reject and even condemn the unfamiliar or different. The implications of this tendency for people, progress, knowledge, and growth are frightening, rightly so. They have slowed us down and hobbled us, all of us, for thousands of years.

Certainty is comforting and, as we shall see later, that need for certainty is built into our brains and expresses itself through Confirmation Bias. We actively look for confirmation of our beliefs and even fail to see contrary evidence when it is right under our noses. I'll be mentioning this bias throughout the book because it is such a huge factor in our perception of differences between the sexes. We'll particularly look at it more closely in Chapter 16: My Mind is Made Up.

This is one of the first experiences you had that ensured everyone knew you were a girl. Even if your parents didn't think you needed pink, almost everyone else did. Labels are an easy way of sorting people and, for everybody, the first label is your sex, boy or girl. Apart from the bits under the nappy, boys and girls look pretty much the same. What to do? Code pink. For boys, it's blue. At least nowadays. There was a time not so long ago when pink coded boys and blue coded girls. Pink was considered too robust for girls, so cool blue was considered more appropriate. Despite this, there are researchers today now trying to prove that baby girls are "naturally" drawn to pink. The desire or need to prove inherent differences between the sexes is powerful, even to the point of ridiculous. If your parents managed to avoid the colour coding, your hairdo probably provided a clue.

Once you were colour-coded, everyone knew how to talk to you, and about you. They knew whether to say "he" or "she", "his" or "hers". They knew how to treat you and what to expect of you. They even knew what gifts to buy you even though you hadn't expressed any likes or interests yet.

The neuroscientist Gina Rippon, author of *The Gendered Brain*, shared an anecdote that helps demonstrate just how soon children can be exposed to gender stereotypes and the negativity towards the female.

It was the birth of her second daughter in 1986. – the night that a footballer named Gary Lineker scored a hat trick against Poland in the men's Football World Cup. There were nine babies born in the ward that day, Gina Rippon recalls. Eight of them were called Gary. She remembers chatting to one of the other mums when they heard a loud din approaching. It was a nurse bringing their two screaming babies. The nurse handed her neighbour a "blue-wrapped Gary" with approval – he had "a cracking pair of lungs". Rippon's own daughter (making exactly the same sound) was passed over with an audible tutting. "She's the noisiest of the lot – not very ladylike," the nurse told her.

"And so, at 10 minutes old, my tiny daughter had a very early experience of how gendered our world is," Rippon says.

But let's check out what probably happened to you and those around you in order to keep everyone else happy and comfortable while you were growing up.

You live in what we believe to be one of the most progressive times for women, at least in most Western cultures. Many laws that once kept women constrained in what they were permitted to do, have been changed. Much of this has happened within my lifetime. But laws are not enough. Laws can be ignored or surreptitiously got around. Attitudes, expectations, customs, culture, religion and the need to conform and the need to be loved, all play a powerful part in a child's development. And in families and communities, attitudes and customs frequently remain unchanged. Through adult attitudes and the teachings of religion, children are moulded and taught to obey customs created hundreds to thousands of years ago.

These teachings and customs are passed down from generation to generation. They are reinforced through child-raising, peer pressure, social expectations, media representations, religious edicts, and that primal need to conform.

For most of us, there is the need to belong to and be part of a group, to conform, to fit in and to avoid rejection, to know who we are and where we belong. We watch and learn from parents, grandparents, friends, kindergarten, school, movies, TV. We are surrounded by images, guidance, and insistence on how we should behave, dress, talk, play, and work. And most of us do conform to expectations of our social class, our religion, our ethnic origin, our parents' belief and requirements. The one universal pressure is to conform to "gender" expectations.

As you grew up, you may have noticed that beliefs about girls and boys, men and women, their treatment by others, and expectations of them, are quite different. Many of the beliefs about the two sexes have been proved wrong, but most people still continue to believe them.

Newspapers and magazines will give lots of space to research findings that claim to find differences between the sexes, particularly if they show that men, on average, are superior. Researchers themselves have commented on the fact that when their research proves any of these theories of gender difference to be wrong, the story is either not reported or buried in a tiny paragraph at the back of the newspaper.

For women, the focus is on appearance and attractiveness. The word "attractiveness" is the key here. It points to our designated major purpose, to "attract" a male. Most but not all people want to "attract" a mate, but in the male/female relationship, men are still expected to do the "choosing", to take the lead in the mating game. Women may manipulate it, but it must be subtle. There are women and men who want to change this and many other gendered behaviours, but while laws and lip service have changed, for many the reality is still rigid, and appropriate behaviour is maintained through ridicule or disapproval. In some cases, through punishment.

While men have many other goals in life as well, the hetero-sexual woman's goal is to be "chosen" by a man. We tell little girls they can be anything they want, but society makes that difficult. We burden females with the expectation that they will care for the children, the sick, the elderly and provide the home services that make everyday family life run smoothly. We expect women to continue to give birth and raise children to replace the population. We tell women and girls they can do and be anything but fail to value what they already do and fail to provide adequate childcare or support to help with the feminine "carer" role, or encouragement to males to step up and do their share. And the final insult is that the underlying critical judgement of the woman without a man or children is always just beneath the surface. "Childless" or "barren" are derogatory terms for such a woman.

This is a sure-fire way of ensuring women keep having babies with the bonus of giving men access to consensual sex with women. Win-win: the species continues, and heterosexuality is protected.

"But," you may say, "Girls can be anything they want." Perhaps, while performing two-thirds of the world's work, much of it unpaid and unrecognised, performing with superhuman energy and strength and maintaining the patience to put up with the unfairness of it all. Hold that thought. We'll check it out in Chapter 3: Are We There Yet?

There are thriving industries trying to prove that not only are women and men extremely different, but that those differences are "natural". As if religions maintaining the required place and behaviour expected from the female, was not enough, the prophets have been joined by the profit-makers. There are industries working overtime to convince you to buy their products and services that will help you demonstrate just how different from the opposite sex you are. Now that just shows how ridiculous this all is. If you need a product to make you a "natural" woman, doesn't that indicate that the characteristic isn't natural to begin with?

Being male and female like the other animals was not enough for humans. Oh no. We took the whole idea into our own hands and embellished the natural order that other animals experienced. Some animals who lived in herds or packs had developed dominance and subordination, often based on sex. Males are dominant over other males in some species usually based on physical strength. Males competing to gain the female's favour is a common form of behaviour in many species. Females are dominant in other species. And some animals who live in pairs just get on with the sharing and caring. Male dominance over all females is not that common in the animal kingdom. It wasn't usual in human societies either until very recently as we shall see in Chapter 2: The Story so Far (A Primal Dream).

Humans took it to a whole new level – as you'd probably expect given our large brains and opposable thumbs or whatever it is that makes us think we are the superior species. As the wonderful Robert Brault quipped:

Humans have been voted the most intelligent species on earth by all the animals who returned the survey.

But probably the most relevant development that gave us the concept and enforcement of inequality was the Cognitive Revolution. At a particular stage in human evolution, around 70,000 years ago, we developed the capacity to think of things that didn't actually exist and to believe them to be real. We became capable of imagination. This enabled us to create stories, myths, gods, and religions. We believed them to be as real as the trees and grass.

This ability to create and believe things in our own minds added a new dimension to power and status, control and inequality, and we figured out ways to make ourselves believe this was all ordained by non-human powers that had to be obeyed – or else. We invented gods and religions. A grand plan that didn't even need brute strength to maintain. We'll also investigate this in Chapter 2: The Story So Far (A Primal Dream). But let's get back to you.

Making the Difference

The first thing that we notice about anyone is what sex they are. Once the baby's sex is assigned, that little person's destiny is pretty much decided. Almost everyone starts to assume and look for *the differences.*

Societies assume that little boys will be more active, rougher, tougher, and adventurous, and later they will be good at Maths and Science and will grow into men who will be strong and in control, and good at sport and perhaps a bit aggressive and authoritative and take charge of things and be explorers and pilots and plumbers and doctors and lawyers and carpenters and prime ministers and presidents. Now, all those things are true of some men and boys some of the time. We probably all know men and boys who have some of those qualities. We also know others who do not.

On the other hand, we assume that little girls will be gentler, better behaved, more docile, sweet, and pleasing. Because they are girls, it's assumed they will be less active, and not interested in, or good at, Maths and Science: *Allergic to Algebra* as one T-shirt available for girls proudly proclaims. They will grow into women who will take care of people. They'll still get a job. Many of them will also have babies and look after the house and children and husband. They may need to get part-time or casual work, so it doesn't interfere too much with looking after the house and children - and the husband if they are not single parents.

To fit in, women need to be feminine, to be likable and to be loved or desired by a man. Most of the requirements to fulfil this image are external. They involve your bodily appearance, looking pretty, being sweet, and, in Western civilization in the current era, being slim. Then there's feminine behaviour to conform to: not being loud or "opinionated", being pleasant, non-aggressive and slightly diffident, caring for other's emotional and physical needs, and smiling. These are all part of the feminine job description. Never upstaging a man is also a subtle requirement. It makes everybody, particularly the man, feel very uncomfortable if a woman does this. The upshot of all this feminine preparation for "the male gaze" is the assumption of the inevitable rivalry of women. We'll explore this in Chapter 12: Women are their own Worst Enemies (Let's You and Her Fight.)

Not a moment to be lost then. The lessons begin as soon as you arrive. What you learn will stick better if they get you when you're young. Until the age of six, our minds have no filters. We believe what we receive. The Jesuits, way back in the 1500s, knew this when they said, "Give me a child until he is seven, and I will give you the man". Aristotle said it even before the Jesuits, about 2,400 years ago. The beliefs we learn before the age of seven are embedded in our minds. They resist all logic and any efforts to shift them. Depressing really.

Like training young elephants. Baby elephants are tethered to a stake when they are young and small. They pull against the tether, but they cannot break free. As they grow bigger and stronger, they give up trying and, by the time they are strong enough to pull the stake right out of the ground, they still believe they cannot. The same tether they were tied to as babies, still holds them in place despite their enormous strength as adults.

Tethering Elephants

Figure 1: Get 'em Young. And our belief controls our behaviour from within our own brains. No need for external force. © Veronica Schwarz

Similarly, with us. We could break free and risk the consequences, but most of us don't even know we have been tethered. As the great German writer, Goethe, put it:

None are more hopelessly enslaved than those who falsely believe they are free.

Every culture is created by the people who once lived in it. Our cultures, yours and mine, are based on the needs, the fears and the beliefs of people who lived more than a thousand years ago and, in many cases, two to three thousand years ago. Their knowledge and understanding of the world around them were only just evolving when they began to create their imagined world full of rules and requirements, fears, and conformity. It's quite remarkable that we base our modern societies and our lives on their rules. But that's what most of us do. The good news is that, since people created societies and cultures, people can change them. This means those of us living today can change societies and cultures to make them fairer and kinder, richer and happier. If we want to. Of course, that doesn't mean it's easy.

First, we must "see" that "the way things are" is not set in cement or even written on tablets of stone. Sadly, parts of our own brains are lagging behind. Human brains are still operating in ways that kept us safe in the Stone Age. We react more strongly to fear and uncertainty than we do to reason and even reward. Our brains also look for things that confirm what we currently believe. We fear, deride, or fail to notice things that contradict those beliefs.

We need to "see" that much of our potential is hidden from our view. Our enormous potential for growth, and contribution to our societies are, for most of us, kept hidden beyond the horizon of our cultural limitations. The possibilities opened up by a wide range of experiences, joy, learning, and understanding, are hidden from us, both male and female. In many cultures, they are even forbidden to us.

As the cognitive scientist Alexandra Horowitz put it:

Even as we develop from relatively immobile, helpless infants into mobile, autonomous adults, we are more and more constrained by the ways we learn to see the world.

As author and entrepreneur Tim Ferris put it, the common-sense rules of the "real world" are a fragile collection of socially reinforced illusions. And yet they seem so right and reasonable.

These constraints apply to groups of people to varying degrees. The result is gross inequality which is currently worsening around the planet. These inequalities are not related to anything that individuals have personally done. They are almost totally the product of the randomness of birth into different circumstances, particularly to which sex you are assigned and what colour your skin is.

Almost 500 years ago, the great German astronomer and mathematician, Johannes Kepler, noted that his mother's intellect was not inferior to his, but their lives and circumstances were as different as night and day. He made the perceptive observation that the difference between the fate of the sexes is not in the heavens but in the earthly construction of gender as a function of culture. It was not his mother's nature that made her ignorant but the lack of opportunity for intellectual growth, learning and development of potential. Her gender ensured her fate was as fixed as the stars. Today, 500 years on, we are still fighting to have that fact recognised with more than lip service. It's also worth noting that, in 1615, this famous man set aside his career, risking condemnation himself, to spend six years defending his elderly widowed mother against charges of witchcraft. Imprisoned and chained to the floor of a cell, Katarina Kepler did not burn at the stake like the many thousands of women and men in Europe who did. At the end of those six years, her son's rational and well-argued case won her freedom. A rare event. Sadly, she died six months after being released. You can read her story in Ulinka Rublack's book *The Astronomer and the Witch*.

As Kepler observed, it's patently obvious that not all males are cleverer, more intelligent, or more competent than all women, but cultures are structured as if that were the case.

Almost all cultures on earth are now hierarchical. Power, status, wealth, privilege, and respect are mainly allocated to designated groups. Individuals are given specific privileges, or deprived of them, generally on the basis of group membership rather than individual merit.

The most basic grouping of humans is that of sex, female and male. No matter what other group you also belong to, rated by skin colour, religion, caste, or social class, males are almost universally granted higher status than females within every other group.

How did it happen? Let's check out the story so far.

2

The Story So Far
(A PRIMAL DREAM)

When men are oppressed it's a tragedy; when women are oppressed it's a tradition.

Letty Cottin Pogrebin

Men look to destroy every quality in a woman that will give her the power of a male, for she is in their eyes already armed with the power that she brought them forth, and that is a power beyond measure.

Norman Mailer

DO you ever wonder why things are the way they are? Why some people have so much, and others have so little? Why some groups control most things and other groups are powerless?

Why do we persistently do things in a certain way when there are probably several ways at least of doing them? Some of them more efficient, fairer, or kinder.

Probably one of the major reasons for the ongoing nature of customs is that we tend to believe that the way things are is the natural way they have always been. And as anthropologist Ruth Benedict pointed out in her seminal work, *Patterns of Culture*, even though these "right and natural" ways of doing things differ across cultures, each society believes its customs to be the "right" way to do things. Grouping and ranking people, however, is common to almost every culture, if not all cultures today.

The most basic grouping is that of sex – female and male. Both sexes are members of the human race, *Homo sapiens*, even though one group – males – disputed that concept for centuries in some cultures including Western culture.

Homo sapiens is an interesting term. It means "wise man"! We modestly gave ourselves that name. We got away with it because none of the other humans was left around at the time. It's possible that we had killed them off. Other humans? Yes.

Let's just take a little detour here and look at our ancient sisters and brothers from all those years ago. Why? Because we are so convinced that the way things are, is the way they have always been. Knowing there were other humans before us, might be a refreshing wake up call to break free of the cementlike nature of our beliefs.

We are part of the species *homo* which means person in Latin. We've been here for 300,000 years but we weren't the first, although so far, we are the last.

Homo habilus (meaning "handy man") was one of the earliest human species as far as we know. A fossil was discovered in

Tanzania, Africa between 1960 and 1963. It turned out *homo habilus* had been around for at least 1.44 million years. The debate still rages as to whether or not *homo habilus* is a true member of the species *homo*. Another discovery, also in eastern Africa, proved to be another species of human, called by us, *homo erectus*. These humans had been around for at least some 1.55 million years. This would indicate that the two types of human could have co-existed for hundreds of thousands of years. We always think of ourselves as the top of the evolutionary tree, the only one above all the other animals. The story is much more interesting than that. Check out *Sapiens* by Yuval Noah Harari, probably one of the best books available on the subject of us.

When *homo sapiens* came out of Africa, around 300,000 years ago, there were at least six other versions of humans roaming the earth. The number is debated, as is the categorisation of some fossils as in or out of the species *homo,* but the major point is we were not alone. These were species we have since named as *homo neanderthalensis, homo erectus, homo denisova, homo soloensis, homo florensi* (the hobbit). They either died out of unknown causes, or we wiped them out. Some of us still carry their DNA, so there must have been a bit of mixing, mingling, partying, and breeding going on between the different types of humans, specifically *homo sapiens* with the Neanderthals and Denisovans. Their DNA can be found in humans today. So, let's get back to us as we are today.

As we touched on in Chapter 1, there are many social setups that ensure inequality based on difference. Two of the greatest are Racist and Sexism. Others include ethnicity, religion and ability. We go even further and divide and judge people by castes, social classes, and type of work done. Many individuals are affected by more than one power division. This is called "intersectionality". In this context, it means being hit by a double or triple whammy. People may be grouped by their sex and gender, and by the colour of their skin. Then in no particular order, it's their religion or their ethnicity or their body shape. Or something else. Then they may be judged or discriminated against on any or all of the stereotypes related to those groupings simultaneously.

However, the one division of power that cuts across all others is Sexism. It is the use of sex and gender to decide who does what, and who gets the most reward and the most say. It culturally gives power, dominance, respect, visibility, and control to males over females across all other divisions of people. Religions, rituals, beliefs, attitudes, language, and even humour support this hierarchy of dominance. It's been like this in Western culture in particular for 5,000 to 10,000 years. Colonialism and predominantly the Christian religion spread it globally. It was not always like this. It is not natural or inevitable that males should dominate females regardless of race or religion.

Let's look at how things came to be the way they are. Not because I think we should dwell on the past. The dead opposite in fact. But I do believe we can learn from the past to understand the present. It can even help us break free of outdated or unfair customs.

So how did it come about? It's worth knowing, because most of the myths, beliefs, and attitudes that rule our lives today, have their origins in the past, and usually, the distant past.

Based on the fact that women have the babies, and the belief that men are stronger and more competent than women, we tend to assume that gender roles developed as a rational division of labour. We believe this is normal and natural and has always been the way things are. The story goes like this:

Hunting and Gathering

Only females become pregnant, give birth to, and breastfeed the young of the species. To date, men cannot. Also, the human male, like most mammals, is usually stronger than most of the females. So, we believe that our pre-historic ancestors organised themselves accordingly. The men hunted the big animals. Women stayed close to camp and gathered, foraged, and caught small animals. Naturally, they looked after the children. Easy peasy, gender roles naturally developed. Or so the story would have it.

But that explanation does not explain all the facts. Why didn't women who were not heavily pregnant or caring for an infant, join in the hunt? Why did men who were unable to hunt, for reasons of age or disability, not help gather and forage. If this division of labour is indeed factual, the tasks seem to have been assigned by sex rather than on actual ability or agility.

Kevin Reilly noted this puzzle too in his book, The West and the World: A History of Civilization,

He wrote: *It is a common practice among hunting-gathering societies to assign different tasks to men and women. These separate assignments go far beyond what is required by the differences in size or strength between men and women or the need of women to carry and nurse infants. In fact, some jobs are thought of as "masculine" in one society and "feminine" in another.*

It seems creating different roles for the sexes is the true aim of this division of labour. Ability, skill, or potential are not the primary factor. It is sex.

It is perhaps even more important to cultures than good sense, better results, or even survival, as we shall see when we check out modern society's divisions between the sexes. Nowadays, we still divide societies by sex in spite of changes in technology, infant welfare, and the lack of a need for brute strength in many tasks. We do this, often unconsciously, and automatically, regardless of the fact that today this has proved irrational and detrimental to society as a whole.

But this division of Man the Hunter and Woman the Gatherer, may not have been universal. An article in *Science Magazine (November 4, 2020,)* by Ann Gibbons, reported a recent find in the Andes. Archaeologists discovered the 9,000-year-old grave of an apparently highly respected hunter. The skeleton was found to be female. Graves of other female hunters were also found, leading to the conclusion that early big game hunting may have been gender neutral.

We also know that many tribes used a team effort to hunt big game. Women and children participated in driving animals over cliffs. The indigenous people of Australia worked together to drive animals out of the bush with noise or fire, while others waited to club the animals as they tried to escape.

In addition, the gendered view which focused on Man the Hunter, hid the contribution of women in earlier societies, making it all but invisible until recently. We now realise that almost all hunter-gatherer tribes relied on the gatherers for up to 85% of their food on a daily basis. The hunting of larger animals provided meat very irregularly and was often cause for great celebration when it happened.

Scientists now say our concept of prehistoric humans and their behaviour might be based more on our own sexist assumptions than fact. Earlier palaeontologists seem to have brought their modern beliefs about gender roles and male dominance to their research. They interpreted their findings through a modern gender-biased lens.

Pennsylvania State archaeologist Dean Snow stated in an interview with National Geographic: "There has been a male bias in the literature for a long time. People have made a lot of unwarranted assumptions."

Scientists who study hunter-gather tribes still in existence find most are remarkably egalitarian.

Mark Dyble, lead author of a report on a recent study of existing hunter-gatherer tribes summed it up. *There is still this wider perception that hunter-gatherers are more macho or male-dominated. We'd argue it was only with the emergence of agriculture, when people could start to accumulate resources, that inequality emerged.*

Anthropologists have found evidence that women probably hunted too. Their conclusion is based on skeletal injuries found on the bones of females similar to the injuries found on males.

Some skeletons have been found with hunting tools buried with them and were erroneously believed the skeletons of males. More recent testing methods have revealed that the skeletons were in fact female. One notable skeleton, found in the Andes in Peru, was buried with many hunting tools, and was assumed to be a great hunter and chief until the skeleton was revealed to be female. The significance of this is still contested.

Anthropologists who assumed that men did all the hunting, also assumed that the men did all the artwork in caves since so many of the paintings involve animals. This too is a myth. Seventy-five percent of the paintings of hands found in caves are female. Women certainly had contact with animals and perhaps as we have just seen, participated in the hunting of them. If they were in the cave, painting their hands on the walls, it's reasonable to assume they also painted animals and other things.

In Erie, Pennsylvania, Mercyhurst Archaeological Institute's Director James Adovasio suggests that the idea of Palaeolithic men as the strong, fierce hunters and of women staying away from danger, may derive more from our own modern culture than from the actual evidence.

Anthropologist, Margaret Mead, noted that all existing early cultures differed in their gender roles, but the more the men separated themselves from the women and children, the more warlike, aggressive, and combative the men were. In those tribes and groups where men were more involved in caring roles, men and women had more equal status and influence and worked together. The tribe members and particularly the men, were more co-operative and peaceful.

Women fulfilled another vital role in early societies. They were links between tribes. By interbreeding with males from other tribes, women not only brought valuable variations in genetic material to the tribe, but they also contributed to the union of families, the expansion of territories, and the prevention of territorial disputes and wars. It became the custom among men to "give" women as gifts to other men from other tribes. This was the beginning of marriage. We still see the remnants of this custom in traditional marriage ceremonies when the conductor of the ceremony asks, "Who gives this woman?" and usually the father of the bride hands her over.

Why have we downplayed the importance and contribution of women, and given the men the power and the glory? We'll explore our modern reasons in later chapters. For now, let's look at our ancestors' path that transformed Woman from Partner to Property.

Phallus in Wonderland: Fatherhood, Religion and Property

In the early days of human development, both women and men were unaware of men's role in conception. Because women gave birth to the children as if by magic, being female was important and valued. The Great Goddess was the most powerful of the gods.

Once men became aware of their contribution to conception, it seems to have gone to their heads. They assumed the women were merely the soil in which their seed was planted. The penis or phallus became an object of worship. The Great Goddess was overthrown in a frenzy of envy and resentment. In many cultures, she was then depicted as evil and was torn or cut into pieces. Her place was taken by a male god. This fundamental status shift from the female to the male appears in many mythologies around five to ten thousand years ago, corresponding with the development of agriculture, the end of nomadic existence and the beginning of possession of property.

Men did not see fatherhood as giving them equality with women but rather as proof of male worthiness, superiority, and dominance. Women's status plummeted and the chief gods became male, finally culminating in the One God, invariably male. Men created THE god in their image, then declared that they themselves were created in the image of God, and women were an inferior offshoot.

Since the male was made in the image of the god, woman was the sexual contrast, the polar opposite, the "opposite sex". Not even fully human. And so, developed the Taboo of Sameness, to use Gayle Rubin's apt term. Whatever men were, women were not and should not be.

Here we see the beginnings of our modern child-raising mantra to men and boys: *Never do anything like a girl*. Even today, men are belittled if they behave in a "feminine" way. Men who knit. Men who stay home and look after their children. Men who prefer poetry to football. Trivial examples but revealing.

Men embodied all the human skills and abilities. Women were the half-formed, inept opposites, servants and property of men, and incubators for the next generation. Humans entered the age of Phallus in Wonderland to use Rosalind Miles' phrase. We are still in that state with male dominance and gross inequality of the sexes, after more than five to ten thousand years.

For too many men, the penis became a weapon of dominance rather than an instrument of desire or love. Rape is still used as a weapon in war. It is seen as the best way to humiliate the male enemy. Violate his "property", his females, in the most intimate way possible. It is also used as a weapon against women in "civil" society. Fear of rape constrains our movements and our whereabouts even today.

Once early humans developed agriculture and domesticated animals, they stopped being nomadic. The irony in all this is that, since most women gathered and foraged for plant foods and killed smaller animals, it was probably women who invented the farming of crops and domesticating of animals, sealing their fate. With the development of farming, ownership of property became important. Men wanted to be sure the sons they passed their property on to, were in fact their sons. Ensuring their wives were not impregnated by some other interloper became of top importance to them. Female virginity at marriage became a requirement. The balance tipped further to male dominance and female secondary status. It led to more and more constraints placed on women's movement, behaviour, and especially their sexual activity.

Not all humans developed an agricultural lifestyle. Some groups continued as Hunter/Gatherers and others domesticated animals but herded them nomadically rather than settling down and owning land. There is some evidence of women in those societies enjoying more freedom, equality, and a place in the decision-making of the tribe, than their farming sisters. There is the Biblical record of Deborah who was a judge of the Israelites for forty years and organised them in battle against the Canaanites. She rode into battle with Barak, the commander she had summoned to lead the army. The men and women of the hunter/gatherers in the Kalahari Desert of southern Africa, also held equal status and decision-making powers until the arrival of European anthropologists.

But the majority of humans became owners of property and settled primarily in one place to grow crops and raise animals. And women were confined, constrained, and controlled.

Other theoretical explanations of male dominance include the development of the alphabet and the increasing dominance of left-brain activity right up to the present day. Left brain activity exhibits characteristics associated with, but not confined to males.

Women's subordination may have been a combination of all these factors. Anthropologists and scholars agree that the status of females took a nose-dive several thousand years ago. Women have not yet regained their place as equal fellow human beings anywhere on the planet since then.

From the time of the development of agriculture, gender roles became much less egalitarian. They became a matter of power and possession, and it was always favourable to men – to their wants and needs. Women went from being partners with men to the property of men. Women were taught or forced to conform to what men wanted, what they wanted women to be and do for them.

This was achieved through culture, custom, brute force, religion, philosophy, science, law, and social pressure to enforce and maintain the role of women "in their place". Both men and women have colluded in this enforcement. They still do, in many countries today – including yours and mine.

There was one marvellous exception in the darkness. Sometimes Sexism and misogyny can get very depressing so let me tell you the story of Lilith, the first rebel, just for fun.

Long, long ago there was a man named Adam who lived in a garden. His wife's name was Lilith. Adam loved having sex. So did Lilith for that matter, but she never seemed to be satisfied. Finally, she refused to have sex in the "missionary position".

"It's a put-down," she told Adam. "Why should you always be on top?"

But it was a bit like talking to the proverbial brick wall – if there had been any in those days. Finally, with no compromise from Adam, she walked out.

Poor Adam couldn't understand it. What went wrong? Hadn't he always brought home the berries. Well, no, he hadn't. She had -- but that's no reason… So, he complained to God who sympathetically sent three angels to bring her back.

The angels looked high and low and eventually found Lilith by the Red Sea partying on with several horny little demons. When the angels finally managed to turn the music down and make themselves heard, they told her to go back to Adam immediately and she told them -- just what you'd expect she'd tell them.

Adam moped and whinged and generally made every other animal in the garden thoroughly miserable. So, God created Eve to be everything that Adam could want or need. And for a while there she was the apple of his eye. However, it seems even that little romance met its snake in the grass!

Lilith is still laughing.

Now that's a myth worth holding onto. But sadly, reality was not like that. Once the boys put themselves in charge, there seemed to be no stopping them.

There are records of some women rebelling against some things. There may have been more, but since history was recorded by men who, at the time, did not value women very highly, there is not much about women in it.

One of the first written records of a woman addressing misogyny and the devaluing of women not just at a personal level but at a cultural and societal level in Western culture, was in 1405 C E. Christine de Pisan was a medieval writer who wrote *The City of Ladies* to counter the ferocious misogyny in the works of male writers of the time. Her writing included poetry, novels, biography, and autobiography, as well as literary, political, and religious commentary. Her work is considered to be one of the earliest of feminist writings - over six hundred years ago! It is still available – in modern book form.

A less well-known philosopher, composer and poet from Mexico was the Hieronymite nun, Sor Juana Ines de la Cruz (Sister Joan Agnes of the Cross in English). Her outspoken opinions and writing earned her the names of "The Tenth Muse" and "The Phoenix of Mexico" Beginning her studies at a young age, Sor Juana was fluent in Latin and also wrote in Nahuatl (a part of the Uto-Aztec language group) and became known for her philosophy in her teens. She educated herself in her own library, which was mostly inherited from her grandfather. After joining a nunnery in 1667, she began writing poetry and prose dealing with such topics as love, Feminism, and religion. She turned her nun's quarters into a salon, visited by the city's intellectual elite. Her criticism of misogyny and the hypocrisy of men led to her condemnation by the Bishop of Puebla, and in 1694 she was forced to sell her collection of books and focus on charity towards the poor. She died the next year, having caught the plague while treating her fellow nuns.

After fading from academic discourse for hundreds of years, the Mexican poet, writer, and diplomat Octavio Paz re-established Sor Juana's importance in modern times. Scholars now consider Sor Juana as a "proto-feminist", and her writings are used in modern discussions of themes such as colonialism, education rights, women's religious authority, and Feminism.

I'll bet some of you are saying right about now, "Hey! Wait a minute. It's not like that anymore. Sure, it's not perfect but we've come a long way since those days." Some of you are probably also muttering, "And Feminism has gone too far. It's men and boys that need a fair go now."

OK. We can't let those questions hang around unanswered so let's pause the journey with our ancient ancestors. We'll return to it later because not only can we learn from the past but also as James Baldwin proclaimed, "not everything that is faced can be changed, but nothing can be changed until it is faced". In addition, much of the progress for women has only been achieved since the 1960s, a good deal of it in my own lifetime, and already it is slipping backwards. It only takes a couple of generations for us to take our freedoms for granted and forget how fragile they are.

But for now, let's ask if we have really achieved the goal of equality for the sexes and genders, as many people claim. Are we there yet?

3

Are We There Yet?
(ILLUSION, DELUSION, OR JUST PLAIN CONFUSION?)

There is an incorrect aura of it 'all being sorted' … It's like taking most of the antibiotics course and then stopping because you feel better… but the last few really resilient bugs might still be there. In the case of Feminism, these little hangers-on are gender stereotypes.

Lucy May Doyle

Sexism is like poison ivy. It's deep rooted: you weed the rampant stuff, but it pops up again.

Dominique Browning

PEOPLE TELL me women and girls can now be and do anything they want to. Women are treated equally to men. Women have equality, and Feminism is not needed. Feminism has probably gone too far, and now men and boys are disadvantaged. Men's rights groups have sprung up with angry men asserting that they have been discriminated against and badly treated. Their grudge is usually triggered by anger at an ex-partner or wife, and a perception that the law and society have favoured women's rights over theirs.

If you believe this or know someone who does, and you would like to know the facts one way or the other, information is readily available. On a grand scale of half the human population being ignored, excluded, or not even considered at every level of human activity, you can't go past Caroline Criado Perez's book, *Invisible Women: Exposing Data Bias in a World Designed for Men* published in 2020. This is a mind-blowing summation of how every aspect of our lives from our safety to our convenience and everything in between is planned around the needs, habits, characteristics, and measurements of men. From transport to office air conditioning temperatures, from seat belts to assessment of merit, from medical research to occupational health and safety, designs of work clothing and equipment, and designs of recreational space as well as public toilets, and the design and location of public housing. It's all based on the needs of men, or data compiled by research on male bodies. This is far from trivial as Caroline Criado Perez shows in the inconvenience and damage to, danger for, and deaths of women as a result.

Similarly, Marilyn Waring's book *Counting for Nothing: What Men Value and What Women are Worth.* demonstrates how the wealth of nations, the GDP, doesn't even include much of the work done by women because it's unpaid. This is discussed at greater length in Chapter 14.

Humane reasons, economic rationality, and decent fairness are all ignored in retaining the status quo of male dominance and women's second-class status. In spite of all evidence that dealing fairly with women would enhance societies for everybody in every way.

These examples don't even touch on the customs and constraints of culture that confine and discriminate against women. Nor does it deal with the issues of contempt, hatred, cruelty, and violence women are subjected to by many men. We have not even touched on embedded internal biases against women, or the language and symbolism that render them invisible. Nor does it deal with the problem of health, fatigue, and constraints of education, recreation, and time for oneself, all of which affect women disproportionately because they provide two-thirds of the world's labour.

Why is equality for women so difficult to achieve? One reason could be loss aversion. We will fight harder to protect what we already have. This means that modern day conservatives are going to fight brutally hard to maintain societies and cultures as they are. To the privileged, equality feels like oppression.

Once a year on 8 March, many of us observe International Women's Day. This inevitably raises the question by those who believe women have equality or even that women are better off than men: "So, why don't we have an International Men's Day?" they ask.

The late Pamela Bone, journalist for the Melbourne newspaper *The Age*, responded way back in 2001 with the following comment:

The answer is that when baby boys are killed at birth for no other reason than that they are male, when boys are routinely denied food, education, or medical attention, when men are two-thirds of the world's illiterates and 5% of the world's heads of state, there will be one. We promise. Pamela Bone, *The Age*, 8/3/2001

To add to Pamela Bone's comment, we could similarly say if the current sex and gender situations were reversed, and the statements and statistics referred to the disadvantages, suppression and death of men, the situation would look something like this:

(Warning: the following section contains prejudice, cruelty, injustice, violence, and just plain stupidity, and may cause distress to some readers.)

- Most of the world's wealth would be in the hands of women.
- Almost all governments, organisations, and institutions around the world would be run by women.
- Men's skills, talents and contributions would be largely undervalued, unrecognised and undeveloped or inaccurately credited to women close to them.
- Men would perform at least two-thirds of the unpaid work in households and communities and this enormous contribution would be excluded from the GDP of all nations because it's not worth a dime.
- In mixed company, men would be constantly interrupted by women, patronised, ignored, or kindly explained to about things they already knew.
- Men would be harassed, belittled, groped, and threatened as they walked in public places or travelled on public transport.
- Men would be attacked and raped in public places and then blamed for the attack because they shouldn't think they have the right to use public space. And what were they wearing?
- Men would be routinely beaten and/or murdered by their wives, or their wives' relatives, and law enforcement would at best appear unable to stop it, and at worst indifferent.
- Men daring to express an opinion on almost any topic on social media would be trolled by women, and subjected to obscene hatred, threatened with rape or murder and hounded, in some case for years after they withdrew from social media.

- Men would be forced to provide sexual gratification to women as part of seeking or maintaining employment.
- Men would spend many hours and many dollars on constrictive clothes, cosmetics, and grooming, to be considered attractive enough for social acceptability, for jobs or for attracting a mate. They would also spend time and money on diets and cosmetic surgery, including genital surgery, to attain a mythical body shape, appearance and weight, and they would suffer various illnesses, physical and psychological, resulting from these efforts.
- Men would change their family name to that of their wives on marriage. Their children would have their wives' family names.
- Unmarried men would be pitied and pilloried.
- Men without children would be pitied or blamed for being selfish.
- Shopping for food, cooking, cleaning the house, and washing and taking care of the children, the sick, and the elderly would primarily be done by men.
- Thousands of men and boys would have the entire foreskin and the tops of their penises ritually and often brutally removed so that they could not enjoy sexual pleasure, in a custom touted as ensuring men's "purity". Commonly referred to by its opponents as Male Genital Mutilation.
- Young men's half or totally naked bodies would be posted everywhere, to sell everything and anything.
- Social humour and banter would continually focus on sexualising or denigrating men.
- Men would disappear from our history books and most sections of the newspapers.

There is more, but I'm sure this is already quite enough. You bet we'd have an International Men's Day.

And of course, #notallwomen would treat men like this.

But wait, that's not how it is for men, is it? But it's very real for most of the world's women. And – International Women's Day was not intended as a day of celebration of women's achievements, but a day to remember that women still do not have equal respect, equal pay, or freedom from sexist objectification, harassment, and violence. A day to raise awareness that the struggle is not over, and massive change is still to be achieved. Men and women are not from different planets, but they live in different atmospheres.

Let's be clear here. Sexism is not unique to males. As we'll see in Chapter 12, many women have internalised Sexism and wield it with a vengeance against other women.

It is an observation of sociologists that, when two groups live in an interdependent relationship, the lower status group will often adopt the beliefs, and identify with the needs of, the dominant group. There are many women who have internalised Sexism – after all they've been taught since birth - and you will find them attacking or criticising or denigrating other women in a sexist manner. They will deny the existence of Sexism and defend men when the issue is raised. Many women spring to the defence of men. Some women say we should all leave the poor blokes alone and get on with more important things.

Many women have declared to me that they have never been discriminated against in their lives. They have made these statements in spite of the fact they were working before Equal Pay legislation, and they were legally earning only two-thirds of a man's salary. Even when they had to resign if they married, or they could not apply for certain managerial roles because only men were eligible, it all seemed so normal that they hadn't noticed it as discrimination. But those were the good old days when times were bad – weren't they?

Yes, they were. Some of us still remember them. Nowadays, where laws and rules have changed, sadly the facts, figures, and research show that reality has not changed much and, even when it did, it slips backwards within a decade or two. The beginnings of change and awareness were refreshing and beneficial in the 1970s and 1980s. They began to slow in the 1990s and not only has there been little change since, but knowledge and awareness of the existence and strength of Sexism has declined, and some countries and States in the USA are repealing laws that protect women. In fact, the USA, the land of the free and the home of the brave, has never been able to get its Equal Rights Amendment ratified, so strong is the opposition in that country to women's equality.

Many younger women feel that they have equality. They have worked diligently at school and, in many cases, outclassed the boys. They head out into a world in which they feel confident of being welcomed wherever they choose to head. They have not yet realised that the diligence for which they were rewarded in school, is not what results in recognition, reward, and promotion on the job. There's something else. They have not yet encountered the boys they outclassed at school being given the promotions ahead of them, being paid more, listened to more, and at the end of it all, having way more superannuation to retire on than they do.

Older women may not feel overtly discriminated against if they remain in the appropriate gender role or career. They are conveniently constraining themselves, self-monitoring in fact. They have not recognised the Sexism in their lives. The world around them is much the same as it always was so everything appears "normal". And yet, everyday Sexism is all around us. Like gravity, Sexism controls our every act. Like gravity, we do not even notice it until we defy it. The results can be painful.

Tangible signs that Sexism and inequality are alive and well are still evident. Modern technology makes their revelation and public sharing more possible than ever before. It is not so easy to censor or filter out women on Social Media as print and audio media controlled by men have managed in the past. Once on Social Media, however, the trolls mercilessly attack and intimidate women, hounding many of them back into the silence desired and required of women for thousands of years.

Today's social media was used to good purpose when author Laura Bates invited women to respond online with stories of Sexism they had experienced. The replies poured in. The sheer accumulation of what women put up with on a daily basis is staggering. Women from countries around the world, of different social classes, all ages, religious or not, employed or unemployed, and of different gender orientations, responded to her invitation to tell her their experiences of Sexism. The patterns across all cultures were similar. Also similar was the belief of many women that it was somehow their fault, and they should never tell anybody. What was and still is usually overlooked or unacknowledged is the fact that everyday harassment, groping, touching, cat calling, abuse, and whistling, are one end of a continuum of men's attitude and entitlement to women's bodies. Laura Bates published the results of her Everyday Sexism Project in 2014. Her book is a powerful indictment of the behavior of too many men and has shocked other men into realizing what women are subjected to daily. For the most part, women do not complain and accept it as part of life on earth for women.

Ms Gulliver and the Gender Ties

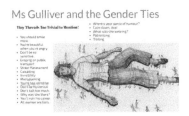

Figure 2: Ms Gulliver and the "Trivial" Ties of Gender.
Each thread is tiny but enough of them make the
difference. © Veronica Schwarz

To ignore these so-called "trivial" behaviours is to ignore the underpinning of men's assertion of power over women, which culminates in violence, incest, rape, and murder. More on this later.

Another revelation made possible by the modern technology of Social Media, the #metoo movement has brought out into the open the commonality of so many men's sense of entitlement to women's bodies and their exercise of that "entitlement" over women who are invariably vulnerable to them.

Since the age of eight, I have been touched "inappropriately", fondled, and groped by males including a cousin, a great-uncle, a doctor, a chiropractor, a gynaecologist, several employers, and random strangers on public transport. I have also been raped by two men who refused to accept the word "no". And yes, not all men are like that. In fact, as I was growing up, most men I encountered were not like that. The fact that I considered myself "lucky" that most men are not like that, only indicates the normalization of this type of men's behaviour.

In later life, I began to talk about it with other women and almost all of my friends had experienced the same violations, several of them much worse than mine. We none of us had spoken up at the time. We instinctively knew that we would not be believed or, if we were, we would also be blamed. And who do you complain to when it's the boss doing the harassing? Laura Bates' book provides the overwhelming evidence that this behaviour is mind-boggling in its enormity and the fact that it still continues. Proclaiming that not all men are like that is a pointless and selfish retort unless the men who are not like that, are prepared to believe women and help do something about it. Nor does it deal with the impact of that behaviour on women's lives.

In recent years, women have begun sharing their experiences with one another, and we are now aware that way too many of us have been treated in this way. In the 1970s, we had consciousness-raising groups where women shared their experiences and, for the first time, began to see the common patterns across the lives of most women. We learned that we were not alone, our experiences were not unusual or unique, and it was not our fault.

So how can this male behaviour continue? Why isn't there more determination from both men and women to change it?

It's complicated. Let's, for now, just say we're all in this together. What's stopping us from changing it? Two things. Our outer world and our inner world. We'll also look at this in greater detail but for now here is a taste of what I am talking about.

Our own minds keep us tethered, and our societies teach us to conform. As noted in Chapter 2, members of every culture on earth tend to believe that their culture is the "right" way to think, act, believe, govern, even eat, dress, and wear our hair. We also tend to believe that the way things are is the way they have always been and are, therefore, quite "normal" and "natural". The situation of women in most societies has remained static for thousands of years with only the last 150 years showing a slight shiver of change. To call it pathetic would be praising it up. Women's position in particular is always perceived by the majority in a culture, both male and female, as "natural", the "natural place" for women which leads to it being unquestioned by most people. The stereotypes are clear, and we must fit in. Customs insist on it. Religions, society, and families reinforce it. And certain groups benefit from it.

"A woman's place" is a term which applies to all women. There is no such term which applies to all men. Women are still perceived as a group, with the same characteristics, the same skills or lack of them, the same needs, and the same behaviour patterns. Men, within their own culture, are mainly perceived as individuals. We'll look at this and the harm it does, in more detail in Chapter 13: Does it Really Matter? (Let Me Count the Ways.)

A major factor in maintaining the myth of equality is the fact that many women do not identify with other women. They tend to perceive incidents as unique or specific to the individuals involved. They do not see patterns of overall treatment of women. In addition, the women who are harassed, beaten, and raped have learnt that it was probably their fault, and society reinforces this with a blame-the-victim (more accurately a blame-the-woman) response. Again, we'll look at this and the reasons behind it in greater detail in Chapter 12: Women are their own Worst Enemies.

Occasionally, whole societies protest, and an outcry is raised at a particularly horrendous and brutal rape or murder, and cries for reform ring out to the politicians and law-enforcers. Feathers are ruffled, heads are shaken, promises are made. For example, thousands marched in the street in Australia, quite justifiably, when Jill Meagher was raped and murdered in Melbourne. Then the dust settled, and life went on. Till a month or a year or ten years later, it happens again. We see the same cycle of protest and promise in the Black Lives Matter movement. Each time we think *This is the tipping point. Enough is enough. This time things will change.* But, at the time of writing, 2021, they have not.

I believe that many women and girls survive in this world by denying that they are living in patriarchal societies which are designed for men and run by men, or that Sexism and misogyny exist. The awful truth of the position of women may well be just too painful to bear. Any deep study of women's position is so depressing as to raise despair and anger in anyone who faces it squarely. It seems so horrific and hopeless that it feels totally overwhelming.

To quote Gandhi in his struggle to gain independence for India from the British, he said:

If I had no sense of humor, I would long ago have committed suicide.

In writing this book, I too have felt that hopelessness, over-whelmed by the enormity of it all. I took a year off researching for this book in order to stay sane - and ended up writing a book of mostly cheerful sometime humorous quotes in that year. Returning to this book - I have tried to present the facts, the reasons, and some possible solutions. I have also tried to remain upbeat for most of the time. Moving on -

I've been tossing some words around at you as though I expect you to know exactly what I mean by them. I shouldn't make that assumption because we often have different interpretations of, and reactions to, some words. By way of a kind of light relief, let's just check to see if we're on the same page. In the next chapter: What's in a name?

4

What's in a Name?
(WHATEVER CAN YOU MEAN?)

When I use a word," Humpty Dumpty said, in rather a scornful tone, "it means just what I choose it to mean—neither more nor less."

"The question is," said Alice, "whether you can make words mean so many different things."

"The question is," said Humpty Dumpty, "which is to be master—that's all."

Lewis Carroll *Through the Looking-Glass, 1871*

IT'S SUCH a waste of time or energy to disagree with each other because we are using words differently. I'd like to tell you what I believe some crucial words mean so, even if you don't agree with my definition, you will at least know what I am trying to say. Let's give it a go.

The ones that are important to define are *Sexism, misogyny, Feminism, sex* and *gender,* and occasionally *Patriarchy.* Let's start with

Sexism.

Sexism

Sexism is defined as discrimination and prejudice against any person based on their sex. Sounds straightforward.

But the Sexism that women face is more complex than that. It is the belief that males are superior to females, and males should, therefore, rightfully dominate in the home, and in society. Sexism against women is built into the culture, the language, the expectations, the structure of society, and the existing privileges and entitlements of men. It is taught to children of both sexes from birth. It is so normalised that even its worst aspects are excused or ignored by most of the population. It's like water to a fish.

We are like the two young fish, swimming along together. An older fish passes them and says, "Hello there. How's the water today?" They reply, "Fine, thank you." As the older fish swims away, one youngster turns to the other and says, "What's water'?"

Figure 3: What's Water? Sexism - like fish in water - all around us and so much a part of our lives, we don't even notice it.

So, it is with Sexism. Quite "normal", all-pervasive, and invisible.

That's the nature of Sexism, often invisible and unremarked. Like the air around us. Sexism is unnoticed because it's so common. Once we recognise this, we can begin to deal with it, because once we see it, we can never un-see it.

In her ground-breaking book *The Feminine Mystique*, Betty Frieden spoke of the "problem that has no name". She was speaking of the sexually determined, stereotypical, social roles of women. She labelled it "the feminine mystique". At that time, she was right: the problem was unrecognised, and it had no name.

The word "Sexism" was probably coined in 1965, by Pauline M. Leet. The word gets to the heart of the matter in the same way that "Racism" does.

Racist literally means discrimination against, and belief in, the inferiority of a person based on their race. It's possible for a white person to experience Racism in some non-white countries, but from the days of colonialism and slavery of black and indigenous people, the term not only refers to the inferiority of non-white people but was also built into the laws and the social structure of societies run by white people. South Africa and the United States of America are historically the most blatant examples of institutionalised Racism.

Sexism against women is the same. It has been institutionalised for centuries and is only now being slightly shaken but not overly stirred. However, dictionary definitions of "Sexism" lag behind our growing understanding of the systemic, subterranean nature of the problem. Most dictionaries define it as prejudice or discrimination based on sex, with the occasional addition of the words "especially discrimination against women".

However, we are now aware that Sexism is far more complex than "prejudice or discrimination based on sex". Sexism, like Racism, was until recently institutionalised through our laws, but we have learnt that changing laws doesn't change minds. Sexism is still embedded in our attitudes, our beliefs about men and women, our language, our humour, our customs, our clothing and our actions. In many nations, it remains embedded in law as well.

Fundamentally, like Racism, it is about the exercise of power.

It's about the power of one group, men, over another group, women, a power that is granted, openly or subtly, by the society we live in – not legally in Western culture, but in so many subtle and subliminal ways. It pervades the entire system that makes up a society and a culture. In spite of changes to the law, Sexism rolls on like the giant ugly idol it is, crushing spirits, ambitions, potential and understanding. Since the 1990s, it has become more pervasive, more violent, and more subtle.

Why then is it so hard to eradicate? Short answer: It provides men with a range of privileges that, for the most part, go unnoticed because the entire concept is built on the belief that it is all "natural".

It also provides many women with a sense of being sheltered and shielded by a male Protector, without analysing the fact that the need for a male Protector is founded on the imbalance of power between the sexes. The male Predator she requires protection from, is himself also a product of the imbalance of power between the sexes.

In addition, many women enjoy having men open doors for them, and see it as good manners or respectful. Yes, it is good manners and perfectly reasonable for either sex to do it. But to consider that a good reason for maintaining the status quo in the relationship between the sexes is like the Biblical story of Esau.

Esau came home one day exhausted and begged his twin brother to get him something to eat. He willingly agreed to give Jacob his birthright, his recognition as the firstborn and the prestige and inheritance that went with that if Jacob would bring him a bowl of lentil stew.

To me, giving up the right to be treated as an equal human being, with all the opportunities and status available to men, giving up the right to be free of fear and violence, to receive equal recognition and reward for equal contribution, in exchange for the opening of doors, seems as mind-boggling as Esau's deal to sell his future inheritance to Jacob for a bowl of stew. By all means have doors opened for you, but this is not an either/or situation. The sum total of freedom to be fully human, is not located in a doorway.

Sexism is expressed in a variety of ways from benign, through social or customary, to malignant, but they are all part of a continuum of attitudes and behaviours based on belief in male superiority, competence, dominance and even entitlement.

At one end of the continuum, they are benign or benevolent, even chivalrous, and at the far end of the continuum, they are hostile, cruel, violent, and murderous. Sexism of one sort or another is taught to and believed by most men, but it is also internalised by women and used by them to teach their children and to monitor other women.

Parts of Sexism, although based on prejudice, are socially accepted and go unremarked. Remember the two little fish in water. Surrounded by it, they could not see it.

Benevolent or benign Sexism describes men's "positive" attitudes and actions towards women which appear respectful, protective, and courteous. The hidden Sexism here is that women who do not fulfill the feminine stereotype are not offered respect, protection, or courtesy. As many women also find out over time, even behaving in a feminine manner does not automatically ensure chivalry.

Social or customary Sexism finds its expression in patronising, mansplaining, not listening to females, sexist jokes, sexist language, and language that does not even acknowledge the very existence of females.

Also customary is judging the same behaviour positively for men and negatively for women, for example taking charge, expressing an opinion in a confident manner, or expressing anger. Men are respected for these behaviours. Women are labelled bossy and bitchy for the same thing. Another example is the outcome of regular sexual activity which results in a man being referred to as a stud, while a woman is a slut. Hurdles for women also include stereotypical assumptions, social and political invisibility, expectations of different careers, forms of dress, behaviour, and niceness.

And the icing on the cake: both men and women have internalised the sexist myth that men are more competent, capable and knowledgeable, even more intelligent than women.

Not far to go from there to valuing the work men do more highly than the work women do. Unequal pay, although not legal, is still the reality achieved by manipulation of the label/title or valuing a man's education for his career more highly than a woman's, or valuing and paying more highly, occupations where men cluster in greater numbers, mainly "blue collar" work, while paying so-called "pink collar" occupations less, or burdening women with a far from fair share of nurturing and caring and housekeeping and social and health responsibilities for the family, ensuring women, through exhaustion or common sense, choose less responsible positions, casual or part-time work. Or, right from the outset, allowing good old subconscious gender bias to give men but not women the benefit of the doubt in assessing their capabilities.

Also, in this category of "customary" Sexism, there are street harassment, catcalling, touching, or rubbing against in public places, and non-consensual touching or kissing in social situations.

Malignant or hostile Sexism is overt and threatens, intimidates, or abuses women and girls. It perceives them as objects to be used for the pleasure and service of men. It begins with disrespect and slides from denigrating, humiliating, abusing, coercing, controlling, and raping, to physical harm and murder.

As we move from benign to malignant Sexism, society's acceptance moves from perceptions of normality to realising things are not quite right but there's not much we can do about it. From there, as the intensity, control and impact heighten, society begins to take notice, round about the point of actual murder of women and children. Society then takes it seriously and finally declares the situation intolerable and illegal. In other words, not until the extreme is reached. Why do we turn a blind eye, find excuses, disbelieve women, or blame the victim to protect men who behave in these ways? At the beginning, we use the "boys will be boys" meme and let it slide on from there. There is no clear point at which we call a halt until a death is staring us in the face.

Benevolent or benign Sexism is the carrot, and hostile malevolent Sexism is the stick that, between them, whether consciously or unconsciously, keep women in their place. The Predator ensures the belief that women need a Protector.

To ignore, accept or excuse the seemingly harmless even benevolent expressions of Sexism is to pave the way for men who perform or express its malevolent extremes. These behaviours are all expressions of a set of beliefs that devalue and disrespect women.

I have turned the concept of a continuum to an upright position in the following diagram, forming a funnel. This is to emphasise the downward slide and the deteriorating outcomes. This is not a procession of behaviour from one side of a spectrum to the other. It is a downhill slide into violence, cruelty, and murder.

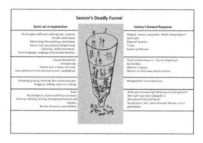

Figure 4: Sexism's Deadly Funnel. Trivial everyday Sexism, disrespecting, diminishing, denigrating, and objectifying women is a slippery slope toward malicious, malignant, and murderous misogyny. Preventing the currently acceptable forms could prevent the slide into malignant Sexism and toxic masculinity. © Veronica Schwarz

This funnel demonstrates how, at the top, most men have subconsciously learnt to be sexist as part of their training in masculinity. We will discuss the tragic consequences of this further in Chapter 9: Boys will be Boys, particularly when we look at the Man Box and explore the concept of a "real" man. We need good men, not "real" men. We need men (and women) who are decent human beings, capable of a range of attitudes and behaviours including empathy, courage, kindness, caring, and people who value ethical and co-operative behaviour.

As we slide down the funnel, fewer and fewer men are involved, but the devastation and grief are very real and both men and women need to work at every level of Sexism to eliminate it.

On the occasions when men feel they are unfairly treated because of their sex, it is usually because of society's sexist attitudes towards women. Here are just two examples of sexist attitudes to women, disadvantaging men:

- Child custody and parental payment arrangements: This has, in the past, favoured women because of the feminine gender stereotype. Women are considered the natural nurturers but not great money earners, thanks to the structural educational, pay and superannuation disadvantages they have suffered because they are female.
- Military conscription: Men, not women are conscripted into the army in most but not all countries, because women are perceived to be incapable in battle or a distraction to the male soldiers.

Yes, men can be disadvantaged by Sexism in its basic form of discriminated against on the basis of sex or gender. They can be mocked if they look after their own children, accused of lack of commitment to their career if they take family leave, ridiculed if they sew, knit, or perform other crafts associated with women. They can be objectified as hunks or studs. They can be discriminated against in divorce proceedings because of the patronising but favourable attitudes towards women that are still held by some of the legal profession.

Sexism for women is far more complex than discrimination on the basis of sex or the sexual objectification of individuals. Both of these actions are deplorable when applied to either sex. Men are right to challenge discrimination when it happens to them.

When a good-looking male actor complains that he has been a victim of Sexism because he has been turned into a sex object, his experience is different to that of a female actor similarly objectified. First, it is not the only way he is judged of value as an actor or in any other aspect of his life. It does not symbolise a lack of power or show that he is inferior to females. It is not a culturally encouraged behaviour as the same treatment of females is. He is not lessened by it. It is a one-off individual instance affecting him, a barefaced and pragmatic attempt on the part of the film maker to increase profits based on sexual attraction.

Women on the other hand, are seen and treated as one "group" with stereotypical characteristics assigned to all of them. As are other groups such as Jews, Muslims, Aborigines, and other people of colour, in the presence of Racism. Or as people of different sexual orientation or gender from the straight male/female "norm" are, in the face of homophobia.

MISOGYNY

Another word that is often used these days in reference to women's status and experience, is "misogyny". This word's been around for hundreds of years but had disappeared from most people's vocabulary. When Julia Gillard, Australia's Prime Minister at the time, used it in a parliamentary speech in 2012, people were scrambling for their dictionaries. Much of the discussion seemed to conclude that the word was similar in meaning to "Sexism". It isn't. It is actually a hatred, dislike, or mistrust of women. That is different from a prejudice based on a belief in men's superiority which Sexism covers. Sexism does not automatically involve hatred or mistrust. It simply sails along on the sublime assumption that women are just not as clever, competent, intelligent or able as men. Misogyny is a horse of a different colour. It's been said that most men hate women some of the time, and some men hate women all of the time. It is the latter group that misogyny refers to.

Misogyny has become a basic creed for Men's Rights Activists who believe women's rights have run roughshod over men's rights. Misogyny also fuels the destructive actions of the Incels (Involuntary Celibates) who hate and blame women for denying them sex. There also seems to be a strong element of misogyny in the White Supremacist movement. And the latest addition to the choir: The Red Pill Men. More on these later.

SEX AND GENDER

Sex is a physical characteristic. *Gender* is a behaviour pattern.

Yes, gender is used interchangeably with sex these days but that's not its original meaning. Following our passion for duality, we label genders of females and males *feminine* and *masculine*. There are other ways of being male and female, but we cling to the two. Masculinity and femininity are cultural constructs and vary from society to society. They are taught. If gender were inborn, it would be the same across all cultures, and all social classes. It would be common across all humans. It is not.

Your sex is the type of body you were born with. Male or female. The primary sex characteristics are all related to reproducing our own species. Ovaries, uterus, vagina if you're female. Testes, prostate, and penis if you're male. With animals, it is the same. They are male or female according to the parts of their bodies associated with producing more of their species. Today, many people use sex and gender as if they were the same thing. They are not.

Initially, the word *gender* came from Latin meaning "a type of something" or "a category". *Gender* was initially and still is used in grammar to classify nouns as masculine, feminine or neuter or some other category.

In the 1950s, the word *gender* was first used by John Money in his ground-breaking work on socialisation of the sexes. But the idea didn't take off till the 1970s when the Women's Liberation Movement began exploring the nature of femininity.

Using the word *gender* to mean the sex of an animal didn't begin until the 1980s, when animal researchers began referring to the sex of animals as *gender*. In 1993, the American Food and Drug Administration (FDA) began using *gender* to refer to the sex of a person. The FDA reversed this decision in 2011 and now more accurately uses *gender* to refer to an individual's presentation (behaviour and dress) of themselves as being male or female.

Official forms still ask for a person's *gender* and insist on a choice between M and F. Some allow the option "Prefer not to say". Those who present themselves in some other way from the traditional masculine or feminine, or those who are born with genitals that differ from male and female and would like to state the fact that they do not fit the options offered, usually have no choice.

The bottom line is that sex is not gender even though they are frequently and even officially used interchangeably. Sex is your body relevant to having children. Gender is your behaviour, the way you present yourself to the world. Feminine or masculine or some other way of dressing or behaving.

Obviously, the two sexes, female and male, are different. No rational person would argue otherwise.

The actual biological differences are that females ovulate, menstruate, gestate, and lactate; males ejaculate.

Secondary sex characteristics are physical differences between the sexes that are not related to conceiving and birthing babies. Males have more facial hair, more body hair, and Adam's apples. Females have larger breasts which produce milk. Incidentally, the size of the breasts is not relevant to the amount of milk produced.

This does not account for people who are born of indeterminate sex or intersex characteristics. Some are born with genitals that are not completely male or female or have a combination of both. About one in 250 babies are born with variations to their genitals. We are so insistent on people being one sex or the other that many of these babies are surgically altered so they "look like" one sex or the other.

The point is that sex is a physical characteristic. Gender is behavioural.

Gender is a cultural idea and differs across cultures, social classes and throughout time. Upper class masculinity differs from working class masculinity. Italian masculinity differs from Germanic. Nowadays the term "toxic masculinity" is often used to describe a type of rigid, macho, stereotypical, even violent extreme expression of being male. It is only one form of many expressions of masculinity and does not refer to all forms of masculinity.

Sex and gender have been used, like skin colour, to differentiate, discriminate against and even oppress more than half of humanity, those who are not identified as male.

Men and women can both do everything that's humanly possible. Yes, we'll talk about physical strength later but remember some things are beyond the strength of men too. That's why they used their brains and built machines.

However, there is one exception. Women have babies. So far, men can't. And that is the main difference. Some male writers have even suggested that early men's jealousy of this fact, may also be the reason for men's insistence throughout history that women are incapable of doing almost everything else.

Patriarchy

This word is not used by many people outside of feminist or some activist circles but it's a good shorthand word to refer to a particular type of society, in the same way as we use *democracy, republic,* and *dictatorship.* Patriarchy is a way of structuring a society. The type of society it refers to, was created by people and can and has been changed by people. It is not "natural" or inevitable. The word comes from the Latin word *pater* meaning "father". Initially, patriarchy meant the rule of the father as the head of the household and the term "patrilineal" means the inheritance of a family passing through the male line. A matriarchal society, from the Latin word for "mother" meant that the mother ran the household, and a matrilineal line meant that inheritance passed down through the daughters. There is no evidence throughout history of any matriarchal society morphing into a system that oppressed, enslaved, or denigrated men.

Patriarchy, however, as we saw in Chapter 2, morphed into something more oppressive in which males came to dominate and control and even enslaved or claimed ownership over females.

Today, we live in a social structure created by our ancestors a long, long, long time ago. Men still dominate, are allowed to dominate, and are considered less than "masculine" if they don't dominate. This has been sustained for so long through the clever myths of Sexism.

FEMINISM

Those opposed to the equality of the sexes and genders, have twisted the meaning of "Feminism" till it is almost the opposite of the truth. Humpty Dumpty would be proud.

Some amazing contributions to the anti-feminist tirade come from conservative Christians. Here's one example that gives the flavour of the attack. It's from Pat Robertson, American Christian televangelist:

(The feminist agenda) is about a socialist, anti-family political movement that encourages women to leave their husbands, kill their children, practice witchcraft, destroy capitalism and become lesbians.

What is Feminism?

Feminist philosophy calls on societies to recognise the full and equal humanity of females and males, and to structure their societies accordingly. It opposes those beliefs, attitudes, actions, institutions, and social structures that hinder the achievement of that goal.

There appear to be several types of Feminism, interrelated with a person's political ideology or, in some cases, linked to the marginalised group they belong to. You will find feminists from some sections of society attacking middle-class white feminists. This, to put it mildly, is far from helpful. It's true, if we're not experiencing intersectionality or various forms of discrimination and disadvantage, we're probably not very aware of it. Surely women can talk to one another and discuss their differences and work towards solutions for all.

Some men, while not experiencing misogyny themselves, have been able to see what women are being subjected to. Many of them have stood by their wives, daughters, and sisters, to support their fight for equality. Others of them have written some excellent feminist books, poetry, and treatises. John Stuart Mill, Walt Whitman, and Michael Korda, just to name three.

Here is what I believe Feminism is about. I very likely haven't covered everything, but I hope it will give you the flavour.

I will begin with the things Feminism is opposed to because I think identifying the problems gives you a good starting point to change things for the better. If you know what you want to change, you know where you need to start and can begin planning its reversal.

I believe Feminism is opposed to:

- sexist prejudice,
- sexist discrimination and bias,
- inequality of access to power, influence, privilege and financial reward based on sex or gender,
- women's (and marginalised groups') relative invisibility in history or news, literature, or sport,
- violence against women or anyone else,
- the straitjacket of gender stereotypes imposed on both females and males.

These are very broad-brush areas, and part of the purpose of this book is to drill down into the supports and propagation of these practices.

Feminism is about giving all men and women regardless of skin colour, social class, ethnicity, or ability an equal opportunity to gain respect, responsibility, dignity, knowledge, fulfilment, social contribution, influence, and money based on their individual merits and talents.

What's there to disagree with? Partnership not Patriarchy.

Feminism is a philosophy so, since both sexes are capable of philosophical thought, in my opinion, both sexes and all genders can be feminists.

I want to end this chapter with an explanation of why I focus mainly on women in this book. There are probably people who will attack this approach because they believe that Feminism should take on board the fight for justice and equality of all the oppressed of the world. In fact, by including all men and women within the concerns of Feminism, it does just that. But the sexist bias is unique as I will explain a little further on. Hence the focus on it.

Women's concern for all disadvantaged people and their willingness to fight everybody's battles have not to date helped women. We will see how the French revolutionaries suppressed the women's movement within the revolution, saying that the revolution was for everyone. It was not.

We will also see how the Russian revolutionaries attacked the women's movement within their revolution, telling the women the revolution was for all workers and it would achieve justice and equality for everyone including women. It did not.

During the fight for liberation of the slaves in the United States of America, those fighting for women's suffrage were told to get behind the cause of black freedom and their goals would be achieved later. Women including white women were at the forefront of the fight for emancipation of the slaves. After the slaves were freed, black men were given the vote. No woman, regardless of skin colour, could vote until fifty years later.

I am not saying we should not help the fight for justice for all. And many of us will. What I am saying is that there is a need to focus on the unique nature of the fight for women's liberation because history demonstrates that the outcome of most freedom fights, involve women in the battle but ignore them in the victory.

As I write this, there is a much-needed global push to support the "Black Lives Matter" movement which is a result of the killing of black people in America by usually white officers or vigilantes. It is horrific that in 2020 the world is still fighting this battle. Not unexpectedly, a counterargument has arisen with the slogan "All Lives Matter". Of course, this is true. The Black Lives Matter is not saying only Black Lives Matter. It is saying Black Lives Matter Too.

Similarly, with the feminist movement. It's not about "Women First". It's about "Women Too". Women's situation is unique as it involves the defining of identity as "Not like the Other". Masculinity defines itself as being not feminine. The uniqueness of women's position also involves the intimate relationships of the two groups involved, men are our grandfathers, fathers, sons, grandsons, friends and lovers, people we usually love and defend, nurture and admire. And perhaps most intimate of all, the complexities of sexual relationships and their many modes of expression. Although Sexism entwines itself within all forms of discrimination and prejudice, it has these unique aspects. This makes it necessary to focus on aspects that are not common to any other form of prejudice. The discrimination faced by women within many marginalised and oppressed groups, is harsher because of their sex and gender. But the inter-sectionality of their experience sometimes blurs this distinction. Here are a couple of examples.

Recently, the President of the USA attacked an Asian press reporter because she had dared to question him on an issue to do with the pandemic of the time. The global reporting of the incident called it a racist attack, and then went on to describe the fact that it was another example of the president's inability to accept strong, confident women! I suspect it was both racist and sexist, an example of intersectionality, but the focus illustrates the way we tend to ignore Sexism, but most of us do recognise and deplore other forms of bias and prejudice. The Sexism remains invisible because it is still so normalised.

I have experienced this with female work colleagues who feel they have been discriminated against. They have put it down to their ethnicity. They have not noticed that I too, although a member of the "favoured" ethnic group, have also suffered similar discrimination, while their male colleagues of their ethnic background have not. Yes, Racism is alive and well and needs to be stamped out. I heartily agree. What I am saying is that for women the situation is often more complicated, and the extra dimension of being female needs to be teased out, and the Sexism dealt with as well as the Racismt. And some of the solutions will very likely not be the same. If we fail to recognise or acknowledge the hidden Sexism, we will never root it out.

There it is. Now wouldn't every fair-minded person be a feminist? If you believe in fairness for all people, then that includes being a feminist – unless you think women aren't people.

Partly as a result of the assault on the meaning of Feminism and the ridiculing and denigrating of feminists, we have many women of all ages who declare they don't need Feminism. We've been fighting for a long time and we still have a long way to go. That leads us nicely into the return to our time travel which we put on hold in Chapter 2.

5

Earth Women Are Revolting
(YOU AIN'T SEEN NOTHING YET!)

One of the things about equality is not just that you be treated equally to a man, but that you treat yourself equally to the way you treat a man.

Marlo Thomas

Male domination is so rooted in our collective unconscious that we no longer even see it.

(Pierre Bourdieu)

IN CHAPTER 2: The Story so Far, we left the human race at the point when women's status took a serious plunge. From partner to property. This coincides with the beginnings of agriculture and the development of established settlements. Religions changed from female to male gods, and men ruled the earth. Over time, not only were women the property of men but also, they were considered inferior to men and not quite human, as men were.

That's not as silly as it sounds, or maybe it is, but a lot of people have believed it. This concept that women are not quite as fully human in the way that men are, has been with us for a long time. It has underpinned most of our laws and customs for a few thousand years. Men are the actual humans. Women are an inferior sort of man. Women are somewhere between children and men when it comes to full adulthood.

Let's return to our trip through time and see just how powerful this idea has been.

The one thing that the various institutions of evolving societies agreed on was that man should rule over woman. Religious teachings dictated, laws enforced, philosophers pontificated, and science proved unquestionably that women were childbearing machines and should be protected from intellectual activity that could damage their ability to produce children.

Here's a taste of what some of these worthy gentlemen came up with:

Religion

Jewish men learned to pray "Blessed be the God that has not made me a heathen, a slave, or a woman."

Hindu scriptures state that "a woman must never be independent".

In Buddhism, being born female is believed to be the result of bad Karma.

In Christianity, we read that St Paul basically told women to sit down and shut up.

In the Muslim Koran, the value of a woman is "half a man".

To be fair, some of the original teachers of these religions, did not make these statements. Successors introduced these ideas of women's inferiority after the death of the founder. But this has not lessened their impact. Even though, for example, Jesus is depicted as including and supporting women.

Philosophy

In China, Confucius, who lived from 551 BCE to 479 BCE, put in his two bits worth with his statement: *One hundred women are not worth a single testicle*. How's that for pride in one's equipment?

Greek philosophers got in on the act around the sixth century BCE. Pythagoras linked the left side of the body with femaleness and evil, the right side with masculinity and goodness.

The great Aristotle declared:

Man is active, full of movement, creative in politics, business, and culture. The male shapes and moulds society and the world. Woman, on the other hand, is passive. She stays at home, as is her nature. She is matter waiting to be formed by the active male principle ... Man consequently plays a major part in reproduction; the woman is merely the passive incubator of his seed... the male semen cooks and shapes the menstrual blood into a new human being...

His views of female nature and inferiority influenced Western thought for a thousand years. The application of his ideas kept women subjugated until the sixteenth century – some 1800 years after his death. Now that's power!

It's said that prejudice is the offspring of fear. In 195 BCE, Cato the Elder said: *Suffer women once to arrive at equality with you, and they will from that moment on become your superiors*. He sounds more than a bit nervous, don't you think? (You'll probably see lots of men who share this fear today.)

Science

As scientific method grew in popularity, it too was co-opted to "prove" women's inferiority. We find statements on the brain size of women, the wandering wombs of women, fearful teeth in the vagina, and hysteria. Science told us that educating a woman would shrink her uterus and make her incapable of having children.

Law

Women were not permitted to participate in politics or be elected to parliaments or even vote. This meant that all the laws were made by men. These laws were based on the dictates of religion and philosophy and science – all developed by men. Not allowing women to vote or participate in politics, was fundamental. Educational courses such as medicine were barred to them. In addition, when women married, they legally lost their individuality, their property, their right to earn and keep money, their right to keep their children after divorce. Rape in marriage was not a crime and still isn't in some countries. And men had the right to punish their wives if they were displeased with them, such punishment included beating or flogging.

There would seem to be a strong case for keeping women "in their place". Certainly, it allows men to continue with some comforting beliefs about their own superiority.

The process of keeping women in their place is so powerful that many women have internalised their own culture's Sexism. They police other women and teach the customs and beliefs to their daughters.

But not all women. There have been some women who have fought against these constraints, and more women nowadays who do. And there have been thoughtful and fair-minded men who have supported them.

Both men and women began to throw off the yoke of the tyrannical power of kings and aristocracy in the eighteenth century. Great revolutions brought great changes but change for women has rarely been part of the general struggle for equality, in spite of women's attempts to be included.

The first great revolution of this kind was the American War of Independence in 1776. Even then, women began to question their role (or lack of a role) in the forming of this new society.

Abigail Adams wrote to her husband John Adams in 1776. He was away helping to draw up the American Declaration of Independence. You can easily read the full content of these letters on the internet.

Abigail wrote asking her husband to "remember the ladies" and to give them a say in the new government. She also asked that less power be given to men over their wives.

Brave words from Abigail Adams. Although she and her husband had a loving and apparently egalitarian partnership in their marriage, the thought of equality of the sexes was too much for her husband. He replied Original spelling and punctuation retained): *As to your extraordinary Code of Laws, I cannot but laugh. … Depend upon it, We know better than to repeal our Masculine systems.*

When the Declaration was ratified on 4 July 1776, it contained the famous words:

We hold these truths to be self-evident, that all men are created equal, that they are endowed by their Creator with certain unalienable Rights, that among these are Life, Liberty and the pursuit of Happiness.

This is one of the best-known sentences in the English language. It acts as an inspiration to all marginalised people. The word "Man" and "men" is said to include women. We know from John Adams own words that it did not. (It also did not include many other people who are still struggling for equality including indigenous people and people of colour.)

The French Revolution in 1789 also aroused women to fight for a better position in society. Women had no political rights. The women of the Revolution demanded equality with men and an end to male domination. They formed women's clubs and distributed pamphlets. They were cruelly crushed by their fellow male revolutionaries who then abolished the women's meetings and arrested their leaders in 1793. The men had no intention of sharing *liberté, egalité, fraternité* with women. Ten years later, the Napoleonic Code legally confirmed women's second-class status.

In 1792, Mary Wollstonecraft wrote *A Vindication of the Rights of Women*. It's a calm and reasoned call to treat women as fellow human beings. For this she was hated, despised, and labelled a "hyena in petticoats" by both men and women alike.

The Subjection of Women is the title of an essay written by John Stuart Mill in 1869. Mill credited his wife Harriet Taylor Mill with co-writing the essay. Some scholars insist that it was the sole work of John Stuart Mill. Giving major credit to a male involved in any project a woman participates in, is a well-docu-mented bias and continues today. It's been acknowledged that some of the arguments in Mill's essay are similar to Harriet Taylor Mill's earlier and almost unknown essay *The Enfranchise-*

ment of Women. She published her essay eighteen years before her husband's, but the people of the day refused to believe the ideas were hers.

John Stuart Mill was a remarkable man in taking up the plight of women and rightly maintaining his wife deserved credit for co-writing "his" essay. The essay outraged European society at the time. It was an affront to European conventional ideas on the status of men and women.

The Russian Revolution began in 1917. Women fought to include women's equality in the general fight for equality of the Russian people. They were considered to be undermining the effort of the revolution. Alexandra Kollantai became the most prominent female member of the revolutionary government. Initially, she struggled to gain rights for women through the revolution. She and other fighters for women's equality were told to support the main revolution because it was for everybody including women. Kollantai bowed to this demand. She died in exile a disappointed and disillusioned woman. The Revolution failed to lift women to equality with men in Russia or the Soviet Union.

Women in the struggle for equality for African-Americans in the USA, also found themselves marginalised by their male fellow fighters. Many men treated them as sex objects and providers of coffee and comfort. During his fight for civil rights for African-Americans, Malcolm X was asked how he saw the position of women in the struggle. He replied with a single word: *Prone.* Presumably, he meant "supine", but the meaning is clear. On their backs. To his credit, over several years of travelling the world, he changed his mind. He realised that the most basic requirement for equality of all people, was equality of women.

Democracy is defined as government of the people, by the people, for the people. This again was a half-truth. Democracy began in Greece and did not include women or slaves. Much the same as the American constitution in 1776. At the end of the nineteenth century, except for New Zealand and South Australia, democracy still did not include women, nor did it include other marginalised people.

As Rosalind Miles summed it up in her excellent book *The Woman's History of the World:*

All democratic experiments, all revolutions, all demands for equality have so far stopped short of sexual equality.

Revolutions and "democratic" governments totally failed to achieve equality for women. Women then turned their attention to one tangible goal, achieving the right to vote. They were not referred to as "Suffragists", which is the term used for people fighting to achieve the right to vote. They were immediately belittled as "Suffragettes" meaning "little Suffragists", not to be taken seriously.

In 1893, the colony of New Zealand became the first self-governing country in the world to give women the right to vote. However, this did not include the right to stand for election to parliament.

In 1894, the State of South Australia granted women the right to vote and stand for election to parliament.

In 1902, most Australian women won the right to vote in Federal elections, but indigenous Australian women and men did not have that right until 1962.

The vote for women was won in Finland in 1906, Norway in 1913, Denmark in 1915 and Canada in 1917. Indigenous Canadians, male and female did not win the vote till 1960.

Austria, Germany, Poland, and Russia followed suit in 1918, the Netherlands in 1919.

In the United States of America, women began fighting for the right to vote in 1848. Women's fight for the right to vote was long and hard and they were often imprisoned and cruelly treated for their "uppityness".

As we saw earlier, in 1870, the vote was rightfully extended to African-American men. However, no woman in the USA, no matter what her race or skin colour, achieved the right to vote until 1920. Fifty years later.

Sweden saw the light in 1921 but Britain and Ireland lagged behind until 1928. It took Switzerland until 1971!

The great struggles for equality of all people, massive revolutions and social change for many, may not have resulted in equality for women. But the picture began to look brighter for some women in the twentieth century, and no organised revolution was involved.

The year 1968 can be seen as a watershed. The Americans and their allies mired themselves in the Viet Nam "War". There was a major shift in people's attitudes to acceptance of the way things were. There were protests, marches, lifestyle changes, awareness of gross injustices in America, the land of the free, in particular, and the Western World in general. The so-called Women's Liberation Movement, and second wave Feminism were part of that social mind shift.

This fact was largely ignored by most historians, politicians, and the news media. For them, what women said or did was secondary and not universally relevant. It is what men say and do that is universally relevant to history, human affairs, current affairs and for our understanding of the past. Women's demands and needs were seen as merely "women's movements" or "women's issues".

We saw this bias in the writings of palaeontologists about our Stone Age ancestors, and it is both male and female writers who have this gendered lens. Not just men. It is a socially universal myopia - a bias and a blindness. The incredible invisibility of women. And, probably more depressing, their blindness to their own absence. But we've been well taught. Give me the girl before the age of seven, and I will give you the woman.

We also saw this attitude of women's needs being limited and secondary in the history of major revolutions. The dismissive attitude towards them, and even suppression of women's attempts to be included in fights for equality and liberation from the oppressions specific to females, and there were and are plenty of those. They were laughed at, violently supressed, imprisoned and always told to support the wider movement which was liberty and equality for "everyone".

The outcome was always the same. No change for women. Sexism and secondary status remained firmly in place.

In 1968, across the Western world, in those places where democracy had spread, women and men took up the fight for Women's Liberation. This was dismissively dubbed "Women's Lib". Can you imagine referring to the Palestinian people's struggle for nationhood as Palestinian Lib? Or the fight for equality for black Americans as Black Lib? As with the term "Suffragette", ridicule and belittling terminology were the default reaction to women's attempts to break free of gender roles and stereotyping.

If ridicule didn't work, the next step was scaremongering. They were labelled "man-haters". Better yet, the label became "hairy legged man-haters". This was a reference to some women's refusal to conform to the "feminine" requirement to remove body hair. It wasn't long before they were also labelled Lesbians.

Mahatma Gandhi summed it up in reference to his own struggle for India's freedom from British colonialism. He said first they ignore you, then they laugh at you, then they fight you and then you win.

But women are not taken seriously enough to be "fought" as equal combatants. Bullying is the usual default position. Ridicule, belittling, and name calling are familiar tools in the bully's arsenal. And bullying, harassment and violent words and actions, are the usual responses of opponents to women's equality. A kind of undeclared guerrilla warfare.

However, with the emergence of the Men's Rights activists, the Incels, and the Red Pill Men, we are beginning to see some misogynists are prepared to openly fight to keep women "in their place". More on these later.

From the 1960s onwards, the works of Simone de Beauvoir , Betty Frieden, Germaine Greer, Gloria Steinem and others, inspired many women to shake free of the beliefs, expectations and rules that kept them in their place as second-class citizens with limited life choices. The old order of patriarchy (the rule of men and male-organised institutions) was shaken to its roots. The Women's Liberation Movement was becoming a force to be reckoned with. Something had to be done to control and reverse the momentum. Right on cue, the backlash began. The bad news is that progress has stalled, and, in some areas, women's rights are going backwards.

Social media trolls invariably use violent threats of mental and physical violence to attack any woman who raises her head and questions or disagrees on social media.

The group calling themselves Incels applaud the massacre of women and even other men.

The Red Pill men have drawn up a constitution in which women are seen as very little other than man-pleasing robots. And sadly, there are women who have joined them, begging to know how they might better please their man.

The Russian parliament has repealed the law which made rape in marriage a crime. Different states across America are clawing back women's access to abortion. Fundamentalist Christians are attacking and twisting the concept of Feminism as evil and destructive. Several states in the USA, during the Covid 19 pandemic, declared church attendance an essential service but abortion was non-essential.

The struggle for women's equality of opportunity, citizenship, and recognition as full human beings, has been a long and difficult one. Its history makes for inspiring but depressing reading. Equally interesting, has been the fight **against** women's freedom and equality. There has been a steady but determined move to ensure women never regain their place as partners in the human race. Some women, in some countries, have made gains towards that goal, but no country has achieved this. Laws have been changed but custom, culture and internalised Sexism persist. The opposition has been powerful, relentless, often underhand, and deceitful. It has been perpetuated by women as well as men, and it continues today. What could they be afraid of? What are they protecting?

Why is the opposition to women's equality so strong and so persistent? It's been going on for ten thousand years, give or take a few thousand. It continues, despite reason, science and evidence of wanton waste and harm, both human, economic, and environmental.

Despite vitriolic and even violent opposition to women's equality, in recent times, in some societies, women have gained greater freedom. As a result, they now have broader educational opportunities and more career choices. Some, but not all, have control over when and if they have children. In some societies, women have the right to own property. They can legally divorce and keep their own children. Equal pay for equal work is recognised but not a reality, particularly in private enterprise. Rape within marriage is now recognised as a crime in some societies.

Five powerful forces undermine change in the status of women:

- Most people fear and resist change of any sort.
- Changing laws does not change hearts or minds.
- Companies and corporations make huge profits based on the gendered way things are.
- People who enjoy privilege, even if they are unaware of it, feel the coming of equality as oppression rather than fairness.
- A belief acquired before the age of seven is very hard, although not impossible, to shift.

There is a huge body of research showing that most of the beliefs about the differences between men and women are not true or biological. They are taught. Yet, most people do not read research. Researchers themselves have noted that the popular media readily reports on research that appears to uphold the stereotypical beliefs about women and men. When such findings are disproven, there is very little prominence given to the fact. It appears most people prefer the myths despite the injustices and wanton waste of talent.

Gender roles and stereotypes remain stubbornly difficult to change. Prejudice and bias against women exist in hearts, minds, homes, and the wider society. Discrimination (often unconscious) against women still exists in the institutions and structures of society. We'll look at these in greater detail in following chapters, but the truth is there has not been a level playing field for women in ten thousand years.

Why? How is it achieved? Let's have a look at the core of the matter – making the difference through gender stereotypes.

6

Making the Difference

There is strong and completely convincing evidence that girls and boys are not very different emotionally, physicaly, or psychologically when they are born, but that we systematically train girls and boys to be different.

Paul Kivel: *Boys will be Men.*

Follow me here: your brain will begin to change as you do.

Alexandra Horowitz, cognitive scientist

IN CHAPTER 2, we saw that around five to ten thousand years ago, women's status plummeted. We believe that one of the reasons was the realisation of paternity. Another was the desire of men to ensure their property was passed on to their own sons. To do this, they had to control women, particularly women's sexual activity. And control them they did. We saw how women went from partner to property. This was reflected in the change within religions – from a Great Mother goddess to the supremacy of male gods. Reinforced through law, custom, philosophy and science over centuries.

Now this has been going on for five to ten thousand years in most developing cultures. Men took over control of running the show, as well as control of women to ensure women had their babies and not someone else's. How was it done, and how is women's secondary status maintained right up to today?

The key to understanding inequality in any form, is difference, not necessarily real difference but perceived difference. Inequality requires a perception of difference. If two things are seen to be alike, there is no inequality. If you want someone to be your subordinate, someone you can clearly see is not your equal, you need difference. If there is not much difference between you, then you'll have to create it or take minor differences and blow them up to be much bigger differences.

Inequality requires comparisons and assumptions based on differences. There is considerable evidence that women and men are not all that different, and we will be gathering that evidence throughout this book. So, why do we see men and women, girls and boys everywhere behaving so differently? We took a brief look at this in Chapter 1 when we looked at your birth and childhood.

Let's now set the scene for a wider look at societies in general because inequality between the sexes has, for centuries been based on the belief that men are better suited to run pretty much everything because they are just naturally better at it. They possess the necessary characteristics and talents for this. Women are better suited to provide the caring and back up services. "Naturally".

It's true that, a few hundred years ago, women began to object to the patriarchal system in some countries. Individual women and some fair-minded men began to argue that women were fellow human beings and should be treated as such. But it's been a difficult road and, as we have seen, it hasn't actually gone as far as some people claim.

We have seen too that women as a subordinate group in almost every culture on earth are in a unique position. They live in the most intimate of relationships with the dominant group. This makes institutionalised Sexism different to other prejudices although it is also present in all prejudices.

Males are our fathers, lovers, brothers, husbands, sons, and grandsons. Consequently, we relate closely to several males much more than we relate to a foggy concept of Sisterhood. This is one reason, if we needed one, that it is preferable not to blame men, but for both sexes and all genders to change our behaviour and our customs and our society. Blame won't work anyway. It only leads to defensiveness such as the #notallmen response. It rarely results in change for the better. Besides, it is important to see that men have been socialised to think and behave the way they do just as women have been.

In addition, the "women-have-equality-now" believers are quite rightly able to point to changes in legislation, at least in Western and other advanced societies. Yes, women have the vote, they are entitled to education, to own property and to divorce. They can enter any career of their choice. The reality of women's lives is not so rosy. Even where the laws have been changed; attitudes, beliefs and behaviours still limit or influence women's freedom of choice, development of potential and financial equality. We have looked at much of this in previous chapters.

We have also seen that changing the laws alone does not change some men's sense of entitlement or dominance and their often-fragile egos. Women in relationships with such men are constrained mentally, physically, emotionally, and financially. In a so-called free society, these women are far from free. Until recently, domestic situations were considered a private matter, and we still see evidence of that belief in some of our politicians and police and even some citizens of both sexes.

We need to face the fact that society moulded the men who enslave women, or brutalise them, or denigrate, harass, and belittle them. As a society, we will all benefit from helping women harmed by such men, as well as helping those men to change if possible. Perhaps above all, we need to ensure that we do not continue to re-produce them in the next generation. Consequently, we need to be more aware of what we are doing when we raise girls and boys, and the way we ourselves are influenced by gender stereotypes. We need to change the way we raise girls and boys to reduce or eliminate the imbalance of power and agency. Agency, in the sense I mean here, is the ability to act on or affect the world around you. We particularly, need to change the type of masculinity we thrust upon many boys from babyhood to manhood.

As we explored in Chapter 4, put simply, sex is a fact, gender is an act, not a pretence but a performance. We are born and labelled male and female depending on the shape of our genitals and reproductive organs. This is true of all human beings. We are taught to "perform" our gender according to our culture. This is not uniform across all cultures. It can vary from culture to culture, and what is considered "masculine" in one culture may be considered "feminine" in another. The variable nature of it, indicates immediately that it is teachable and not inborn and unchangeable.

In Western culture, for example, masculinity can vary across social classes. Working class men perform masculinity differently from middle- or upper-class men. Working class men might even consider other men somewhat soft or effeminate in their performance of masculinity.

While "femininity" with all its trappings and its expensive maintenance is an obsession in Western Culture, it does not seem to have the same extreme forms in some other cultures.

The unique thing about humans is that we aren't born with an inbuilt "nature" or a raft of common instincts. We aren't born knowing how to behave or how to do particular things. We have to be taught. This is different from most other creatures. The spider is not taught how to spin a web, but all spiders of the same species spin the same type of web. The birds are not taught how to build nests, but all birds of the same species build the same type of nests. Humans cannot even speak without being taught.

In *Sapiens,* Yuval Noah Harari's powerful study of the human species, he writes:

Most mammals emerge from the womb like glazed earthenware emerging from the kiln – any attempt at remoulding will only scratch or break them. Humans emerge from the womb like molten glass from a furnace. They can be spun, stretched, and shaped with a surprising degree of freedom. This is why today we can educate our children to become Christian or Buddhist, capitalist or socialist, warlike or peaceful.

There's a lot of argument over Nature versus Nurture when it comes to discussing the different roles of women and men. I think it's really fairly straightforward. They are both involved.

Nature gives us needs. Nurture gives us the means of acquiring them. Here's a simple example. Nature tells us we are hungry when our bodies need sustenance. Nurture and culture and custom and belief teach us, or more often dictate, when we can eat, what we can eat, who will catch it, gather it, grow or breed it, or buy it, who will prepare it, how it will be prepared, what implements we will use to eat it, who we will eat it with, who will clean up the mess afterwards and who will swan off and relax with a full stomach.

We glibly speak of "human nature" as if it were universal to all of us, unchanging and predictable. Not so, the relatively new neuroscience demonstrates that our brains are moulded by our experiences; they are not set at birth. This neuroplasticity allows the brain to change and adapt. Apart from some survival techniques, based in our lizard brain, there is no universal nature. Thankfully, there is so much more to our brain than the primitive part. I mentioned the Cognitive Revolution in Chapter 2. You may recall that around 70,000 years ago, we developed imagination, the capacity to think of things that didn't exist and believe them to be real. That developing part of our brain also allows us to think, imagine and make decisions on so much more than fear or prejudice or bias or imaginary evil in others.

We have to learn how to be human, and it is the accident of our birth involving place, era, culture, including belief systems and social status, and our experiences of life, intertwined with genetic potential, that will shape the human we will become. None of us is identical. None of us is possessed of a universal human nature. We have basic needs that require fulfilment. But we determine how or even if they can be fulfilled. More on this in Chapter 13: Does it Really Matter? (Let Me Count the Ways.)

Looking around, we see many different skills that individual humans have. Some are good cooks, some are great sculptors or singers, others help and heal, some teach and inspire. While we recognise some people, if not all, have inborn talent, we do not have talents that are uniform for all humans. We are all different. There is little that is naturally common to all of us when we are born. Fear of falling, fear of loud noises and the ability to suck are among the few we are born with – but very little else. If this were not true, people would not vary in their beliefs, and the behaviours based on those beliefs, across different societies, cultures, and religions.

We accept the culturally embedded gender stereotypes that have been handed to us. We are taught from childhood to conform to them. Before the age of seven, we have very little choice. Our brains work against us. In later life, you will see women and men conforming to stereotype and teaching their daughters and sons to do the same.

The bottom line, at least in early childhood, is that most of us tend to imitate the same-sex parent. Unless our parents are non-conformists, we will probably get our first lessons in gendered behaviour at home. And this is where the initial solution lies.

But, and this is a big "but", we have a fairly strict Taboo of Sameness. The two genders have specific characteristics assigned to their performance and never the twain shall meet. We get pretty twitchy when a member of one sex starts presenting the characteristics of the other. When a man behaves with confidence, expresses opinions, has new ideas, takes a leadership role, he gains praise, promotion, power, higher pay, admiration, and sexual partners. Women behaving in the same way are often seen to be bitchy, bossy, hard, unlikable, and unlovable. It's the old Catch 22 for women. Damned if you do and damned if you don't. But it happens to boys too. When a boy begins to show an interest in ballet, his father and probably his grandfathers are likely to be decidedly twitchy and not always particularly supportive. Taking up knitting, well, just don't let the neighbours see.

Full marks to the men who support their sons and grandsons in gender non-conformity. And to the men who support their wives and daughters to branch out of the constrictions of the feminine stereotype. We need more of you.

Each of us has qualities and talents and interests across the spectrum of human possibilities, regardless of sex, gender, colour, ethnicity, religion, or any other category. We are, on the whole, taught, encouraged, or even coerced to develop and perform only those deemed appropriate to our gender in our culture. We are moulded to be as similar as possible in our gender performance: males to be masculine, females to be feminine. The giant powerful cookie cutter of culture shapes us in an attempt to ensure that we all come out just the same. There are pink ones, and blue ones... as Malvina Reynolds wrote in her 1962 song about suburbia, made famous by Pete Seeger a year later.

Throughout this book, I am speaking about the stereotypical gendered behaviours expected of us based on our biological sex. I want to be clear here that I am not saying that women should stop being feminine or men should stop being masculine. All of those behaviours are human, and like Samson with the pillars of the temple as you'll see in Figure 6, we have pushed them in different directions with tragic consequences.

What I am saying is that all humans should have access to all human possibilities.

It is wildly illogical to praise behaviour in one group of people and condemn the same behaviour in another group. Behaviour should be judged by its outcomes not by the biology of the performer. Behaviour should be judged by it its results. Is it helpful or harmful?

If women want to wear makeup, that is their right but not their obligation. If men want to wear makeup, that should equally be their right. In past cultures, powerful men have worn makeup, grown their hair long, worn high heels, lace, and bright colours. It did not hinder their ability to lead battles, explore unknown lands, invent wondrous cures or machines. And it did not prevent them from siring children.

If a woman is permitted to do or be or have something, then men should equally be permitted those things. And likewise, if men can do or be or have something, women should also have the right to those things. Neither should be obligated to do or be or have anything. Especially the high heels. As Roxanne Gay astutely commented: they are designed to slow you down. But the choice to wear or not to wear, should be yours, man or woman. We don't have to all come out just the same as Malvina Reynolds sang nearly sixty years ago.

Figure 5: Breaking Free: From the Cookie Cutter
©Veronica Schwarz 2020

Right now, instead of seeing each person as human, individual and unique, we teach them to conform. And, sadly, that's very easy.

Most humans have a strong desire to conform in order to be accepted. Belonging to a family or a tribe was essential to survival in the early days of human development. To be rejected or cast out meant death. Conformity was a survival technique.

We belong to a group because of some external similarities such as sex, or because of accidents of birth such as ethnic, national or religious groupings. All other people who are seen as different, do not belong to "our group".

Grouping or categorising people or things leads to comparison and inevitably to value judgements. As with Racism and other categories of prejudice, identifying difference leads to evaluation. Evaluation frequently results in the belief that one's own group is "better" or "superior".

This is done in the case of males and females, first by labelling them according to their genitals, and then by assigning "opposite" characteristics to them regardless of individual talent or interest. The outcome is rigged. Allocate the powerful, strong, admirable, leadership characteristics to males and gentle, nurturing, compliant characteristics to females, then teach them from birth or force them to conform. Yep, there I've said it. It's rigged. The outcome is pre-determined – not by natural differences because those that exist are not sufficient, and those that could lead to independence and agency are naturally distributed across both sexes. The outcome is rigged to ensure "men on top".

But even that is not enough. Males performing "feminine" characteristics must be ridiculed, labelled homosexual, sissy, effeminate or punished, even murdered. They are despised and even hated and often cruelly persecuted. Such men are breaking ranks in not maintaining the masculine power structure.

Females performing "masculine" characteristics must be labelled "bitchy, bossy, unnatural, unattractive" and ridiculed or punished. And no man will ever want them. Or so they are told.

It's a twisted process. First select human characteristics present across all humans and divide them into two types – those that involve action, independence, confidence, assertion, and agency in the wider world, and those that involve nurturing, caring, compromising, self-denial and attention to daily requirements to keep the family and community in harmony. This is not an exhaustive list but gives you an idea of the process. It also varies across time and across cultures.

Second, label the former constellation "masculine" and the latter "feminine", even though they are attributes found in both sexes. Then declare them "natural", "god-given" attributes of males and females. Look for the appropriate behaviour as soon as the child is physically identified as male or female.

Thirdly, encourage the appropriate behaviour for the sex. Frown on it if it doesn't fit the requirements of the culture the child is born into. Play on parental fears, use the child's desire to fit in and need to be cared for, sanctify the plot with religion, develop laws to enforce it, use force, ridicule, punishment, ostracization and culturally sanctioned murder such as honour killings to enforce the required behaviour.

And voila – he's masculine and she's feminine – and they were made for each other. Societies then have a built-in domesticated class in the form of feminine women, and a deterrent to male homosexuality in the form of the masculine man.

This allocation of different expected behaviours to each sex, pretty much guarantees who is going to be in charge and who is going to provide the support staff.

Societies for thousands of years, have been structured on the myth that women are very different to men and that those differences prove their inferiority, and justify their subordination.

Women were told their brains were not designed for deep or reasoned thought because they were smaller than men's. What then are we to make of the fact that Bottlenose dolphins (Tursiops truncatus) have an absolute brain mass of 1,500–1,700 grams? This is slightly greater than that of humans (1,300–1,400 grams) and about four times that of chimpanzees (400 grams). Women were also told that too much reading, learning, or use of the brain would stunt the child-bearing capacity. Shrivel the uterus. Grow fungus on the ovaries. No, I am not making this up. Women were also told they needed men to protect them and look after them as they were not fully mature human beings like men.

Most experts in the field agree that there are little to no sex differences in the average level of intelligence (Nisbett et al., 2012) However, men tend to overestimate their intelligence while women underestimate theirs. And many men consider themselves more intelligent than women regardless of their own level of intelligence.

The phenomenon of "mansplaining" demonstrates how most men believe they always know more than any woman on almost any topic. The term is applied to a man explaining something to a woman without first finding out if the woman actually knows anything about it. I personally would be fairly wealthy if I had a dollar for each time a man has done this to me. And most of my friends tell the same story. The classic example was of a man explaining a book to Rebecca Solnit who was actually the author of the book he was explaining. Someone else finally enlightened him. The author herself had been unable to get a word in to tell him this. The irony of it was the book's title is *Men Explain Things to Me*.

My own unforgettable experience of this occurred like this: I was having a conversation with a fellow camper and, as I had just arrived in the area, I asked him what local sights to see in that outback town. He was suggesting I visit a site near the local lake where the indigenous people had camped for centuries; still today, the remains of the feasts could be seen in the packed sand. "Oh, a midden," I said. A local man was standing by listening in, and he promptly interrupted our conversation. Turning to me, he said, "It's called a midden." I thought perhaps he hadn't heard me, so I replied, "Yes, that's what I said. A midden." He looked at me disbelievingly, and asked, "Do you know what a midden is?" "Yes, that's why I used the word," I said. To my amazement, he persisted. "You really know what a midden is?" At that point, I turned back to the man I had been talking to, and he continued to tell me the local must-see sites.

Yes, it's trivial, but so much of it is. Remember the tiny threads that tied down Ms Gulliver. Or the tiny grains of sand that, with enough of them, can bury a city. Each act is tiny but, day in day out, we are subjected to them. As one woman said to me, it undermines your sense of worth, and after a while you begin to doubt yourself. In a domestic situation, this behaviour is now considered subtle abuse and a form of control. But it happens everywhere, all the time.

It is the trivial things, the things we say are "not so bad" that are all the more dangerous and insidious for that reason. One ant doesn't ruin a picnic but try setting up your sandwiches on an anthill.

Why do so many men think women are incapable of intelligent thought or acquiring useful or interesting knowledge? To be fair, some women do talk drivel, but then so do some men. Guys, stop and listen for a change. And if all you hear is still drivel, it's time to widen your social circle and mix with a few more women who are more interesting to talk to. They are out there.

Even today, research also continues to try proving there is a difference in female brains and male brains. They never give up it seems. The truth is brains are different. There are some differences between the sexes. But what is labelled as a feminine brain, can be found in both males and females. The so-called masculine brain can also be found in males and females.

It's a bit like the way we label bits of plumbing, or electrical plugs, one part that fits into another part, as "male" and "female". We do this because they complement each other and fit together as do the female and male bodies in sexual inter-course. Similarly, we have labelled attributes of the human brain in ways that fit our stereotypical allocation of attributes to males and females, and some media have subsequently trumpeted the welcome information that the brain is gendered.

With these gendered differences firmly in place, and most of the population unconsciously conforming, the stage is set. By valuing some human characteristics more highly than others and labelling highly valued characteristics as "masculine", we are then able to value males more highly than females. Big prob-lem. Note, the allocation of high status is usually given to males, rather than to a person who has the desired charac-teristics.

If a female possesses the required valued characteristics, you would think that would confer distinction and reward on her. Oh dear, no. She is rarely rewarded, admired, or promoted. Rather she is seen in a negative light, and she is not valued. As mentioned before, she is seen as bossy, bitchy, or uncaring when she performs the same behaviour and language patterns that bring a man respect and admiration. As a result of this deviation from the expected, she is often disliked by both men and women.

Women and girls have known for decades that they must down-play their intelligence or knowledge so as not to frighten off the men. The story is that such women are to be pitied because they are "unfeminine". In the past, they were labelled "spinsters" because they couldn't get a man. They were labelled "blue stockings" as a term of derision for an intellectual woman. When I was growing up, the women's magazines were full of "helpful" advice on how to get and keep your man. They always included hiding your intelligence, massaging his ego, and being pleasing in every way possible.

The Taboo of Sameness rode roughshod over any inborn interest or talent. Play the game. Get the man. Even today, many men still don't like smart women. On the other hand, many young women are refusing to play the game. And quite a few older women have seen enough to know it just ain't right. So, yet there is hope.

7

The Taboo of Sameness
(NOT LIKE A GIRL!)

Far from being an expression of natural differences, exclusive gender identity is the suppression of natural similarities. It requires repression: in men, of whatever is the local version of "feminine" traits; in women, (the repression) of the local definition of "masculine" traits.

Gayle Rubin, 1975

THE CONCEPT of the Taboo of Sameness was introduced by cultural anthropologist, Gayle Rubin. It had been staring us in the face since Biblical times. Deuteronomy 22:5 tells us: *A woman must not wear men's clothing, and a man must not wear women's clothing, for whoever does these things is detestable to the LORD your God.*

Strong words. But the push to ensure the sexes were never to be similar, goes much further than clothing or cross-dressing. A large section of masculinity could almost be defined as never doing anything like a girl. And it is quite clear that doing anything like a girl shows a man to be weak, inferior, and effeminate.

This gender push is a bit like the blind Samson pushing the two pillars of the temple apart. The Philistines, having captured and blinded Samson, brought him into their temple for their entertainment. Hundreds of them gathered to taunt their enemy. Samson asked the guards to place his hands on the pillars of the temple to steady himself. Then, with one hand on one pillar and the other hand on another, with all his returning strength, he pushed the pillars apart, and the temple collapsed on top of the crowd. He killed more with his own death than he had when he was alive.

In my illustration below, Samson, playing the role of culture and society, demonstrates the Taboo of Sameness as he pushes the pillars of male and female apart, each towards their designated gender role:

Figure 6: Samson and the Pillars of Gender - The Taboo
of Sameness. © Veronica Schwarz

Males and females are the two necessary and equal pillars maintaining societies. Push them apart and you destroy the balance and the strength that both contribute. We have created "opposites" with only one half in control, and that half has been robbed of much of its potential to be fully human. As we shall see later, destroying the equal strength and contribution to society of males and females is, particularly today, detrimental to health, prosperity, and the entire planet. You can't get much more destructive than that.

The Taboo of Sameness brings us to the heart of the gender myths. It tells us that male and female must be different from each other. Hence the mantra for masculinity: never do anything like a girl. The two sexes must perform differently, look different and meet different expectations. Not just different. Opposites. The opposite gender: masculine and feminine. This allows us to enhance and romanticize the male/female bond with tales of soulmates of the opposite sex and finding "the one who completes us". And, of course, we all know, opposites attract.

Here's an interesting piece of history.

Most people in Western societies have heard of Joan of Arc, and any picture of a woman in armour on a horse is usually Joan, or La Pucelle (Maid or Virgin in English) as she called herself. Most people also know she was burnt at the stake. Why was she burnt? Well, she did have the audacity to lead the French army to defeat the English, in the Hundred Years War. This was the first time the French had defeated the English in an embarrass-ingly long time. As you can imagine, the English were more than a little upset at being beaten by a girl. They used to scream insults at her from behind their barricades. The terms they used sound remarkably familiar. Yes, they called her "slut", "whore", and similar derogatory sexual terms. This, in spite of the king and the priests having her examined numerous times to try – unsuccessfully - to prove she wasn't a virgin. Nothing much has changed today. Rejected, angry men still scream those very words at women.

But most people will tell you she was burnt as a witch. Yes, the trial judges tried the witch theory, but they couldn't make it stick. So, they turned to the charge of heresy because she insisted on obeying angels instead of priests. But that one was hard to prove too because the wretched girl was so devout.

And then they found the solution. During her time serving the Dauphin of France, she wore men's clothing. Practical I would think. In the beginning of her journey, her companions suggested male clothing as a disguise while she was travelling across war-torn France. She was riding a horse, fighting battles, raising sieges. I'd like to see any man try doing that in a long skirt. Not even Braveheart would give it a go.

When questioned by her judges about it, she explained the practicality, the need to avoid rape and to avoid arousing sexual desire in any of the thousands of soldiers she slept side by side with on the battle fields. We know her male garments had been fitted with twice the normal amount of lacing to make it difficult for anyone to undo them.

She had returned to wearing female clothing while in prison in accordance with biblical requirements. While she was asleep in her prison cell, they removed her clothing from beside her bed and left male clothing in its place. When she awoke in the morning, she saw what they had done and begged the guards to return her dress. Finally, she had no choice but to put on the male clothes. Snap. The trap was closed. She had reverted to her old ways and was therefore a relapsed heretic.

They dragged her out and burnt her, cruelly, so high the executioner could not strangle her first as was the "merciful" custom. When she was finally dead, the executioner raked back the fire so the 10,000 spectators could see her naked body and see for themselves that she was a woman. Many people did not believe that a woman could do the things she had done. Then he stoked the fire back up again and let it completely consume the body. She was only nineteen.

The Taboo of Sameness is powerful indeed. Having the two sexes different also makes it unambiguous when rights and responsibilities, privilege and power are being handed out as we grow to adulthood.

But across cultures, we have seen that what is masculine or feminine is not consistent. In some cultures, it is acceptable for heterosexual men to walk down the street holding hands. In other cultures, it is unacceptable for men to cry. Anglo-Saxon culture is particularly strong on this one!

We can also see that rigid gender roles can be quite malleable when it is expedient. In times of war with men away fighting, jobs which had previously been declared beyond the competence of women, were magically suddenly okay for women to do. And do them they did. Very well too. But, on the return of the men, the women were pushed back into the homemaker role, and women's magazines went into overdrive to convince them that wife, mother, and homemaker were their appropriate and most fulfilling roles. Many of those magazines are still today playing to the stereotype of what women are expected to be interested in and should be doing. Magazines aimed at young and not so young women still mostly emphasis family, food and fashion, or beauty and boyfriends.

The beliefs about what women couldn't do bordered on the ridiculous. Here's an example. In 1973, I took up taxi driving to pay my way through university as a "mature-age student "in Melbourne, Australia. At that time, the State law had deemed that only men could be taxi drivers A shortage of taxi drivers led to an expedient change of the law which removed the sex barrier for drivers. Six women, in the entire State of Victoria took up the job, including me. I loved it. I love driving and I enjoy talking to people. What's not to love. However, at the time, it was considered unusual if not impossible, for any woman to fill up a petrol tank. No, I am not making this up. "Real women don't pump gas."

As a taxi driver, I obviously had to fill my own petrol tank. On my first day, in the middle of winter, I drove into the taxi depot where the petrol pumps were, and all the male drivers came over and lined up to watch me, laughing and joking amongst themselves. To their amazement, I did fill the tank successfully. They looked me up and down in my navy-blue taxi driver uniform, including long trousers, and one of them said, "Oh well, come Summer, we'll see if she's got good legs," and they all walked away.

Almost every society on earth believes males to be superior to females in every way except apart from child-raising and domestic tasks. This results in males being valued more than females. In several cultures, female foetuses are still aborted, or female babies are killed at birth. Most societies pass inheritance through the male children no matter how many female siblings they might have. If you're feeling smug because these things don't happen in your culture or society, don't forget that valuing males more than females, while less physically abhorrent than infanticide, is starkly demonstrated by the gender pay gap: unequal pay for equal work. Pay the boys more than the girls in professions, in entertainment, in sport. Even prize money still varies between the sexes although change is occurring.

With this process of "masculine" and "feminine" characteristics being allocated to each of us appropriately, and value and status applied accordingly, we have carefully and deliberately built a sexist society that appears perfectly "natural". The boys are in charge and it's God's will. Suck it up, Princess.

No one is ever born with sexist beliefs or any other beliefs for that matter. No one is born knowing how they should look, behave, or speak. They learn these from the people around them.

As we saw, when a child is born, and its sex announced, parents, family, friends, and neighbours start looking for and remarking on the expected differences.

Not all children are born with genitals that make a declaration of sex possible. This confuses almost everybody involved. What do you mean, you don't know what sex it is? Changes are made surgically. Or decisions are made for the child, and it is given a sex label anyway. We don't like uncertainty, and we especially don't like it when it comes to sex or gender. Having given a child one of the two acceptable labels – male or female – we then move on to reinforcing the label and instilling the correct gendered behaviour.

I have mentioned the toys and books most children receive, and the clothes children wear. Look at the way their hair is done, even before they have much hair. Watch the different ways adults speak to little boys and little girls and what they talk to them about.

Pity the little boy who chooses to play with a doll - unless it's called an action figure. He'll be whisked outside and handed a football so fast it will make his head spin. People won't get quite so upset (just yet) if girls choose to play with "boys' toys".

Meanwhile, out there in the garden, street or park, the little boy is learning a few more lessons. With his bat or his ball, he'll pretty soon learn he must not "throw like a girl, hit like a girl or run like a girl". And he definitely must not "cry like a girl".

What do you think this is teaching him about girls? And in later years, about women? Is it respect? Is it admiration? I suggest he's learning that what boys do and the way they do it, is superior to what girls do and the way girls behave. They won't say it aloud, but the inference is there. He's learning that females are different, and those differences make them inferior to males.

Here's an interesting story: When cricket was first played, bowling was underarm. An English cricketer, John Willes, is credited with being the originator or reviver of "round arm" bowling in the nineteenth century. He was practising cricket at home with his sister Kristina. She was filling in as bowler. Kristina threw the ball over-arm to avoid getting tangled in her long skirt. Willes realised this was an improvement and used the method in a match. He was promptly penalized. The method was banned, and Willes quit the game in frustration. Over-arm bowling was finally accepted and legalised by 1835. To be fair, men have added a lot of energy, speed, and strength to bowling since then. As have their female counterparts in women's cricket. The women also dress more sensibly these days. But those boys are still throwing like a girl. And it's an improvement!

Entire societies are structured on the cultural compliance of women to fulfil the caring, nurturing, serving roles for the rest of humanity. If all else remained the same, societies in their current form would collapse if women refused to accept their designated place. No wonder there is such resistance to women's equality.

It's possible that the world would be a gentler more peaceful place, if men refused to accept the rigid masculine role imposed on them too. Many of the disadvantages that groups such as Men's Rights Activists complain of, can be traced back to the sexist prejudices towards women. Much of male suicide can be linked to the repression within men of all things "feminine", and the rigid "masculine" expectations imposed on them. Despair, a sense of inadequacy and overwhelming "masculine" requirements, no doubt leave many men with a sense of hope-lessness.

For women, "gaslighting" is a tool used by many societies to keep them in their place. They are told that men are there to protect and support them. Women are repeatedly told they perform the most important work in the world. They give birth to and raise the next generation. If it really were considered the most important job in the world, it would be highly paid, highly applauded and acknowledged, bring considerable power, and probably men would be doing it.

Around the world, women perform their allotted role for free. They rarely have power or wealth, certainly not from motherhood. Their lives are governed by rules made by men. Their sons are taken from them to fight the wars usually decreed by powerful men. They are frequently powerless to save their daughters from the predatory or abusive behaviour of sexist or misogynist men including those men closest to them. They work and serve all their lives. There is no retirement from their tasks. No great reward for a job well done. For too many older women joining the ranks of the homeless, I think it was writer and journalist Jane Caro who summed it up, "Thanks for caring for everybody all your life. Now go live in your car.".

The rare women who are wealthy or powerful, have not achieved that status because of their fulfillment of the feminine role. They are the ones who have stepped out of that role and taken on roles usually assigned to men. Some may have used so-called feminine wiles in the process, but what a perfect camouflage. No one would see them coming. Duplicitous, yes. But when the cards are stacked against you, you use what you've got. And before you start naming powerful women to disprove the lack of women in power, remember most people can name or point to powerful women because, compared to powerful men, there are so few of them.

Women may hold up half the sky but down here on earth, the world operates on the backs of unpaid women. Their contribution is not even included in the sacred GDP of nations. Much of women's work is invisible because it is unpaid, or could it simply be because it is done by women?

Most men fulfilling the breadwinner role, would be unable to do that if they did not have a woman looking after their children and sick or elderly relatives, cooking, shopping, or gathering, washing, cleaning, organising the medical appointments and the family social calendar. All unpaid. The value of her work contributes to the value of his work, but hers is not counted. There are still men who consider that what they earn is their money, and she is only entitled to the amount he chooses to give her. They totally dismiss the unpaid contribution she has made to the family and his opportunity to earn money outside the home. The irony is that in any other context, this would be called slavery.

How has this been justified and maintained for thousands of years? The answer given over the centuries and still everywhere you turn is – because men and women are so different – and it's natural.

The story goes like this: Women are designed to have babies and look after the home. They are physically weaker than men and their brains are smaller than men's. Men are designed to be the hunters and warriors, providing the food, and protecting the territory. Males and females complete each other, two halves of a unit seeking its mate. Now that's romantic. It sounds good. Is it true? Or could it be the greatest case of gaslighting humans have ever pulled on one another?

And we're still living with it. I know. There'll be the usual protests that women have equality now but, if I'm doing my job correctly, you at least are beginning to see that perhaps that's not quite true. Men do still run the world, and they run it in their own interests, and I believe this is quite often unconscious because when most men think about people, they actually think about other men. Women are invisible except in their relationship to men. In addition, many male politicians, following the macho gender stereotype, are more interested in having the latest missile, than having the best health system in the world. Appearing strong is more important to them than being compassionate. Qualities associated with women are not seen as useful in running a country or a company.

The truth is, it is not that men rule the world but rather that men demonstrating "strong" masculine qualities run just about everything. They are often referred to as Alpha males, as though we were still a pack of primates thumping our chests and roaring our sense of superiority to the stars. But we are no longer those simple primates, and perhaps it's high time we grew up and realised that we are indeed amazing creatures capable of so much more than chest thumping and humiliating our competitors or sending young men into battle to grab more territory to boost the chief primate's ego.

We know that co-operation beats competition hands down in any effort at survival. And yet we continue to glorify competition. Nothing wrong with healthy competition, but we have misinterpreted Darwin's theory. It is not "survival of the fittest". It is survival of the most adaptable, the ones willing and able to change. The creatures who are able to adapt to changing circumstances are the survivors. Sadly, we have let the Alpha boys run our lives for a very long time, and our planet is teetering on the edge of catastrophe. There are men and women who can and have contributed greatly to our progress, our enlightenment, our health, and our joy. Unfortunately, they are not the ones who seize control or, when we have the option, they are not the ones we put in charge. Most of us, we the people, if we have a choice, still appear to want Big Daddy to look after us, to tell us what to do, to show strength and toughness when we think it's needed. Flexibility and the ability to change in the face of further information are not seen as leadership qualities, but rather are labelled weakness. Confrontation and winning rule the day. Good "masculine" qualities apparently. Women who do gain power are seen as weak if they do not demonstrate these qualities and, if they do perform with these "masculine" qualities, they are often judged totally unlikable, and an unnatural abomination.

The glimmer of light is there, however. Some countries have elected leaders who have compassion, caring, intelligence and a vision that involves their citizens' well-being. At the time of writing, in New Zealand, Jacinda Adern has gained the admiration of many people around the world with her acts of compassion, strength (no chest thumping involved) action, and care for New Zealanders. Justin Trudeau of Canada is another light shining in the political darkness. Many of the rest of them could be seen as a disgrace to humanity. And yet we go on supporting and electing them.

Why am I going on about world politics when I said this book is primarily about women? Partly because we tend to see those things that appear to relate only to women as "women's issues", secondary and limited. Anything relating to half the human population cannot be relegated to a sealed off compartment which does not involve "the rest" of the human race. World politics very much affects women, and women can and must be involved in world politics. There are women who are highly suitable and willing, but the barriers of bias and the perception of needing a "man" for the job, have kept many of them out of the job. And the disgusting treatment many of their fellow male politicians heap upon them makes the likelihood of their remaining in politics problematic.

The other reason for discussing world politics in the context of "women's issues" lies in the type of human characteristics that we choose to hand power, status, and reward to. Those Alpha masculine qualities have been running human affairs for several thousand years now, and even many men admit it's been a bloody mess.

This is not a call to let women run the world. They're not all saints either. It is a call to change our attitudes to masculine and feminine characteristics. This would require valuing more highly many of the characteristics currently labelled "feminine". And, secondly, seeing them as human characteristics, possible of expression by almost all humans, female and male.

The cornucopia of human possibilities for the most part lies untapped. If we drew together the best human characteristics to teach our children regardless of their physical sex, we would finally have a human race worthy of living on this planet. Far from making everyone the same, removing the Taboo of Sameness would unleash a myriad of different human beings, vital and life-loving as they realise their potential and put it to work for their own growth, the benefit of others and a harmonious relationship with the planet.

8

Stay as Sweet as You Are.
(FEMALE IS A FACT. FEMININE IS AN ACT.)

I myself have never been able to find out precisely what Feminism is. I only know that people call me a feminist whenever I express sentiments that differentiate me from a doormat or a prostitute.

Rebecca West, British author and journalist

In order to please others, we lose our hold on our life's purpose.

Epictetus

Women are the only exploited group in history to have been idealized into powerlessness.

(Erica Jong)

LET'S have a closer look at the Western version of what a woman should be.

Over the centuries, quite a few books were written by men telling women how to behave. They quite openly stated that the most desirable behaviours for women were designed with the sole object of being pleasing to men and of useful service to them.

Virginia Woolf summed it up in her book *A Room of One's Own* when she wrote:

Women have served all these centuries as looking-glasses possessing the magic and delicious power of reflecting the figure of man at twice its natural size.

In the twentieth century, the popular women's magazines took up the task of telling women how to behave to be pleasing to men. One of the key pieces of advice was to hide your intelligence and to focus only on making "him" feel good. This advice is still handed out on certain dating websites and workshops. And is part of the creed of the Red Pill Men.

In more recent times, some women have taken up writing these types of books. It's hard to understand a woman who wants other women to behave like doormats. The Red Pill men consider it Woman's natural state, and there are women who agree with it. They call themselves Red Pill women, and you'll find them on the Internet begging to be told how to please their man.

In Chapter 1: Maid or Made, we began to touch on the marvellous way in which the genders are created. It could be summed up as: A man's gotta be a man but a woman's gotta be – a lady. Now what's that all about? It's like he's gotta be – what – himself? But she's gotta be something else.

She's got to be a lady! And definitely "feminine". At least in Western culture. And particularly in some social classes. We all have an idea of what feminine looks like and we certainly recognise it when a woman is not feminine. Other cultures have different ways of requiring women to behave, but all of them attempt to control females, physically, intellectually, and sexually. Women's expected roles not only prevent most of them from having agency outside the home sphere, but also cunningly prevent them from wanting it.

Controlling women's ability to have agency or power outside the home is achieved in a number of ways:

- physically, through restrictive clothing, particularly shoes and tight garments, discouragement from developing muscles, constantly policing of appearance, and expectations of ways of moving and speaking or preferably, not speaking at all.
- sexually, through shaming, blaming, and focussing on male pleasure to the exclusion of the female's, or even acknowledging the female's capacity for pleasure,
- intellectually, through education or prevention of it, encouragement of appropriate "feminine" interests through toys and books and magazines,
- spatially, in public places, through fear of harassment or violence,
- Timewise, through the allocation of most of the caring, social, family and people- oriented activities performed for free (the second shift).

If you're an adult human female, you're a woman. That's a fact. If you're a lady, that is not solely a fact; that's a value judgement of your behaviour based on society's expectations of you.

Interestingly, the word "lady" was originally the female version of "lord" as in lords and ladies of the court. It was used as a form of address as in "Good morning, my Lady". It referred to aristocrats and royalty. Every other adult human female was a woman, but quite a few customs of the upper class have been taken on by the rest of modern society, particularly in the middle class.

Nowadays, "act like a lady" has morphed into "femininity" and "being feminine" with a touch more sexual allure. Note the word "act" in "act like a lady". It's the clue. It's a performance not an inbuilt characteristic.

Culture and Femininity

Societies, cultures, and religions went to considerable lengths for thousands of years to control women and keep them in the power of men. Perhaps one of Man's greatest achievements is the "domestication" of Woman. As we have seen, it was achieved through a range of constraints. But it is not just men who have enforced the subordination of women. Many women have been the conveyors and coaches in this control of genera-tions of women through teaching their daughters to conform to their culture's expectations, as well as raising their sons differ-ently by teaching them to conform to whatever the current version of masculinity happened to be.

Femininity was the constellation of characteristics required to survive in a society where you were totally in the control of men; your comfort, happiness, and even life were dependent on your pleasing them.

The expected characteristics of the feminine personality are to be affectionate, cheerful, compassionate, not using harsh language, not saying much at all actually, eager to soothe hurt feelings, easily flattered, gentle, loving children, loyal, sensitive to the needs of others, shy, soft spoken, sympathetic, tender, understanding, warm, yielding, modest, controlled in physical movement. There is also an expectation that women are emotional, cry when sad or distressed, and are prone to hysteria, and panic in a crisis.

I can't stand watching those actresses in movies cowering in a corner screaming uselessly while the hero is left to deal with the villains. I can just hear the director saying to her, "Louder! More! Keep screaming". Puhleeeese. I just want to yell at her, "Damn it, woman, pick up a brick and help the guy!" But she wouldn't be feminine then, would she? And his masculinity and ego would probably be dealt a severe blow – more harmful than the brick on the skull of the villain. The movies that do break this stereotype are a rare breath of fresh air. Watching a man and woman team up to achieve something as equals, is a great joy to behold.

Traits the feminine woman definitely must turn off include being aggressive, dominant, forceful, independent, individualistic, self-reliant, self-sufficient, and any signs of a strong personality.

Even the word "woman" still gives the impression of coarseness to many people, and they shy away from calling a woman, a woman. They prefer to use the term "lady" or "ladies". Or even "girls".

One interesting example of this shying away from the use of the word "woman" can be seen in the discovery of the oldest human skeletons in Australia.

In 1968, geologist Jim Bowler discovered the bones of a human female around the now-dry Lake Mungo in south-western New South Wales, and subsequently discovered that she had been cremated and ritually buried. Even more startling, her skeleton was one of the earliest anatomically modern human remains discovered anywhere in the world – 40,000 to 42,000 years old.

Then in 1974, continuing his search, Jim Bowler found the remains of a male skeleton older than the female - 35,000 years older than the prophet Abraham.

The male skeleton is known as Mungo Man. But the female is not Mungo Woman. These days, she is labelled Mungo Lady.

The word "woman" is more frequently used as a putdown. For example, "woman driver", "stupid woman", "silly woman", "Listen, woman". On the other hand, calling a male, however young, a "man" or even calling a boy a "little man", is a positive expression, even a term of praise.

However, being feminine requires a lot of work and spending a lot of money on the multitude of products offered to ensure we remain "feminine". Some women are very proud to be labelled "high maintenance" which plays into the hands of the profit motive of big business driving the gender role rigidity.

"Gender", as Cecilia L. Ridgeway put it in her book *Framed by Gender*, "is more than a trait of individuals, [it's] an institution-alized system of social practices."

Silencing Women

Research shows that when a woman talks one-third as much as a man in mixed gender settings, both men and women perceive her to be talking too much. Some women really talk too much and so do some men. Remember, men and women are not really very different in most of their characteristics.

But we often hear the stereotypes about women who talk more and too much. Most people find it hard to believe that men dominate speech, speaking up to 75% of the time in mixed gender deliberative groups and very few people, male or female, notice. A woman speaking for that length of time, would have been interrupted long before she got that far.

History also records the many ways men have tried to silence women in public for more than two thousand years. In her manifesto, *Woman and Power*, Professor Mary Beard, examines the consistent efforts of men to silence women in the Greek and Roman worlds, the major basis of Western Culture. One charming method of preventing a woman reporting her own rape was to cut her tongue out. Preventing women from speaking in public is attributed to St Paul in the Christian Bible and is evident in reactions to the Suffragettes when they fought for a voice in Parliament through the vote. Processes may have changed, but the intent to silence women is still there, even if it is less obvious or at a subconscious level.

I have heard men shouting in parliament for as long as I can remember. It seems the norm for parliamentary debate. One day, in 2018, I was listening to the broadcast of a session of the Australian parliament. On this particular day, a female member of parliament was addressing the House. She was quite passionate, and her voice was raised. Personally, I wouldn't have called it shouting, but it was close. To my astonishment, the Speaker of the House interrupted her with the words, "May I remind the Honourable Member that her microphone is working." Almost everyone present laughed uproariously. Men shouting goes unremarked.

Women are also frequently interrupted more often than men, in parliaments, courtrooms, professional meetings, social gatherings and private conversations.

In February 2017, Senator Elizabeth Warren, while quoting the words of Coretta Scott King as part of her speech in the United States Senate, was silenced on a technicality by a vote along party lines. Later, two male Senators read the same letter into their speeches without interruption. The historic words of justification in silencing her, "She was warned. She was given an explanation. Nevertheless, she persisted", went viral on the internet. "Nevertheless, she persisted" became a feminist battle cry – for a short while.

Not only have men tried to silence women, but it's a commonly observed phenomenon that men don't listen to women or, for the most part, do not consider women worth talking to. I know, there are men out there who are not like that, but I'm betting many women reading this can identify with it. It is totally evident at social occasions when the men gather together and talk to each other. It used to be quite an inbuilt process in the upper classes for men to withdraw after dinner for port, cigars, and manly chat. It hasn't changed much. Watch a man enter a room where the majority of people are women. You'll see him look around until he spots a man or group of men, and head straight for them. The sex division at an Australian BBQ or party is a standing joke: the men around the keg of beer or the BBQ, the women in the kitchen.

My husband and I once tried to put a tiny dint in this practice. He went and talked to the women, and I went over and talked to the men. It didn't help or change anything. Everyone thought I was a flirt, and he was a "poofter".

It seems the women have nothing to say that is worth listening to. Or are men afraid? And if so, of what?

In her article, "Are you a Man-Talker", author Kasey Edwards highlights a fact of life that many women regularly experience. The man who ignores the woman and speaks to the man, even when she is the one asking the questions, or even the one who will be paying the bill. He ignores her and addresses his responses to the man. This even occurs in interview panels, when a female panellist asks a question of the male job applicant, he will frequently address his response to the male panellists. It's as though the women are invisible.

Women really begin to feel invisible in meetings of colleagues. Many are familiar with being ignored by the person chairing the meeting. There is also the experience of putting forward a suggestion or idea only to have it ignored or rejected. Then ten minutes later, a man will put forward exactly the same idea and is greeted with acceptance, praise and appreciation. The first time you experience this, you'll think you were imagining it, it was just an accident. But looking beyond the individual experience to the experiences of others and research done on the topic, you find it is quite a pattern and happens all the time.

This is true of almost all Sexism. Its power lies in its invisibility because it's so all-pervasive. Says the fish, "What's water?"

But there's more.

Anger

Anger is one of the few emotions publicly acceptable for men. They are almost invariably shown in movies and TV series as showing anger through physical violence. They smash a fist into the wall or throw over the furniture or knock everything off the table or desk. Frequently, it culminates in hitting someone else. Not your best image of a role model for little boys watching.

In contrast, women must deny anger, bury it, block it, hide it, ignore it, or medicate it. To express it or act on it, is unfeminine. Some men even seem to fear angry women. It does not take much for men to perceive an assertive woman as being overly aggressive. A woman does not have to get very stroppy to be told to "Calm down, dear" or "You're over-reacting". As one writer put it, "Have you noticed that the people who tell you to calm down are usually the ones who pissed you off in the first place?".

In the 1970s and 1980s, the socialisation process, the ways we are taught our gendered behaviour, was discussed, researched and awareness was at an all-time high, much higher than now in some circles. Books were written and courses were run on the topic of helping women become aware of socialisation processes and to break free of the constraints of submissive femininity. Some men too were becoming aware of the prison of their own gendered expectations and behaviour.

During that time, I designed and conducted classes for women at various adult education centres in Victoria, Australia. While designing those courses, I read a little story about two gentlemen dining on the balcony of an elegant restaurant over-looking the Mediterranean Sea. They had finished their meal and were enjoying a couple of glasses of port while discussing the politics of the day. As the moon rose full and brilliant over the darkening sea, a small black beetle appeared over the edge of the table. It began to march confidently across the crisp white tablecloth as both men looked on. Smiling at his friend, one of the men took a pen from his coat pocket and carefully drew a large black circle around the beetle. The beetle continued to march forward till it came to the black line. It stopped, paused, backed away and marched in a different direction. Again, it came to the black line and stopped, paused, backed away, and tried a different direction. Again and again, the little insect came to the black line and could go no further. Its movements became more and more frantic until it finally gave up and lay on its back in the centre of the circle, all six legs in the air, totally defeated. The two men watched in amazement, unable to make any sense of it.

When I read this story, I was struck by the similarity between the beetle's dilemma and the invisible barriers that keep most of us, male and female, within the circle of society's expectations of us. We are held in place by a variety of things, many of which are invisible or even non-existent. For women, there appear to be many reasons we behave in a ladylike or feminine way but there is a common underlying fear hidden beneath them all.

Some examples are:

- I won't show my anger even though it's justified because they'll think I'm shrill, aggressive, emotional, or hysterical – and they won't like me.
- Even though I have more experience in this area than anyone else involved, I won't take charge because they'll think I'm bossy – and they won't like me.
- If I do what I really want to do instead of what they want me to do, they'll think I'm selfish and uncaring – and they won't like me.
- I can't say "no" to doing something that someone asks me to do for them, because they'll think I'm rude and selfish – and they won't like me.
- I can't say "no" to letting him kiss me because he'll think I'm a prude, or he'll feel rejected, or his feelings will be hurt – and he won't like me.
- I can't not go to the movies with them because they'll think I'm stand-offish – and they won't like me.
- I can't say "no" to helping with the fund raiser because they'll think I'm mean and self-centred and unco-operative -- and they won't like me.
- If I stand up for myself or my opinions, they'll think I'm rude and aggressive – and they won't like me.

Do you see the common thread that underpins them all?

In researching and designing those courses for women, I came up time and time again with the observation that being likable and pleasing everybody was one of the constraints placed on women. With many of the things women would not assert themselves over, it came down to the fact that the fundamental fear was that people wouldn't like them.

In her book *Lean In*, Sheryl Sandberg tells how her boss Mark Zuckerberg once told her that her need to be liked would hold her back in her career. Sheryl Sandberg! Even she is infected with this damn "please-like-me" bug. And, I admit, so am I.

The assumptions leading to the conclusion that people won't like us are almost always the worse-case scenario. We ignore the possibility that people might actually respect us more or just move on and ask someone else without a second thought. But almost inevitably women assume the AND-THEY-WON'T-LIKE-ME scenario because it was one of our worst fears. The scenarios listed above are social situations obviously and do not touch on situations where retaliatory violence could be involved. We are looking at the invisible boundaries women put on their own behaviour in everyday social situations in order to please others. Women's compliance through threat of violence is not the issue being discussed here. What I am referring to is the totally invisible, non-tangible line which, like the beetle, we will not cross.

Having pondered the fate of the little black beetle, it occurred to me, since my classes were for women, to turn it into a ladybug or ladybird as we call them in Australia, those cute little beetles with red back and black spots. The final revelation came as I remembered that beetles can fly, a fact the poor little black beetle seemed to have forgotten, but I decided it was time that my ladybird flew. Why would or should a ladybird be confined by such barriers as a line on a tablecloth? She was born to fly. And so are women and men born to be the best that they can be with the talents they have, not confined by fear of not being liked or accepted.

If someone doesn't like us, we will not die. We will not feel excruciating physical pain. We may lose a friend or two but perhaps they didn't really care about us in the first place. In this day and age, the rejection of the "tribe" will not kill us, at least in Western cultures.

Of course, there are people we do prefer not to aggravate. They are people who affect our livelihood, employers for example.

But many women will even go against their best interests so as not to upset or displease people they don't even know and may never see again. We will smile and say sorry and smile again so they won't think badly of us. To waiters, ticket vendors, saleswomen.

Women's conversations are peppered with "Sorry". Much the same please-like-me behaviour can be seen in public situations. Someone sits down on public transport next to a woman. "Sorry" she says and moves over. Someone stands on her foot. "Sorry" she says and moves her foot out of the way.

The girlish giggle at the end of the sentence is also part of the show. It says, "I'm really harmless and vulnerable. Please like me." The self-denial, the self-effacement, the false modesty, the putting everyone else ahead of oneself, all to ensure that everybody likes us. We'll make good wives and mothers for sure. Perhaps women should take a line from "Gone with the Wind" when Rhett Butler firmly declares that "Frankly, my dear, I don't give a damn." Mark Manson said the same thing in stronger language in his book *The Subtle Art of not Giving a F*ck*. Check it out. He has some excellent points including "not giving a f*ck does not mean being indifferent. It means being comfortable with being different".

And here we come to an even more constraining influence on women's behaviour: the belief as mentioned previously, that our main purpose in life is to find a man to love us. We may want everyone to like us, but society expects us to have one man to love us. Our older relatives will definitely perceive us as a failure if this does not happen. Of course, nuns, Lesbians and other genders have bowed out of this pursuit, but for the majority of women it is still a driving force. Not only will they drop their girlfriends like hot cakes to be with "the Boyfriend", but they will spend hours and dollars to make themselves attractive to men. The feminine grooming, dressing, flirting, niceness, are all designed to achieve this. Men themselves and various industries such as advertising, gaming, and entertainment, have turned us into sex objects. On the other hand, we have, as Laurie Penny points out in her book *Unspeakable Things,* turned ourselves into love objects.

All of these behaviours are a form of bias known as "social desirability" which leads us all to conform to the ideas and behaviour of other people in order to fit in.

Of course, not all women do behave like this and some women can be downright rude, crude, and selfish, but it is a significant part of being nice, feminine, and liked which society requires of us. I am not advocating rudeness or ignoring others' needs. I am saying most little girls are raised to be people pleasers and it is often at the expense of their own needs and sense of worth. It can also make them vulnerable to manipulation and abuse.

The classes I taught helped women to examine the trivial but powerful restrictions on their lives, restrictions that had frequently stifled their dreams and wasted their talents. Like the experience of Ms Gulliver, the threads were miniscule but there were so many of them. My classes also raised women's awareness to the many taken-for-granted aspects of their lives which had been artificially created to ensure they put everybody else's needs ahead of their own.

Time and again, the women in my classes came up with the fact that when they did things they really didn't want to do, it was to avoid being disliked. Sad but true. We had all been taught to be pleasing and likable from Day 1.

Perceptions of women's likability, particularly for highly qualified women, can have more influence on their job prospects than their actual qualifications for the job. Research at Ohio State University in 2018 revealed that employers would rather hire a woman who is likable and will fit in than one who is more competent or academically accomplished. I was actually turned away from a job I had applied for after they gave me an intelligence test. The two men doing the interview informed me kindly that I was too intelligent.

Men's job applications are usually judged on the qualifications they have. It's also been found that identical job applications with a male name are judged more favourably than the same application with a female name on it. Both men and women are biased towards the male applicant.

Conformity

References to conformity occur throughout this book. It is my underpinning argument that conformity to the feminine gender stereotype is the invisible prison that keeps women and girls in positions of secondary status in most if not all societies on earth today. Men are similarly impacted by gender stereotype and many good books by men have been written on the topic. We'll look at the impact of various masculine stereotypes on men and the world around them, in more detail in Chapter 9: Boys will be Boys.

We have looked at one form of "social desirability" specific to women, that of being liked. Social desirability is part of the wider constraints of conformity that dictate our behaviour whatever our sex or gender.

We are all aware of peer pressure and its power to get us to conform to the group's expectations. Psychologists know that group dynamics are among the most powerful determinants of our behaviour. Most of us will do or say things we don't even agree with if four or more people in our group do or say those things. Women are twice as likely to do this as men.

Socialisation

Socialisation is the process that turns individuals into "appropriate" members of their culture or group. And remember, it works best if you get 'em when they're young.

As we saw in Chapter 2, Aristotle and, much later, the Jesuits, knew that before the age of six or seven years, we have no mental filters. We take everything in, and we believe what we are told. After the age of six or seven, we begin to question and criticise, but we are subconsciously still controlled by our earlier beliefs. We are totally unaware of this process and for most people, it continues throughout their lives.

You can tell a girl she can grow up to be anything she likes, but the world around her tells her a totally different story. She hears and sees the message coming from every side and every aspect of her life: you are valued for your appearance and body shape, your ability to please people, your attractiveness to men and your ability to have children. Besides, she will observe, all those cool things like action heroes, presidents, principals, people in history books, people in the newspapers, heroes in children's books are usually men or boys, even the principal animal characters in films or stories, are usually male. The fact that we can usually name the exceptions is only testimony to their rarity.

Like the practice of binding the feet of little girls in the China of not so long ago, we take the whole baby girl and bit by bit we mould her, impress her, constrict her, limit her horizons and her beliefs, and consequently her use of her own human potential. She is changed from a full human being with her own individual characteristics to a female impersonator exhibiting the feminine characteristics expected of her by the society she lives in. Most of us are female impersonators. It's been observed that Marilyn Monroe was one of the best. We primp, we preen, posture, and paint our faces. We shave or wax. We hide our intellect. We put the needs and interests of others ahead of our own. And we smile and smile.

Little boys are similarly moulded, constricted, and even more severely policed for "non-masculine" behaviour.

Who are You?

One of the most important questions any human being can ask themselves is "Who am I?" Please notice I am not asking "What are you?" This means the answer does not come down to "I am a wife, a mother, a grandparent, a teacher, a friend." All of those answers place you as a "product" of a relationship to other people. If those other people did not exist, would you cease to exist? So, who are you really? Attempting to answer this question may be the most liberating thing you've ever done; it may also be the most confusing and conflicting thing you've tried to think about, or you may just not think it's all that relevant to "real" life. The choice is yours but please, at least think about it.

Great philosophers have devoted their lives to this question. Historically, women have not been encouraged to think of anything wider, deeper, or broader than how best to take care of their families and provide service and comfort to men. They have been actively discouraged and even prevented from exploring the wonders of their own intellects on the grounds that it would stunt their reproductive capacities. Conceptual thinking has been considered the province of men. But we do actually have the equipment for it so why not use it? **Gentle, caring, and intellectual soaring are not mutually exclusive,** and you just might find they are as inextricably related as joy and love and ecstasy.

9

Boys Will Be Boys

Boys will be boys and do childish things.

The American Heritage & Idioms Dictionary. This expression was first quoted in English in 1589. Its meaning has shifted quite a bit since then.

You've got the brain of a four-year old boy, and I bet he was glad to get rid of it.

Groucho Marx

Why do boys say someone acts like a girl as if it were an insult?

Tamora Pierce, In the Hand of the Goddess

If we do not redefine manhood, war is inevitable.

Paul Fussell

There is a time in a boy's life when the sweetness is pounded out of him; and tenderness, and the ability to show what he feels, is gone.

Norah Vincent

AS WITH THE genderisation of girls, the little boy is similarly bent like a twig to produce the correct shape of a masculine bonsai plant. He learns to posture (in a manly way of course) and compete, to fight to win, to be in control and to never ever behave like a girl. He is encouraged, even pushed, to be a success in the public sphere of his world. He is applauded for sexual "conquests" (a revealing word). "What a stud!" they'll say. And much of his behaviour will be encouraged and excused with one four-word mantra.

Boys will be boys!

The masculine myth maintains that:

- Certain bad behaviour on the part of boys and young men, is acceptable.
- It lets them flex their muscles, spread their wings, and become more masculine.
- It highlights the PRIME MYTH of difference between male and female.
- It reinforces belief in the inevitability of gendered behaviour.

The ideas discussed here and throughout this book, are not about blaming men and boys. It's about identifying beliefs about human males, focussing on their origins, and seeing clearly the damage they cause to men and boys as well as the world around them.

Here are some of the apparently innocent behaviours we tolerate under the umbrella of "Boys will be Boys". We tolerate, accept, and even encourage these behaviours in the belief that it's "natural" for boys and men to behave in this way, and we don't want to squash their budding masculinity.

- He's making so much noise. Boys will be boys.
- He's teasing the girls and pulling their hair. Boys will be boys.
- He's just going through a phase!
- He's such a boy!
- Oh my god! Girls and boys are sooooo different!
- He. Just. Can't. Help himself!
- He's always out with his mates. I don't know what they get up to. Boys will be boys.
- He's drinking too much and fights at the drop of a hat. Boys will be boys.
- He's boasted that he's had sex with a hundred girls. Boys will be boys.

Look at him posturing with his mates, accepting dares to prove himself, demonstrating his anger to show he's no pussy, kicking things, hitting and smashing things. He's a real boy. And he'll learn to despise any boy or man who doesn't behave the same.

Of course, not all boys and men are brought up with the extreme tolerance of the "Boys will be boys" belief. Yet, whole societies tend to go along with it.

It's used by fathers and mothers to excuse a boy's rough behaviour. particularly behaviour that girls or women would not get away with. And that's the whole point. He isn't a girl or a woman. Behaving in this way proves he is not feminine.

It's the mark of a man, or a boy on the way to becoming a man. Masculinity becomes a performance. It's how you show your mates you're nothing like a girl. Teasing girls or disrespecting women you don't know, "proves" masterful masculinity.

The father and grandfather nod and smile at the little boy's rowdiness. They applaud his defiance. He's standing up for himself. It shows he's not a sissy and he's not going to grow up to be a "poofter". Mothers and grandmothers go along with it too.

A large part of learning to be masculine involves male bonding. It's part of sustaining and enforcing masculine behaviour, and it has its rewards. This behaviour maintains team spirit. The boys and men feel stronger and more potent as part of a tribe, or a team or a gang or a platoon.

The most common means and reward for male bonding is entitlement and access to sex, usually with women but raping or humiliating other men from other lower status groups will do too. Female groupies and fans may be persuaded to provide group sex. Rape is an option if consensual sex is not available. The latter is most common in war time but also occurs often in "civil" society. Rape culture is now an ugly part of some of our educational and sporting organizations.

When we say, "boys will be boys", we usually imply a sense of fun, something good-natured. Bending the rules a little but nothing harmful. Boys, we say, need to test their limits to grow stronger and braver, so it's just part of becoming masculine. Boys are expected to be boisterous and noisy.

There'll probably be a bit of physical horseplay, egging each other on. This sort of activity usually involves three or more boys so it's part of belonging to a group, the brotherhood. (Two boys alone may arouse accusations of homosexuality. Safety in numbers.) Such group horseplay is even encouraged in some cases by older men who are responsible for the wellbeing of the boys and young men. The belief is it helps with bonding, working together as a team, beating other groups, gangs, teams, or armies. The boy or young man who does not join in is obviously not part of the group. Worse, he is quickly labelled weak, a wimp, a sissy, a queer and, the ultimate direction all this is heading, a girl.

Boys play with toys that involve fighting and killing, sport and movement. They watch entertainment that glorifies the male hero who fights and often kills. The rare hero of only a few decades ago who could reason and right the wrongs without bloodshed is rarely seen these days. Video games and movies mainly focus on the male as centre stage, physical, and never weak. Their default reaction to frustration or anger is to smash a fist into a wall or break the furniture. Cartoon heroes are often depicted with massive muscles, huge shoulders, and small heads. A telling image. Especially the small head.

Author Kasey Edwards tells the following story in her article "Why I have mixed feelings about teaching my daughter to stand up to boys" http://www.dailylife.com.au/life-and-love/ parenting-and-families/why-i-have-mixed-feelings-about-teaching-my-daughters-to-stand-up-to-boys-20160105-glzn5a:

She was at a six-year-old's birthday party and was watching two little girls playing in a cubby house. Three boys arrived, stood over them and told them "No girls allowed." One of the girls, clearly afraid, left the cubby house. The other girl stood her ground. "We were here first, you can't kick us out," she said.

Kasey Edwards commented: "They weren't my kids, so I gently told the boys that everyone was allowed to play in the cubby house." The boys ignored her and pushed the girl out of the window of the cubby house. The girl fell flat on her back and screamed in pain. The boys ignored her distress and went on with their game in the cubby house.

Ms Edwards took the sobbing girl over to her parents at the party and explained what had happened. The girl's own mother told her that she should have stayed away from the boys. The message to the girl: it was her fault she got hurt because she didn't do what the boys had ordered.

A father of one of the boys laughed and told Ms Edwards that she should have caught the girl as she fell. There were no consequences for the boys. Their violence was so much an accepted part of their behaviour that it didn't even raise an eyebrow. The father saw it as a non-event. His attitude showed the boys that it's fine to use physical strength against females to get what you want.

The message is that boys can hurt girls without any consequences and get what they want into the bargain.

This is only one example. But we can see similar scenarios played out daily in our kindergartens, playgrounds, and primary and secondary schools showing how this attitude to male entitlement over females is ingrained at an early age.

As the boys grow older, we make the "conquest" of women's bodies a measure of masculinity and manhood. Women are expected to put up a fight as part of the "game" so the male can experience conquest and domination. No wonder consensual sex is so problematic. We even use sporting metaphors such as getting to first base, scoring.

Male bonding for businessmen is frequently done on the golf course but it is also often in strip clubs. Here, once again, the female is depicted as a sexual object who only exists for the pleasure of men.

We hear women making excuses for their son's behaviour. "Boys will be boys". We hear women excusing a straying husband and blaming the other woman instead. The media treats philandering by popular or powerful married men as "normal" behaviour. The younger the woman the more admirable the man. Older women with younger men are still frowned on in many societies.

This myth of boys will be boys excuses and encourages selfish and often dangerous behaviour. These acts are often childish, sexist and sometimes violent. There should be no surprise then when a boy grows up to be sexist and homophobic. He will probably be non-communicative and even lack compassion. He will solve problems with physical force. After all, we built him that way, and now we have to live with him.

By denigrating, humiliating, or harming other people or animals, such men show a lack of empathy. This borders on sociopathic behaviour. People with zero empathy are capable of treating other humans and animals as objects. Many men treat women as sex objects anyway. Does this mean such men have no empathy with women? Some men seem capable of treating their mothers or wives or daughters decently but treat all other women as fair game. This would explain the rape, kill, toss away scenario of many murderers of women. This is sociopathic behaviour, and some forms of "masculinity" are dangerously close to becoming that.

But what has this to do with boys having a bit of harmless fun? Or men in sports teams and army groups bonding together? Again, we need to recognise the range of apparently harmless behaviour and attitudes which are one end of a spectrum. Or as I represented it in Figure 4, as a funnel, Sexism's Deadly Funnel. At the bottom of the funnel's slippery slope, exist behaviours that are far from harmless. These include harm and violence against those who are not part of the group. Victims are women, gays, indigenous men, gentle, tender men, and people of other religions and ethnicities. At the extreme end, lies misogyny, Racist, violence, rape, murder.

We know not all boys develop into this extreme of "masculinity," but our prisons are full of men like that.

- Women are afraid in their own homes because they married men like that. These men were so charming in the beginning too.
- Women cannot walk in the streets, cross a college campus, or use public transport without harassment, verbal and physical, by men like that.
- Young men die from a drunken punch to the head because of men like that.
- Dangerous behaviour behind the wheel of a car causes maiming and death mainly, though not only, because of men like that.

The first item in that list should remind us of the "But he was such a good bloke/guy," comment from friends and neighbours that almost inevitably follows the horror of a man murdering his wife and/or his children.

The ready access to pornography by boys and men is twisting their concept of sex and women's role in it. In most pornography, the woman is again an object. She provides several orifices for the insertion of a penis. She exists for the gratification of the man and has no needs or desires for her own pleasure. As a sex object, she loses all humanity.

Male bonding is used as an excuse for behaviour that is usually not acceptable for other members of society. This behaviour of boys in groups or gangs can lead to others around them experiencing fear, humiliation, denigration, or bodily harm.

The boys themselves, have already learnt that a bit of "fooling around" is usually tolerated and even encouraged. They can develop a sense of arrogance and entitlement towards those perceived to be different and weaker than their group. They can even lose sight of the humanity of the victim of their "shenanigans" and go too far. The so-called gang bang is an example. The person, being used sexually, usually a woman but not always, becomes nothing more than an object. Gang bangs may use sex but, like rape, they are more about power and male bonding. The woman is merely the "meat" or "the bun". She has no humanity, and she exists only as a focus that unites the men.

We go to great lengths to "make a man" of our little boys. We even refer to them as "my little man". Toughening them up. Keeping them away from "girly" things. Suppressing their softer emotions and expressions. Boys don't cry.

All men are constantly under scrutiny from other men. They must continually prove themselves as the opposite of feminine. They must never show weakness or lack of control. They must prove themselves to be tough. One man put it this way: "You've got to walk around so your balls clang."

An innocent young boy has the potential to be a complete and wonderful human being. Instead, we suppress and repress more than half of that potential. We do this to produce a "masculine" man. In the case of "toxic" masculinity, we create a mutilated creature whose only acceptable expression is anger.

One of the most basic negative outcomes for boys themselves is the damage done to boys' academic progress. For the stereotypical male, it is not "cool" to be clever at school. This would set him apart from his group. Boys will go to great lengths to conform so they can remain in their macho groups. This includes deliberately performing poorly at school.

Another harmful consequence to come out of the "boys-will-be-boys" development of masculinity is an inability to communicate or express emotion other than anger. Talking about one's feelings or expressing one's emotion is linked to women. The macho man dare not display or share them. With rare exceptions, most men cannot even communicate with their mates when they are emotionally hurting. Tenderness, sadness, disappointment, and tears are taboo for today's "masculine" man. Many but not all Western cultures do not look fondly on boys or men who cry, let alone pour out their hearts. They may cry into their beer at the pub. Mates will see they get home safely but discussing the cause of the tears is not usually a goer.

As a highlight in the creation of OPPOSITE characteristics, we can note that a woman who does not cry when her culture considers it appropriate, is widely condemned.

Women tend to share their everyday experiences and hurts and delights with their friends. They can cry when they feel pain, physical or emotional. Friends will rally round and help them deal with it. This is not because it's a natural female thing to do, but because our culture allows them to express that aspect of their humanity.

When marriages break down, the woman has usually, but not always, been able to discuss her feelings with family or female friends for some time. A lot of her grieving for the relationship has been done before the actual separation. Most men are usually taken by surprise when their wife leaves them. (At least two out of three marriages in Australia are ended by women.) The man is in shock, even though his partner has tried to discuss the issues in their relationship for years. He hasn't heard or listened to her. He has had no analysis or discussion with family or friends. He has lost control of his family and may experience depression, irrationality, anger and even hatred at such a time. Sometimes, he will go to the extreme of physically harming or even killing his wife and/or their children or himself. This is no excuse but a terrible consequence for all concerned when the masculine gender role results in such tragedy.

The underlying assumption is that boys and young men are, by nature, rough, tough, and even bad. This is disrespectful and demeaning to men and boys. Adults adopt a resigned attitude as though bad behaviour in boys is inevitable. Or else they turn a blind eye to it.

The repeated use of this phrase "Boys will be boys", tends to normalise boorish, rude, cruel, irresponsible behaviour.

Even more so if they are white males. It is unlikely that a group of indigenous boys or men, or an out-of-favour ethnic group, would get away with this sort of behaviour.

In his book, *Raising Boys*, Steve Biddulph also makes this point that gender differences are slight. In most people, they are only tendencies and they don't apply to every individual. Most important of all we don't have to accept them as limitations.

There are actually more similarities about the way boys and girls learn than there are differences. Socio-economic factors make a bigger difference to children's achievement than gender does.

How would it look if the situation were reversed? Would we encourage girls to experiment with many sexual partners? Would we want them to drink lots of alcohol? Would we let them start fights, tease boys, hide their emotions except for anger, solve problems with physical violence? Of course not.

Being born male doesn't automatically mean you are predisposed to be rude, hurtful, mean, unpleasant, angry, violent and a bloody nuisance or even a danger to society. To maintain that it is natural and "normal" demeans the concept of masculinity. It is an affront to all human males.

This has been manufactured and taught since men were little boys. Look at the innocence and beauty of a small boy who has been raised in a caring environment. He is trusting and loving. Look at what we do to so many of them in the name of masculinity. It is nothing short of obscene.

Fortunately, not every man has lost a large part of his humanity in this way. And there are men and women who have been drawing attention to the problem of misguided masculinity since the 1970s at least.

There are active programs to help men break free of the rigidity of the role and the negative outcomes of it. The positive aspects of masculinity are not in question here. It is the negative aspects that do disproportionate damage to some men and boys and the people around them.

There are research projects and programs being conducted as concern is growing around a particular set of characteristics which have been called "toxic" masculinity and its harmful impact. To date, most of the work is being undertaken by charitable and private organisations. Governments do not appear to consider it a priority.

One such program in Australia, is an excellent example of work being done. The Jesuit Social Services have for many years helped men and boys who are in trouble or causing it. In 2017, they set up a program called The Men's Project which looked at the root causes of male violence and negative behaviours. They conducted research called "The Man Box" and interviewed

1,000 Australian men from the ages of 18 to 30. Their findings are worth noting – and acting on.

As a result of their responses, the young men interviewed were placed into two categories: those in The Man Box and those outside it.

Those in The Man Box expressed the beliefs that a "real" man must:

- be tough,
- be in control,
- be the family breadwinner,
- have many sexual partners.

Of the 1,000 men interviewed:

- two-thirds were taught that a "real man" behaves in a certain way.
- 47% believed they should act strong even if they were scared or nervous.
- one-third believed that the man should be the family provider.
- 37% believed that they should know their partner's whereabouts at all times.

Those who believed in these rules were considered to be in The Man Box. Like many packages, this one is very fragile. Comparing those in The Man Box with those who did not hold these beliefs, revealed some alarming facts. The Man Box men had poorer mental health, and behavioural issues harmful to themselves and others, particularly to women.

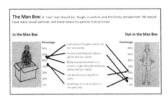

Figure 7: The Man Box. Based, with permission, on research by Jesuit Social Services jss.org.au

While all of these are worrying, the first result would indicate that many of our young men are deeply disturbed, twice the proportion of The Man Box men contemplated suicide but the numbers for the other young men are also disturbing.

Now look at the second, third and fifth results. Almost half of The Man Box men perpetrated physical violence and sexually harassed women they did not know, within the previous month. Compare this with only 7% of the other men interviewed. More than a third of The Man Box men were involved in car accidents within the past year.

In June 2020, an article on the Jesuit Social Services website read:

Sadly, COVID-19 has resulted in a spike in family violence, and we expect an increase in mental health concerns, demonstrating that the work of The Men's Project is more vital than ever before. ... The Men's Project will be launching the "Unpacking The Man Box" report in mid-July 2020, which shows that Man Box attitudes are strongly associated with increased likelihood of using violence, sexual harassment, mental health and binge drinking. In fact, the report shows these outcomes are much more closely linked to Man Box indicators than to other factors such as level of education or occupation. (Article: *The Men's Project Work More Vital than Ever*, Jesuits Social Services, jss.org.au, June 2020.)

We are, I believe, looking at one of the major causes of violence, misogyny, property damage, and harm in our society. Destructive, rigid, antiquated gender role beliefs embedded in the men responsible. Surely anyone concerned with reducing these dysfunctional and damaging aspects of our civil life should be sitting up and taking notice. And then doing something about it. Taking action that would reduce crime, violence, and misogyny, and make the world a safer place for women, children, and other men. Now would be good!

10

Suck it up, Princess.
(WHERE'S YOUR SENSE OF HUMOUR?)

A woman without a man is like a fish without a bicycle.

Irina Dunn

Feminism is the radical notion that women are human beings.

Cheris Kramarae

WOMEN ARE PROBABLY the only stereotyped group that has been taught not only to fulfil the stereotype but to believe it. Some don't necessarily believe it of themselves or other women they know well, but research reveals they still perceive "women in general" as having stereotypical characteristics. And why not? Most women continue to behave in stereotypical ways because they have learnt that that is the way to be liked, admired, loved, and respected as a woman. The fact that it also reinforces women's secondary status, lower pay, lack of public influence, lack of promotion, invisibility in the public sphere, and dependence on men, appears to go unnoticed or perceived as natural.

What they are also probably unaware of is the early childhood embedding of these beliefs and behaviours.

For many women in the 1960s and 1970s, two books stand out as arousing awareness to the programming they were subconsciously allowing to rule their lives. Betty Frieden's *The Feminine Mystique* stirred the sleeping giant of women's awareness. Germaine Greer's *The Female Eunuch* woke it up with a bang. The Women's Liberation Movement was up and running, marching, and standing candidates for parliament. These were heady times. Laws were changing, many women stopped accepting their secondary status and role of perpetual caregiver.

Then it all morphed into Feminism. The term "Women's Liberation" said what it meant. The word "Feminism" had been around for a while and it had several meanings. It was less confronting, more acceptable to the nervous and, as we later found out, much more susceptible to misinterpretation. The term "Women's Liberation" faded from view. Have another look at Chapter 5 for the way changing words minimises their power.

By the 1990s the whole push for women's equality ground almost to a standstill. What was left was a sad dying fire where once a vital life-giving movement had been. Some ashes glowed but the roar had gone out of it, and some progressive changes began to be quietly rolled back, and news was spread abroad that it had all been fixed, and we no longer needed "Women's Liberation" – er Feminism.

And the ugly destructive juggernaut of Sexism rolls on. More subtle, subliminal, and subterranean, and if anything often alarmingly acceptable. Like the air we breathe. Just there. Invisible. Feminism was no longer needed.

The world protested at the savage murder of Jyoti Singh thrown from a bus in Delhi by a group of men, raped with an iron bar and dying days later of her injuries. But we have not stopped men raping and killing women, nor changed the cultural attitudes that ostensibly led to it. Australians marched in the streets in grief and anger at the rape and murder of Jill Meagher, but we have not stopped the random rape and murder of women in Australia or the one woman per week murdered by a partner or ex-partner. The chickens fluff and shuffle but soon settle back on their roosts, and nothing changes.

Why is it so?

Because, even today, I am told to give it a rest. It's all over. Fixed. Get over it. Don't be so sensitive, it's only banter. In spite of the overwhelming response of women to the movements of #everydaySexism, #metoo and #timesup. Thousands, if not millions of women around the world are saying "No it's not fixed". Thousands of dead women and children are testimony to the fact that it's not fixed. The widening, yes widening, gender pay gap, is evidence it is not fixed. The harassment of women in the entertainment industry, and the legal and medical professions, is evidence that it is not fixed. The bullying and harassment of women in parliaments by their male colleagues is evidence that it is not fixed. The next generation of boys harassing and bullying girls provides evidence that it is not going to be fixed for a long time.

Yes, we have changed the laws, but we have not changed the attitudes or behaviours or systemic practices. In fact, more women and men now seem blind to the problem than were blind to it in the 1970s.

People no longer notice the use of language which excluded the female that we became acutely aware of a few decades ago. The overwhelming male presence and importance in movies, tutorials, books, newspapers, children's entertainment goes unremarked by most. Many men will not read or watch or be associated with entertainment that features women as the main characters. These are labelled "chick flicks" or "chick lit". My goodness, just look around. There's an awful lot more "cock lit" and "cock flicks" out there. And women and girls don't disparage that. In fact, they enjoy them.

In countries where steps have been taken to eliminate gender bias in job selection, many more talented women have risen in the ranks. The unexpected bonus has been the removal of mediocre men. While it may be harsh on the mediocre men, it is surely an improvement to have the best people available doing the job, particularly in the upper echelons of government, industry, and large organisations. After all, "the best person for the job" is the mantra we hear constantly, but when it comes to women, it has frequently and unconsciously not been applied.

What is harder to understand are the women who are Sexism-deniers and anti-feminists, the women who attack other women who are fighting for women's rights, the women who gossip about and denigrate other women, the women who continue to support men who are proven harassers and rapists.

Who needs Feminism Now?

I would like to say something to those women who believe they don't need Feminism. I do hope that, by now, people reading this book do not still need convincing. But you might like to pass on this message to those you come across who do. I will preface it by saying, it is tongue in cheek so, when you pass it on, please take it in the spirit it is meant.

To all the women who say," I'm not a feminist", or "I don't need Feminism", here's the thing – how about we start by stripping you of everything Feminism has given you. After all, you don't want to be benefiting from something you despise or deny. We'll start by taking away you're right to vote. In any level of government. Of course, you can't stand for parliament either but that probably won't bother you too much. Oh, and by the way, don't ever speak in public. It's not ladylike.

Then we can go on to insist you only be paid 80% of a male wage for any work you do. Nah, let's make it 75% just because we can. Probably no big deal since most women still only receive this.

Next, we exclude you from any profession other than teacher, nurse, or secretary. As a teacher of course you can't be a principal. because leadership is for men. No, no, no. You can't be a doctor or a lawyer or an industrial chief. Your delicate constitution is not suited to anything other than menial, domestic or caring tasks. Learn to embroider for goodness sake.

Then we go on to give any money you earn, to your husband. You won't see a cent unless he chooses to give you some.

Of course, you won't be able to get a loan for a car or a house or anything unless a male goes guarantor for you. Oh dear, you won't even be eligible for a credit card. Eeeek! Now that is harsh.

You won't be able to get a divorce no matter what your husband is doing to you. Your husband will be able to rape you any time he feels like it, and it will be quite legal. If he divorces you, he will take the children, no questions asked.

Oh, and another thing. If you find you're enjoying sex, stop it immediately. It's not ladylike either and you're obviously a slut or a whore. If you masturbate, they'll probably remove your clitoris. That'll stop you enjoying yourself.

We'll also stop your access to contraception or abortion. That means you'll be continually having children whether you like it or not. Probably about twelve or thirteen, but maybe more.

I could go on. There's a whole lot more, but that's probably enough for now.

So, if you don't agree with Feminism then do you think it's fair to benefit from it. Enjoy your life in the Dark Ages. No wait. It's not that long ago. Many of these things have only changed in my lifetime. Since the 1960s. I remember them well.

As I said, this sad litany is tongue in cheek. I wouldn't wish that on any woman. But - this was the way of life for women before feminists fought and changed things. And, as I said, a great deal of it was in my lifetime.

Women maintain that they have no need of Feminism for a variety of reasons that usually highlight the fact that they don't appear to know what life for women was like until quite recently. And for all the reasons discussed in previous chapters, Sexism is invisible to most of us still. Finally, there is the fact that many people don't seem to know what Feminism actually is. I hope we cleared that up in Chapter 4: What's in a Name?

Sexism is Alive and Well

Here are a couple of research findings just to get us started:

Research has shown stereotypical beliefs can even impact on how doctors diagnose illness by jumping to a particular conclusion based on a stereotypical view of the patient. For example, smokers can be diagnosed as having smoking-related diseases without further questions or tests. A good diagnostician will test an initial diagnosis by checking for evidence against it. The fact that one circumstance follows another does not prove that the first caused the second.

In the case of women, research has shown that doctors do not take women's pain as seriously as men's pain. When they are in pain, women do not receive the same painkillers as men. https://www.bbc.com/future/article/20180518-the-inequality-in-how-women-are-treated-for-pain?referer=http%3A%2F%2Fwww.google.com%2F

They are more likely to be prescribed sedative medication. Symptoms of pending heart attack in women have been ignored or dismissed, usually because they are not the same as men's symptoms and are put down to "anxiety". https://www.health.harvard.edu/blog/women-and-pain-disparities-in-experience-and-treatment-2017100912562

One study showed that women are 59% more likely to be initially misdiagnosed when suffering a heart attack. In Australia, more women die of heart disease than any form of cancer, including breast cancer. https://www.theguardian.com/commentisfree/2018/jun/14/women-with-heart-diseases-are-dismissed-and-its-killing-them

And just to wrap it up, here are a few more barriers to women's acceptance into full peoplehood.

Women's emotional work in the home and society goes unre-marked but is a constant expectation. Any woman who does not provide these emotional services is seen as an uncaring, unnat-ural creature.

Women's perceived lack of the appropriate qualities for involve-ment in the world of men, is said to justify their lower status, pay, influence and visibility in society. A glaring circular and totally illogical observation which mainly goes unquestioned.

It is rather like taking a man, tying his hands behind his back, and hobbling him as well, then bashing him to the ground and declaring, "Look Ma. I told you he couldn't fight."

As long as we teach, promote, accept and believe in these gender stereotypical differences, women's cultural inequality is guaranteed. And finally, **as long as women believe in and perform the feminine stereotype, they will never have equality.**

The key is to break the gender stereotypes that constrain and define women's and men's behaviour. That behaviour ensures, confirms, and justifies our unequal power, status, and recognition.

But supporters of the *status quo* are holding their ground. Attitudes are entrenched. Inertia is the enemy of progress. Besides, changing the laws only scrapes the surface of the problem.

We change the laws, we march against the crime, we draw attention to the inequities between the sexes. The problem we have not dealt with is the underlying sexist culture built on stereotypes. But we still hold the same sexist attitudes and beliefs that justified discrimination and structured society according to those beliefs. They are so normalised that they are invisible to most people.

For the last couple of decades, it has been unfashionable to mention the word Sexism. Many people still roll their eyes and look bored if you do. Feminism has been so distorted by its enemies, that many women shy away from calling themselves feminists.

Sexism is Insidious

Sexism is difficult to combat for many reasons. One of the most frustrating is the perception that most of it is trivial. Everyday Sexism is everywhere. Most examples of it do appear trivial and are difficult to oppose without being labelled humourless or thin-skinned. Each woman experiences everyday Sexism on a daily basis and for some it is so common they do not even notice it. While each experience appears trivial and hardly worth mentioning, imagine the pattern. One woman experiencing one piece of Sexism every day multiplied by the number of women in any society, multiplied by all the days of their lives and that's an awful lot of Sexism. Each "trivial" experience is like a grain of sand but how many grains of sand does it take to smother you, bury you alive. Literally keeping you in your place - "a woman's place". Whole civilisations have been buried by enough grains of sand. Or think of Gulliver and the tiny Lilliputians. The sheer number of them enabled them to pin Gulliver to the ground with hundreds of tiny threads. Gendered trivia holds women in their place every day. Just take another look at Figure 2: Ms Gulliver and the Gender Ties we saw in Chapter 3. Each tiny thread appears trivial, too trivial to complain about. But each is based on a deep-rooted sexist foundation.

I believe that many women and girls retain their sanity and survive in this world by subconsciously denying that they are living in patriarchal societies which are designed for and run by men, or that Sexism and misogyny exist. The awful truth of the position of women is just too painful to bear. Any study of women's position is so depressing as to raise despair and anger in anyone who faces it squarely. It seems so horrific and hopeless that it feels totally overwhelming. There's more about this in Chapter 12: Women are their own Worst Enemies.

In writing this book, I have found the depth of Sexism and misogyny and harm done to women and sheer wanton waste of women's talents and lives as full human beings, to be outrageously depressing. Examining the obstacles and constraints women face, and the treatment they receive by almost every society on earth can be overwhelming. You too may experience this despair, so it is important to focus on solutions and look for the good around us while still refusing to ignore the harm of gender roles for both sexes and genders, and the resultant Sexism.

Instead of focusing on and working to eliminate Sexism, discussions have focused on Feminism and its perceived shortcomings. So, let's turn to the real problem and turn the spotlight on "Sexism".

In spite of changes to laws, and a lot of lip service, Sexism is the cultural "religion" that ensures men's place as the superior and dominant group.

Some quick examples:

Beliefs: Both males and females unconsciously believe that men are more competent and have the power to implement their abilities, while women are seen to be less competent but caring and kind.

Behaviour and Mannerisms: We expect men to walk and talk differently from women, to hold their bodies differently and to posture differently. A man exhibiting movements associated with women is usually the butt of homophobic jokes. Women wear high heeled shoes to exaggerate the thrust of their pelvis and the swing of their hips.

Expectations: Many of us still expect men and women to have different interests, to carry out different gender roles, and to prefer different careers.

Language: Most languages still use the masculine pronoun to mean both sexes. We refer to most creatures as male unless we specifically know they are female. The female is all but invisible in general terminology.

Humour: Women as a group are up there with the Irish as the main butt of jokes in English. Think of women drivers, mothers-in-law, dumb blondes, nagging wives and women who talk too much.

If you're not sure if or why a joke is sexist, here's a simple test. Tell the same joke with the sexes reversed. If it's no longer funny when the joke is about a man, then it's probably sexist.

Yes, to every one of these examples, there are exceptions. This doesn't negate the overall trend, and the fact that we can name exceptions pretty much proves that the exceptions aren't very numerous.

From the Trivial to the Profound

Many of the examples of Sexism that women and girls face every day, are small, trivial even. But therein lies their power. Objecting to them seems petty and is usually met with scorn or ridicule or the charming "Suck it up, Princess!"

For those women who step out of "their place", there are always the tools of misogyny: ridicule, abuse, silencing, ostracising, dismissing, ignoring, trolling, aggression, violence, rape, and murder. While not all men act in these ways towards women, all men, whether knowingly or unknowingly, benefit from the constraining effect on women. In 1975, Susan Brownmiller's book, *Against our Will*, was published. She argued that rape is "a conscious process of intimidation by which all men keep all women in a state of fear." The book caused outrage and, I suspect, it still would. Much along the lines of the #notallmen response we currently see. Susan Brownmiller was attacked by journalists and TV interviewers. Her bestseller was one of the first books to define rape as a political problem rather than an individual crime of passion. Fear of rape or violence is one of the major constraints on women's freedom of movement and sense of autonomy. So too are the "trivial" events such as catcalling, street harassment, through to stalking and trolling.

Women consciously and unconsciously plan their daily actions around the avoidance of male aggression and hostility. We avoid injuring men's egos because we know they can react badly; we choose the times and places we can be anywhere outside of our homes. If we do not, we are blamed for any harm we come to. We know that many men react aggressively to rejection, and we give them what they want when we would rather not. Relenting is not consenting but is used against us as if it were.

A lecturer once posed a question to a class of men and women. He asked the men what steps they had taken on their way to the class, to protect themselves against assault or harassment or rape or violence. The men looked puzzled and had obviously never considered the question. Then the lecturer asked the women. The women responded and the list was long. Being mindful of what to wear, making sure someone knew where they were going, choosing the right well lit, popular streets, not sitting next to men on public transport if possible, holding the keys between the fingers pointing outwards to use as a weapon, and so on. The men looked on in amazement.

Both sexes and all genders, are controlled by Sexism every day of our lives. It defines us, evaluates us, constrains us, and determines our beliefs about ourselves and everyone else.

No other prejudice is as universal in human society. Groups who are intersectionally affected by other prejudices are invariably affected by Sexism as well.

The situation has not changed much as far as most women around the world are concerned and, while women in some cultures including our own, may not be subjected to these extremes of treatment, there is nowhere on earth that the sexes have equality. And yet, many people claim Sexism no longer exists, or women have no sense of humour or can't take a compliment or are making a mountain out of a mole hill or are ruining the lives of men.

There are people, men and women, who appear not to link the prevalence of street harassment, campus rape and workplace harassment with Sexism. Those things happen to women they have never met who, they believe, probably brought it on themselves.

They also appear to be unaware of the links between sexist and misogynist humour with demeaning and even violent attitudes towards women. Nor do they link the entertainment we constantly watch, to sexist behaviour in real life. Life imitates art. The movies, TV series, sports, games, and books over-whelmingly present males as the go-to human for entertainment, talent, action, humour, courage, competence, leadership and skill.

Women still frequently appear in movies and TV series primarily to provide a backdrop and reward for male action. The hero rescues and is rewarded with the affections of the eternal damsel in distress. The damsel has very little agency of her own and spends her time wringing her hands helplessly, screaming irritatingly and uselessly, or looking adoringly at the hero. In this, she fulfills her purpose for being in the film in the first place. To make him look good. Yes, there are movies that attempt to depict women in strong, intelligent, courageous roles. Some moviemakers have begun replacing male heroes with female ones, but they are often met with squeals and howls of protest from apparently insecure young men. It was bad enough when they turned Dr Who into an older man, but then to present the next incarnation of the famous Time Lord, as a woman – the blokes came out of their trees! We are talking about an imaginary character (one of my favourites by the way) who can turn into another form when the current body reaches its use-by date.

If you believe that men and women have equality, how do you account for our representation of the world? Both fact and fiction focus overwhelmingly on the doings, opinions, and achievements of men. Don't believe it? Read a newspaper or flip through a history book or check out children's books and films for depictions of male and female characters. It's mostly all about men, boys, or male animals. Even symbols meant to represent human beings are almost always male. The default human is male. In spite of rigorous debates and some achievements in the 1980s, and some changes, languages once again use the masculine to depict all humans. Women are expected to accept that the word "Man" includes them. They are expected to be happy to be Chairman or Spokesman. On the other hand, the worst thing you can call a man is "a girl" or "lady".

And if anyone claims that everything is about males because it is males that do all the great and interesting things, invent things, write things, discover things, get them to check out the countless invisible women. Women have been here as long as men have, even in the caves painting on walls. Women have fought in battles and led armies, invented products and processes we still use, painted great art, written great literature, explored faraway places. But they quickly become invisible. Or credit for their work is given to men associated with them. On history's page, the man will not be upstaged.

Why is women's work so devalued that, in the absence of women, the lowest status male in a group is required to perform it?

Both men and women, in denying that Sexism and inequality are still very real, point to the changes in legislation but, as Nicholas Farrell in his article "Stand up, all male feminists" pointed out: rights on paper do not automatically mean rights in reality.

The great cartoonist Charlie Schultz had one of his *Peanuts* characters, Lucy, say, "Women are the Ladies Auxiliary of the Human Race". Well said. Women provide the backup services (sexual, domestic, parenting, caring and emotional) that men need to get on with the business of running the world or just having the time and freedom to go fishing with a few mates. Women provide backup services at home to enable male freedom in the wider world. Women who have tried to make it in the public sphere world have sometimes declared, only half-jokingly, that what they need is a wife. There are supportive men out there but not enough of them.

Societies have not stepped up adequately with the provision of flexible working hours and work at home arrangements, or workplace childcare and tax deductions for childcare. We expect women to replenish society by giving birth to the next generation but fail to support them. Society's losses are great. The talents of many women who could not develop their full human potential, have been lost. A talented woman may have been born who, if she had the opportunity, could have developed a cure for cancer or other diseases, could have written words that would inspire or entertain as Shakespeare's do, could have developed a process for eliminating recidivism of criminals released from our penal system. The list is endless. Whatever men have done, women could have done – given the opportunity. This would have doubled our talent pool. Even those who did succeed were often hindered or ignored. Elizabeth Kenny and Temple Grandin spring to mind.

Around the world or around the corner, women do not get a fair go. Feminism has not gone too far. Feminism has never really been tried. For thousands of years, women have been second class members of the human race. Why has it been so long and hard and still we haven't achieved equality of the sexes? What's the catch? What's the hold-up? Read on.

One of the greatest barriers to women and girls achieving equality around the world, not just under the law but in attitude and practice, is the unquestioned teaching of the gender stereotypes and the consequent imbalance of power and status between the sexes based on those stereotypes.

All of the negative actions described above are problems, but they are not the underlying problem. The sexist culture is the problem which fosters those attitudes and behaviours. There is the belief that men and women are totally different and women's "place" as man's helpmate, is absolutely natural. As we will see in Chapter 11, women are told this does not mean we are inferior, just different and wonderful, beautiful and worthy of a place on a pedestal. Don't let it go to your head though. There are conditions. You've got to behave in an acceptable "feminine" way. Step outside the stereotype and you'll be off that pedestal so fast, your head will spin. The fall could kill you.

The reality is that in terms of power, reward, and respect, women are secondary to men. Even a superficial study shows this. Digging deeper reveals that the *status quo* is maintained through unconscious bias, belief in the myths separating men and women, force, fear, media manipulation, religion, custom, collusion, and confusion. And possibly the protection of male ego.

Social and Political Power:

In almost every culture on earth now, men are the dominant sex.

Sure, men will joke that their wives are the bosses at home, and, in some cases, this may be true. This humorous depiction of domestic arrangements is a pitiful and insulting cover up for the fact that women have so little power or influence outside the home, in any sphere of activity. It is yet another example of the gaslighting that women are frequently subjected to.

The classic concepts of equality have included winning the vote and attaining equal pay for equal work. Yes, women in most countries have gained the vote. It was hailed as a tremendous victory which would bring great improvements for women. It has not.

In spite of this, there are men and women who firmly believe that it's all good now. It's either been sorted, or was never a problem, or it's the way it's supposed to be.

We could call them Sexism-deniers.

I can understand why many men don't want the applecart over-turned or the boat rocked. Most of it suits them just fine. However, they do fail to see the connection between many of their own problems and disadvantages that stem from the suppression or oppression of women. And they are often totally oblivious to the privileges they enjoy that women don't. Remember how the Jewish prayer goes: *Blessed be the God that has not made me a heathen, a slave, or a woman.*

But why would women themselves deny their unequal status and even fight to maintain things as they are? Are women really their own worst enemies? We'll explore that later. For now, let's have a look at the human race's greatest attempt at gaslighting. You'll see it when you believe it.

11

But Baby, Different Doesn't Mean Unequal.
(WARNING, WARNING! GASLIGHTING!)

But the sexist myth is the greatest and most pervasive myth the world has ever told itself - at once explaining, condoning, and perpetuating male superiority and female inferiority, meanwhile denying - craftiest touch of all! – that to be secondary in everything is at all inferior.

Sheldon Vanauken, 1968

Inequality requires the perception of difference.

Cecilia L. Ridgeway, *Framed by Gender*

THIS MYTH BUILDS on the PRIME MYTH that men and women are naturally quite different with different roles to play. It assures us that not only are men and women very different but that these differences do not mean that women are inferior. This sounds contradictory to the concept of women as the weaker sex, but it is all part of the swirling giddy-making mythology that keeps women on the back foot. Individual women begin to believe they are the ones going mad. They fail to see the overall pattern of the treatment of women in general.

This myth maintains that in many ways, women are superior to men. Just look at their attributes. Women are:

- more caring about others,
- more sensitive to other people's feelings,
- more communicative and less competitive,
- less violent, less likely to commit serious crimes,
- less egocentric, better negotiators.
- good with children, especially little ones.
- finer, purer, and more sensitive than men.

Not surprisingly, these "superior" characteristics always seem to be in the realm of looking after others or keeping men's house and home in order.

All of this means, so goes this myth, that men respect and love women, even place them on a pedestal, open doors for them and protect them from danger.

Men, on the other hand, according to the myth are:

- more basic physical beings who need women's tender guidance to keep them civilised.
- strong, silent, stoic. Their role is to protect "their women" and bring home the money and provide for their families.

Women provide the civilising influence to keep men from behaving like brutes. After all, boys will be boys, whatever their age. Women are God's Police keeping men on the straight and narrow. The myth basically makes women responsible for men's behaviour, for controlling men's sexual urges by not appearing too attractive, easily available or seductive.

In the 1960s and 70s, there was a song that summed it up:

Man taught Woman to mother his heirs,

To keep him erect, his socks in pairs.

Many women who do not fulfil their destiny in this way, fall off the pedestal and lose men's respect and protection. Whatever happens to them is their own fault. When men behave badly, our default position is to blame the victim. Blame the woman. As the Bible tells us, Adam said to God: "She made me do it".

This particular myth would make Machiavelli proud. Machiavelli lived in Florence from 1469 to 1527. He wrote *The Prince,* a very perceptive book on human nature and the art of governing or controlling people. It is considered the foundation of modern political science or a handbook for unscrupulous politicians. You've probably heard the term "Machiavellian". It means the use of cunning, trickery, and deception in politics, society, and personal life. And this gendered myth uses those in bucket-loads. It convinces women that they are special, respected, loved and protected in the face of blatant inequalities, lower status, lower reward, less influence, stifled ambitions, wasted talents, violence, and harassment, and being overloaded with two-thirds of the world's work, much of it unpaid or underpaid.

The prejudice and discrimination women experience are disguised and sugar-coated by chivalry, romance, flattery, and "affectionate" humour. But just try behaving in a way that is not in the constellation of "Feminine" and you will fall off that pedestal at the speed of light. Respect and protection will be withdrawn, and everything that happens to you will either be your fault and what you deserved, or you are a malicious, lying bitch out to destroy men's reputations and lives.

This myth takes the circumstances of half the human population and turns it on its head. It is so sweet, it's almost sickening. It makes being passive, dependent, putting everyone else ahead of oneself, seem like the noblest way to behave rather than revealing that being a doormat is required behaviour for most women and goes against evolutionary notions of survival. Far from perceiving women as different but equal, all societies amplify and create differences between the sexes, insisting that boys and girls conform to them and then use those differences to prove superiority of the male and justify male dominance.

In earlier chapters, we looked at the ways in which little girls and boys are moulded from birth. Their physical bodies are used to determine their expected behaviour, their talents and interests, and their appropriate role in society.

To sum up our story so far, beliefs, expectations and rules were originally developed to help groups and later, whole societies to survive. With men's growing awareness of their role in the conception of children, combined with the development of agriculture, non-nomadic lifestyles and private ownership of land, animals and objects, men took charge.

From that time on, whole societies were based on institution-alised Sexism – and still are. Male dominance of the family and particularly of the women in it, was written into the law and the religions of most societies on earth.

For the most part, it was and is women who teach or coerce their daughters to comply with the requirements of accepted feminine behaviour. This has been for complex reasons we'll look at in Chapter12: Women are their own Worst Enemies.

Women have been taught to conform, and these expectations and behaviours principally serve to keep societies reproducing children, satisfying the sexual needs of men, and keeping the home fires burning.

To add insult to injury, since most women were not out there becoming great inventors, artists, or generals, they were then told this is proof of their inability to do or be these things. Talk about a circular argument. This one's a doozy.

Before you get upset and reach for social media to tell me "men suffer too", here's the part where the boys come front and centre.

Boys are similarly taught how to be "masculine" with all the privileges and the costs of that.

They are taught to conform to their culture's accepted type of masculine behaviour too. But there's a big difference in the behaviours taught to and expected of males and females. Boys are taught behaviours, confidence, postures, and attitudes that will enable them to take their place in the world of men. To be in control, to have expectations of women and children. Gender roles have changed over time, and the masculine gender role is becoming more rigid, more constraining, and more destructive. For some groups of men, it has become a straitjacket, destructive for them and for those around them. Global and domestic violence against women and girls is one manifestation of this type of masculinity. Brutality and domination in all-male environments are others. Such men also seek power and status and take on roles in government and organisations that affect everyone and everything else on the planet. American historian, author and university professor Paul Fussell expressed it this way: "If we do not redefine manhood, war is inevitable." It is urgent that we give women, and men of a less toxic orientation, the authority to run our affairs and influence society. But before that will happen, we need more people to recognise the problem with "toxic masculinity". As with climate change and climate-change deniers, we have Sexism-deniers, and deniers of toxic masculinity.

But, for now, let's get back to women and girls. If you're a woman, look around you now and you will see that as we grow up, there are many pressures on us to make us believe we should be like all the other girls. All the other girls are being told the same thing. It's creating your character for you, almost like science fiction. A triumph of social engineering, moulding people to be the way they should be. Except it's not fiction. It's real and it's going on right now. It would be funny if it weren't so sad, that as soon as people try to change it, they are the ones accused of social engineering.

Little girls start off being confident and wanting to run and jump and climb just like little boys. They begin to change around the age of six to puberty, and there is reason to believe this change comes about through learning what is expected of them.

In a video demonstration of this, little girls younger than six, were asked to "run like a girl". They ran fast and efficiently as any little boy would do. They did their best. Next, girls and boys in their teens were asked to "run like a girl". All of them performed a version of running that involved knees together, arms flapping uselessly and a lot of giggling. Going nowhere fast. No wonder boys don't want to "run like a girl". The girls all admitted they were running that way because they thought that's what was expected. They were then able to demonstrate that they could in fact run fast without all the acting. Perhaps it should be compulsory for girls and boys to watch women running or playing sport in top level competitions. Most men could not keep up with those women unless they did a mighty lot of training.

One of my personal experiences of this attitude was a time I was having coffee in a food hall with my daughter while my three-year old granddaughter played in the area provided for children. She was running, jumping, turning somersaults, and leaping from object to object with great joy. The woman at the next table leaned over and said, "She should be a boy."

We teach boys and men to perform the characteristics that are needed to take power, status, dominance and reward. Then, surprise, surprise, we give greater power, higher status, dominance, and reward to males.

But why do women let them get away with it?

Gaslighting

One of the most powerful tools of manipulating women's perception of their reality is called "gaslighting". Gaslighting is the attempt of one person to overwrite another person's reality. It is also used at a societal level by governments, usually totalitarian and despotic, but politicians of democracies are also prone to use these methods to deflect attention from their shortcomings. Perhaps more and more these days.

This is behaviour that attempts to manipulate or control a person or a whole group, by making them doubt their own perception of events. It is a form of control and domination, and it is usually done to benefit the person doing it. It involves twisting information or selectively omitting information to favour the gaslighter.

The word comes from a 1944 American psychological-thriller film, adapted from Patrick Hamilton's 1938 play Gas Light, about a woman whose husband changes items in her environment and then returns them to normal, convincing her that she imagined the change. This slowly manipulates her into believing that she is going insane.

Gaslighting, when effective, will actually damage your trust in yourself and your experience of reality. It can change not just a person's behaviour but who they are.

It is mostly used to increase an already uneven balance of power, to prevent someone from knowing what is going on, and to instil doubt and lack of confidence in their own perception of reality. As already mentioned, it is used at a personal level, but it is also used at a cultural or societal level to control or manipulate masses of people.

One of society's greatest gaslighting successes is to hide the overall Sexism and misogyny that maintains the unequal power and status of the sexes. Women are too often drawn to romance, flattery, flowers, rings, weddings, and concepts of chivalry. When these things are found to be short lived, the only consolation is to tell oneself that nothing lasts forever, and the subterranean reality of women's lives is glossed over. If women actually saw the overall pattern of how women are treated and controlled, I would hope all hell would break loose.

For instance, every time an obvious hate crime or sex crime is portrayed by the media or various officials as an isolated case of a man's mental illness or extreme stress or provocation, this is gaslighting. Even when a mass murderer leaves a manuscript or manifesto explaining his actions as hatred of all women because they are to blame for everything that goes wrong in his life, both the press and officials downplay the connection, or they just don't mention it. They tell us it's not because the victim is a woman, nor do they dwell on the fact that this happens to women all the time; they say it's because this one particular man is mad or bad. This provides a smokescreen that prevents us seeing the massive pattern of misogyny and Sexism that is enacted by some men to keep all women in a state of fear, dependent on and seeking the protection of "good" men.

Tim Meagher, the husband of Jill Meagher who was raped and murdered in Melbourne in 2012, wrote an article about just this very attitude. He called it "The Myth of the Monster", pointing out that the perpetrators of these crimes were ordinary men whose neighbours and mates, after the murder of a woman, invariably declared him to be "a good bloke". Or as Anna Arendt put it at the Nazi war crime trials: the face of evil is totally banal, meaning it appears so ordinary that it goes undetected and unrecognised.

People who use gaslighting can be parents, spouses, siblings, colleagues, or bosses. It can occur anywhere. It is a specific tool used by manipulative and abusive people to control and dominate an individual. But its greatest success lies in the public sphere. When women insist they have been badly treated or harmed because they are women, they are usually met with cries of "playing the gender card" or outright denial, derision, or scorn.

Attention is deflected from the possibility that the male murderer is part of a pattern of misogyny and masculinity turned toxic by an institutionalised imbalance of power, and an almost universal sense of entitlement taught to men and boys. Instead, we are fed the usual line that he is uniquely mad or bad – a one-off case. It's happened before, we all know, but we don't dwell on that. We don't look for the pattern, or the underlying causes that led to this one man's behaviour.

As we have seen, social conditioning trains men and boys to feel they must prove their masculinity on the basis of how different they are from women and girls. Never do this or that like a girl. Don't be a sissy. They are taught not to allow expressions of vulnerability or pain, not to cry or express emotions showing vulnerability. Such conditioning can prevent the development of empathy or compassion, and the ability to recognise or understand the feelings of others. This can lead to narcissistic tendencies and, at worst, sociopathic disorders.

This type of masculine socialisation is the perfect breeding ground which will turn a relationship into a power struggle between the sexes. He needs to prove he can dominate his female partner. He feels that if she controls him, he will be emasculated and "henpecked". He must control or be controlled. Forming a partnership of two equals is not what most men have been taught. True, not all men, but many men feel they will be "emasculated" if a woman provides advice or tries to influence them or tell them what to do. They are uncomfortable with female bosses for this reason. They hate to have a woman "beat" them at almost anything. To stay in control, some men undermine the influence of their female partners daily. Many women resort to planting the seed of an idea and then letting the man think he thought of it himself. Manipulative? You bet. It's a time saver and sometimes even a sanity-retaining technique.

As Terry Pratchett put it in Unseen Academicals in response to a character's comment that the female mind is a devious one. "Well, of course it is. It has to deal with the male one."

At a societal level, when women are justifiably angry or hurt by the way they have been treated, they are told to calm down, stop being so sensitive, or trivial, or hysterical, illogical, irrational, or shrill, and to stop over-reacting. When we express annoyance or anger at street harassment, wolf-whistling, or catcalling we are told it's a compliment.

Women are told they have no sense of humour when we don't laugh at sexist jokes or behaviour. Humour often uses the reverse of the truth to disguise the truth. One of my favourite examples of this type of joke is: A sign depicting the location of the toilets/washrooms. "Men to the left because women are always right." Trivial, yes. But remember Ms Gulliver and the tiny threads. The opposite of the truth. You betcha. Ask any woman whose ideas have been ignored, whose advice is dismissed, who has been mansplained almost daily. When I first read that "joke", my immediate thought was: "If that's true, what a pity we don't run the world."

When women are raped or assaulted, the spotlight is turned on them, not the male. Their behaviour or appearance or motives are questioned, and the perpetrator becomes the victim of a woman's provocation or lies.

When women draw attention to the violence and abuse they suffer at the hands of men, they are met with outrage and the cry of "Not all men are like that". The problem they have raised is ignored and self-righteous men (sadly aided by some women) leap to defend their own reputation as if they are personally the victims of false accusations. Feminists are labelled "feminazis' as if fighting for equality of the sexes is an attack on men who loudly proclaim they are the victims of these man-haters. Men's Rights groups may or may not have legitimate grievances, but they frame their outrage as being victims of women's aggression rather than seeing that many of their problems are the result of society's gender stereotypes in which women are seen as inferior and less capable than men. True equality of the sexes would remove most of their problems. I would suggest that instead of responding with cries of #notallmen, the appropriate response is "How can I help change this?"

Language

Language is another way of disguising the fact that what is happening to women is a cultural pattern. There are a couple of ways this trick is performed.

You're probably not reading this book for a grammar lesson, but language is so powerful in guiding our thoughts. George Orwell was definitely on to something. So, please bear with me.

The first one: We use the passive voice to describe that something happened to a woman rather than saying that someone did something to the woman. In case you've forgotten your grammar lessons from school, passive voice is a way of structuring a sentence so that the person who performs the action is left out. Let's assume that the suspected perpetrator is known. We will still usually find he is left out – if he is male. A female perpetrator is pulled front and centre immediately. The passive voice is generally used for male perpetrators, rendering them invisible. Here's an example: "The young woman was raped in the park." Doesn't say who did it. Could've been a Martian, but that's probably a bit harsh on the Martians. It's usually a human male. How about another one: She was murdered, and her body was dumped in the swamp." That must have involved a bit of labour but he, she, or it, whoever did it, doesn't get a mention. It could have been a troll from the forest. We see these types of sentences in reportage of male violence against women, all the time. You could justifiably say that these sentences are used because the perpetrator is not known. However, this sort of sentence structure is used even when he is known.

Another use of language to disguise the male perpetrator is similar to the passive voice. It leaves the perpetrator out of the equation and just makes the woman the subject and the object involved. Here are a couple of examples: "She was a victim of domestic violence."" She was sexually abused at the age of five." "She was continually catcalled and harassed the entire length of the street."

This time it's a sleight of hand with the verb. You'll notice the use of the verb "was".

"Okay, Smarty Pants" I hear you say. "What's your point? How should they say it?"

Glad you asked. Here's how it would appear if we didn't leave the guy or guys who did, it out in the cold. "Men continually catcalled and harassed her the entire length of the street."

"She was a victim of domestic violence." Let's get real and say: "Her husband or boyfriend or partner regularly bashed and abused her."

Courtship and Relationships.

There are at least two other ways that women's secondary status and plain ill-treatment is disguised and sugar-coated in ways that lead a woman to believe she is important or special and, consequently, there are no problems for women in general.

One is the attentive devotion a man is likely to lavish on a woman when he is "courting" her. She is flattered, delighted, and usually won over. However, it is also a form of "glamour" in the original sense of the word. It is an enchantment, magic that leads us to see the world differently. It's probably sexual attraction. He is also a victim of it, and the two of you see each other through rose-coloured glasses. Besides, you're also both on your best behaviour. Women are so rarely the centre of attention in our world that this is a moment to savour. Unfortunately, it can lead to a belief that there are no problems with the treatment of women, or women's status. safety, reward, or recognition. In many male-female relationships, this may be true at the level of their relationship, or even within the circle of their family and friends. But step outside your own personal circumstances, look clearly, and you will see a vastly different scenario. I am talking about the broader picture and the reasons so many women fail to recognise it, let alone do something about it.

Another deflecting technique when women's status and lack of equality are raised, is the indignant response from the sexist man: "But I love women." He may very well love some women, but only if they conform to his idea of how women should behave. His respect and protection vanish faster than dew in sunshine if a woman does not behave as he expects her to.

Then there's the endearing way women are referred to as "the Boss" by their husbands. This may or may not be true within their relationship, but it serves to make the woman feel good about herself and her importance in the relationship. It in no way compensates for the constraints and hoop-jumping that await any woman who attempts to be boss of anything in the outside world.

Another bias we have all been taught since childhood and see as natural, is the belief that males just are more competent, talented, knowledgeable, and authoritative than females.

Along with gender stereotypes and the characteristics embodied in them, we believe women are better caregivers, and men are more competent at everything else. Competence is seen to consist of the skill or knowledge to achieve a goal. On the other hand, agency requires the power, status, and confidence to actually originate or direct actions to achieve the goal. Women are "seen" to be less competent and less able to carry out a task requiring that competence. As we have seen earlier, agency, particularly outside the home, is generally the prerogative of males. A woman exercising agency is usually seen to be too bossy and definitely unfeminine. A less competent male is not seen to be outside his boundaries when he takes control or directs action. He is being manly. It's even possible he will receive the credit over the more competent woman who came up with the idea.

This fits neatly with the assignment of responsibility for wider society to men and within the home to women. The stereotypes tell us men are (or should be) the rulers, the bosses, and the breadwinners. Women are (or should be) the carers, home makers, mothers, cooks, cleaners, and laundry workers. Then comes the final insult. We are told that motherhood is the most important job in the world. What a great example of "gaslighting" that is.

Surveys have shown that, in the mind of the public, housewives and "stay-at-home" mothers have the same low status and perceived lack of competence as the elderly and people with physical disabilities, blithely insulting three groups of people with one swoop.

Men are certainly not flocking to be caregivers, which we are told is the most important job in the world. When employers change company policy to make the workplace more family friendly, men who do step up to do their share of parenting are often ridiculed by workmates or colleagues. They are also considered by management to have less commitment to the job and their promotion opportunities suffer. Ironically, men who do take on a share of the caring role at home, are highly praised as wonderful fathers when they do what mothers do all the time without any praise or applause.

When it is pointed out that men run just about everything outside the house, someone will always point to several female presidents, or politicians, or school principals. As I've mentioned before, the fact that they can name them or even point to them demonstrates how few there are in comparison to males. No one could name all the males running things. That there are a number of women who do succeed to gain status, reward, or acceptance is used to show that the system is working, and women's situation is improving. That also may be true

but at the current rate of change and fall back, women's equality
– if it happens at all – could be achieved in about 250 years give
or take a hundred or maybe a thousand. Impossible to predict.

Meanwhile, you have probably noticed that it is not just men
who maintain the way things are and fight to keep them that
way. We now need to look at the concept that "Women are their
own worst enemies."

12

Women Are Their Own Worst Enemies. (Let's You and Her Fight.)

Abandon the cultural myth that all female friendships must be bitchy, toxic or competitive. This myth is like heels and purses – pretty but designed to SLOW women down.

Roxanne Gay

(Sexism) is not simply something men do to women. It is also something women – products of the same society, after all – do to one another and, most tragically, to themselves.

Jane Caro

THE TITLE of this chapter is a tip of the hat to Eric Berne, author of *Games People Play: The Psychology of Human Relationships*, first published in 1968. It's a brilliant book explaining so much in easy-to-understand ways. One of his "games" is called "Let's you and him fight". A perfect description of focussing attention somewhere else other than where the real problem lies. For women versus women, it's spot on.

Well, are women their own worst enemies? Short answer: Yes and no. Caveat: How could they not?! They've been well taught, and they've been set up. But there's lots more to it than that.

The "worst enemies" myth tells us that:

- Many women are bitchy, toxic and competitive and will tear each other down through gossip, innuendo and just plain nastiness.
- Many women criticise other women for their weight, for their clothes, for non-conforming behaviour, appearance, ageing. Many women are petty, catty and jealous of each other and can't stand to see each other succeed. Many women declare they would rather work for a male boss any time.
- Many women who make it to the top, do not support other women. They see all other female colleagues as a threat.
- Most women are where they are because of their own choices. In this day and age, women can be anything they choose. They just choose not to choose high flying careers, or prestigious positions, or difficult subjects at school, or time-consuming courses, or ask for increased pay or jobs that involve getting dirty!

Sadly, there appears to be a large element of truth in these assertions because we do see women behaving in these ways and good old Confirmation Bias kicks in, and we conclude "See, all women are ….".

We need to acknowledge that too many women do behave like this, but let's explore why and how.

We are now in an era when many of us are as sexist as we were in the 1950s. Just yesterday (in July 2020), a young woman was telling me that her husband insisted on rigid gender roles. It had never occurred to her to negotiate a better deal. Or to tell him to go take a flying leap. She wasn't under threat of violence. She just accepted it. She laughingly referred to it as: "Oh, he's old school". She didn't see it as sexist or unfair. She seemed unaware of any other possibilities for her.

The laws have changed. But in the homes and families, large pockets of society have not changed much at all.

Women's situation in society is little better. A glaring example of this is the Equal Pay legislation fought for and won in the 1960s and implemented in the 1970s and yet women still do not have equal pay. The gender pay gap is at a thirty-year high. Another example is the continuing sexual harassment of, and violence towards, women. If you've read this book from the beginning, you already know many other examples of no change, or even going backwards.

The root causes continue to be acceptance of gender stereotyping and gender roles.

As exposed in almost every chapter in this book, gender roles start in the home with mothers and fathers re-enforcing gender stereotypes for their children. And, if we have aware parents, and we almost escape at that stage, we still have relatives. Family, friends, and television present the all-persuasive binary gendered view of life. By the time we arrive at kindergarten, then school, we are, like the fish, swimming in it.

Many parents and grandparents still buy gender-stereotyped toys for their own children, grandchildren, and those of other friends and relatives. These toys usually emphasise the very different roles, lifestyles and behaviour expected of women and men.

Clothing plays an important role. Many women still dress their sons and daughters very differently. Apart from the constant use of pink for girls, their clothing mainly emphasises looking cute or pretty, especially in dresses that make running, jumping, and climbing difficult. Boys' shorts, trousers, shirts, and shoes are designed to provide protection and freedom of movement. And the underpinning is: the two sexes must look different as well as behave differently. Here we see the Taboo of Sameness at work.

Mothers and fathers grow their little girls' hair long, done up with ornaments, ribbons and clips and a hairstyle that takes much longer to do than their brothers'. This is already setting the stage for the hours and large amounts of money adult women spend on their grooming. It is also the beginning of teaching little girls that they are valued and appreciated for their appearance.

Many schools, both State and private, still insist girls wear skirts or dresses as part of their uniform. Parents and students are pushing for a reform in this area to bring dress code into the modern era. Apart from warmth in winter, and greater freedom of movement, wearing trousers also limits boys' harassment of girls; there's not a lot of fun in sitting under the stairs looking up girls' long trouser legs.

Then there is the constant bombardment of casual comments to girls. "Be careful, sweetheart", "Don't climb that", "Let Daddy do it for you", "Don't get your dress dirty". Caring and concerned? Yes, but also restrictive in a way that boys are not subjected to. Not quite the same as "Get out there and get dirty."

You will hear conversations between little children and parents and grandparents in public places that are perfectly designed to perpetuate gender stereotypes. I don't doubt that parents or grandparents are totally unaware of what they were doing, but repetition drives the point home. They were brought up this way themselves, and all societies pass on the parents' beliefs to their children.

One example will give you the flavour. I still remember a remarkable conversation I overheard on a train.

Grandmother: "What do you want to be when you grow up, darling?"

Granddaughter: "A fireman."

Grandmother: "Oh, a fireperson! That's too dangerous. Wouldn't you rather be a nurse?"

Eeeeek! This is sad in so many ways. First the grandmother changes the word "fireman" to "fireperson". *Well, that's good,* I thought. *She's using gender neutral language.* But then she implies a girl should not do dangerous things. Next, she dismisses the child's opinion entirely and recommends another career. A medical career. *Well, that's great.* But it's not as a doctor. It's still stereotypical female-carer role of nurse. Yes, it's a wonderful career. Yes, wonderful essential hardworking women, and men are doing it these days too, but it is still undervalued and should not be the only option offered to girls. I almost cried right there on the train. Not because of the nursing career being suggested but because of the inevitability and limitation of the choice being offered.

Many women are part of the process that excuses boys' behaviour with the wretched statement "boys will be boys", but insist on their daughters being quiet, polite, helpful, diffident, unselfish, and less active. And, definitely not sexually active.

At this point, we look at our daughters and sons and say "Girls and boys certainly are different. Just look at them." We fail to recall that a lot of parental, family, and societal effort has gone into making them that way. And women are front and centre of the training process of little girls. The tethering of the baby elephants - done with love.

Much of this has been said in previous chapters, and many other books, but it is worth repeating in this context because it is at the child-raising stage that the stereotypical beliefs about males and females are instilled into the next generation.

Remember the Taboo of Sameness.

One set of characteristics give a person more power, confidence, and agency in the world. They are associated with "masculinity" and they are taught to, and expected of, boys.

The other set of characteristics give a person a sense of purpose – to be pleasing, helpful and caring, to focus on home and family rather than the affairs of the world. These are taught to and expected of girls and women and are labelled "femininity".

For anyone who doesn't fit into those two behaviour patterns, the going gets tough.

Girls are mainly taught or expected, directly or unconsciously, to behave in ways that ensure they are not powerful, independent, strong, confident, or highly rewarded for their talents because the talents and skills fostered in girls are not those that society values highly in spite of the constant bleating that tells us we do the most important work in the world, raising the next generation. The characteristics expected of girls are not the attributes associated with leadership, competence, confidence or status. Useful, yes. Worthy of reward, apparently not. What goes quietly unremarked is the fact that society could not function at all without the caring, nurturing, self-sacrificial characteristics of women and girls, but it does not reward them or give them high status. As mentioned before, studies by Amy Cuddy, Susan T. Fiske, and others, have shown that housewives, that is women who devote their life to looking after their husband, children, and home, are perceived to be in the bottom half of social groups in terms of status, lower than blue-collar workers. When people are employed to do the jobs done by women in the home, they are very poorly paid, usually less than a car park attendant.

Women as mothers and grandmothers, aunts and friends, unconsciously play a major role in creating male privilege and female disadvantage and lack of confidence by instilling these differing values in boys and girls. If we do this, we are indeed our own worst enemies, or at least the worst enemies of the next generation of girls. No blame intended. Just awareness raising.

And those pressures are only cemented when maternity services pretty much ignore fathers, the baby change is almost always in the women's washroom and baby groups are routinely adver-tised for mums and toddlers. Men's colleagues are also apt to doubt a man's commitment to the firm he works for when he wants to take paternity leave.

One father, journalist Gideon Burrows, describes his experience of sharing the childcare, and baby rearing equally.

'At playgroups, I've had women sit at the opposite end of the room to avoid me. Outside the pre-school, some women do little to make men part of their world. Out in town with my kids, I'm still asked: "Are you babysitting today? "

He also believes that many men pay lip service to the concept of equally sharing the child-raising, and then come up with a host of reasons as to why it is impractical or even impossible.

He makes the observation: 'Men pretty much run the government, most private companies, the public sector, and the media. If we really wanted a fairer deal (for women), we could make it happen very quickly. We don't because it's not in our interests.'

Women could play a major role in changing the way things are, but first they need to become aware of what they are doing that keeps everything unchanged. There may well be an element of territorialism for some women. Since men still run almost everything in the wider world outside the home, raising the children is one of the few areas that most women have been in charge of. A sort of "Hands off, Buster. This is my area of expertise."

Women's role as the default parent, as well as carer of the sick and elderly, is one of the major factors holding them back in career and money-making – even hobbies and leisure time. The interruption to their career or work timeline disadvantages them in promotion, pay and superannuation. I know. How crass of me to compare motherhood with career and money. But think about it. If men and women shared the caring, both would have a better chance of equality in the workplace. There are other factors involved in ensuring inequality, including Confirmation Bias, gender stereotypes and expectations, male privilege and ego. We have looked at those issues elsewhere. For now, let's address the expectation that women will, or even should, do most of the caring. This firmly puts a woman in a state of dependence on her husband or partner – financially, socially, and intellectually. For the time she spends at home not only impacts on her career, but also on her independence financially as well as her need for adult social contact and stimulation.

We know from numerous studies that this leads to an imbalance of power between women and men in the home. This can, and frequently does, lead to abuse and violence on the part of the man. It's usually the man because society subtly and not so subtly gives him dominance, control, and the expectation that he should be in control. Yes, women can be controlling, abusive and violent, but it's not built into society's expectations of them. Boys and men are expected to be in control, and that includes control of their emotions and, ever so subliminally, in control of women. The one emotion men are permitted to publicly express is anger, and usually in a physical way. How often have you seen an angry man portrayed in the movies as smashing his fist through a wall or knocking everything off the table in front of him. I'm betting he doesn't clean the mess up either. This bang and smash and hit something or someone, is depicted as standard acceptable male behaviour in movies and TV shows. The hero who used his wits and intellect to solve problems, kept his composure under pressure, is long gone. I for one, miss him.

Many women seem embarrassed if another woman raises the issue of Sexism in front of men. And it will usually be a woman who will leap to the defence of the men. When men are accused of Sexism, it appears to be too close to the bone for some women. After all men are our fathers, husbands, brothers, and sons. They are part of our closest relationships. They also run pretty much everything in the world so it's best to stay on the good side of them. These are possible explanations for the behaviour of many women in refusing to recognise Sexism and defending men's behaviour and the way things are.

We can see this behaviour at its most cringeworthy when a public figure (male) makes some outrageous sexist or misogynistic statement, and not only does he still retain his female followers, but they are often the ones who publicly defend him.

When I've asked them why they do this, they usually answer admiringly, "Because he's a strong man". They have obviously bought into the male stereotype and see part of the male role as looking after them, making decisions for them, protecting them from other men and providing for them. In other words, infantilising them. They have learnt to love it and desire it. The Red Pill women mentioned in Chapter 5: Earth Women Are Revolting, are an extreme example of this, but they are out there.

We find some women putting down other women, gossiping and criticising their appearance, their shape, or their speech patterns instead of praising their achievements and encouraging their efforts. Women reinforce the stereotypes by laughing at sexist jokes. They even tell anti-woman jokes themselves, seemingly without realising what they are doing.

Women can be heard to say, "She must have asked for it," when another woman reports that a man or group of men has raped her. They'll say, "Look at that outfit she was wearing," or "She shouldn't have been drinking," or "What was she doing there on her own?"

A woman can even experience a sense of being one of the "in group" if she sides with men against other women. When they are criticising or denigrating other women, perhaps she feels a sense of security, a sense of being "special" because they would not treat her like that. She does not identify with the other woman and may even join in with the taunts or attacks. A uniquely female version of *schadenfreude* with a twist perhaps.

The laws have been changed to give women equal opportunity and equal pay. The attitudes and actions have not, and there is hostility towards discussions of Sexism or misogyny. The "#notallmen" is one such unhelpful response.

As Desmond Tutu said: *If you are neutral in situations of injustice, you have chosen the side of the oppressor.*

In the 1970s, feminists found great enlightenment and support in "consciousness-raising" groups. By sharing their experiences of being female, they began to see that there was a commonality and a pattern to the constraints that society placed on them. Women began to realise that the setbacks and discrimination they each faced and the frustrations they each felt, were not isolated incidents but a sexist system operating across society. More women began to realise that they were not alone or unique in thinking that something was not quite right with "the way things are".

In 1971, many of us were awakened by Helen Reddy singing "I am Woman". Uplifting and inclusive of women and men. Go back and listen again. It's an anthem.

But consciousness-raising groups are out of fashion now, and the women who see through the fog of social programming have had to do it for themselves through reading and talking, learning from others, and thinking it through. As noted throughout this book, Sexism is still alive and well but it is now subtler, more subterranean, and the gaslighting has moved up a few notches to meet the questioning of uppity women. Women are being sucked back into the confining prison or onto the teetering pedestal of gender stereotypes while still being told that of course they can be anything they want to be, they now have equality, everyone is judged on merit, Sexism doesn't exist. And don't forget, the huge profits involved in selling the gender stereotype to both women and men, as well as girls and boys.

But many women themselves are not taking up opportunities or insisting on their rights. Why do many women appear blind to, or accepting of, the way things are and the disadvantages, injustices, and abuses that are part of women's daily lives? Why is this so? The answer is all around us.

Part of the answer probably lies in the intimate, co-dependent relationship between men and women which I have already mentioned. But there is an additional aspect we saw in the tethering of the baby elephants.

It's time to look at internalised Sexism.

This is defined as the involuntary belief by girls and women that the stereotypes, lies and myths about girls and women that are delivered to everyone in a sexist society ARE TRUE. It is one form of internalised oppression.

We've looked at the absorption of everything we are told before the age of seven. We've looked at the ways gender beliefs are presented through language, toys, clothes, attitudes, entertainment, games, and adult reactions. Once past the age of six, we are still bombarded with the gender message. Conformity, gender bias, Confirmation Bias all kick in to continue the affirmation of gender as natural. The sexes are very different and that's the way it should be. They are meant to complement each other, to attract each other, and each has her or his appropriate role and place in the grand scheme of things.

It's predictable that a lifetime of hearing such messages, blatantly, subtly, or humorously expressed, will lead to belief in them.

Tell a lie often enough, and it becomes the truth.

Inevitable really since women and men spend a lot of time and energy in ensuring they perform and conform to their gendered characteristics to the best of their ability.

A man puts his heart into being masculine. He fears the derision of his peers and social emasculation by women.

A woman spends a lot of time and money on the physical aspects of femininity as well as her behavioural performance. She is denigrated if she does not perform the appropriate feminine behaviour of being pleasing, diffidence, not being too self-confident, loud, or bossy. She fears being disliked, unloved, and alone.

The second consequence of these constant messages is that women and girls develop internalized Sexism or even misogyny. They begin to doubt themselves and other females and support or collude with the perpetuation of Sexism. We all, men and women, collude with Sexism when we perform our designated roles and behave in the expected manner for our sex or gender.

In Chapters 3 and 12, I referred to the findings of anthropologists and sociologists who have found that when two groups live in a close or dependent relationship, the least powerful group will, over time take on the values and beliefs of the more powerful, higher status group. This happens even if the values absorbed are disadvantageous to their own group. They will even enforce those values on to other members of their own group including teaching them to their children.

The largest group ever to be conquered and colonised is that of women. Over thousands of years, women have shared, absorbed, believed, and taught their daughters to act in the stereotypical manner that men perceived and required of them. In this way, the views and conventions and stereotypical thinking of men have become the "common knowledge" of the community which the two groups have created in their close relationship. The stereotyping perceptions of the more powerful group have become the shared perception of both men and women.

Most relationships between different groups do not involve living in the same house, growing up together, loving and caring for members of the other group. Groups such as Catholics and Protestants can stereotype and despise each other without such co-dependence and intimacy as men and women experience. White people can and do stereotype people of colour and indigenous people, but the stereotyped groups do not themselves believe these perceptions because they do not usually live intimately with or depend on white people. They maintain their own beliefs about themselves based on their culture, their own experiences and teachings. Women and girls on the other hand, are subjected non-stop to gender stereotypical beliefs about themselves in their own homes, by those they love and care for, in their education, entertainment and in the world around them. And they are taught to behave in stereotypical ways to fit into their group.

Women are not their own worst enemies. Their worst enemy is the structural, institutional society we live in, a society based on gender stereotypes and the constraints of gender roles. It's not all that good for most men either, but although men are socialised into and constrained by a gender role, every gendered society on earth gives males the majority of privilege, power and reward.

Little girls are told they can be and do anything they want to. The reality of the world around them tells a completely different story. Women have internalised the limitations society has placed upon them. So many women have said to me "Oh I couldn't do that". I usually reply, "Neither could anyone else till they tried, male or female". Where did the numerous restrictive beliefs come from? The answer again: everywhere around them.

As Simone de Beauvoir wrote: "… her wings are cut and then she is blamed for not knowing how to fly."

Technically, this is a form of oppression which occurs when one group has more access to power and privilege than another group, and when that power and privilege is used to maintain the status quo (i.e., domination of one group over another).It affects many groups, with different skin colour, customs, religions, ethnicity, minorities, and other marginalised groups. The largest group affected is half the human race. Women and girls.

The dehumanising control of women's potential is far more than physical or social. It is buried deep in our psyche. It has become internalised oppression. What has been done to women and girls is nothing short of a psychological obscenity. This could be likened to a form of Stockholm Syndrome on a monstrous scale.

Women's worst enemies are those who perpetrate and perpetuate the structure. And yes, some of those people are women, but this is a symptom of the system not its cause. Sexist men are similarly a product of their culture and their time, but the associated privileges can make them resistant to the need for change.

Merchandising, marketing, entertainment, some religions, and almost universal unconscious gender bias ensure the system is supported and continued.

At a personal level, women have been taught that their major purpose is to be loved by a man. They have been taught to compete for the favours of men. This obviously sets them up to see other women as rivals.

In the workplace and politics, given that the number of places of authority or status occupied by women is so small, women quite rightly perceive that they are not really competing with men for these positions. They are competing with other women. If they treat one another as the enemy, it is again a symptom of the problem not its cause.

Part of the "women are their own worst enemies" scenario is envy of women who rise above the conventional status. This is an emotion which both sexes experience. It is not unique to women.

Envy can be positive or negative. Positive envy involves seeing someone like yourself succeeding and wanting to be like them. The outcome can be observing how the successful person became that way and trying to learn from that. Negative envy is the desire to pull the successful person down, so they won't be better than you. To take something away from them. This is the nasty behaviour that arises in some women when another woman is successful or popular.

But it is not a uniquely female characteristic. There are men who do this. They are nasty and mean too. Women are no better, nicer, or kinder than men. It is not logical to assume that they would or should be. We are all unique. Women, like men, are all different and individual. We are moulded by our experiences and our reaction to our experiences. For each of us those experiences will be different and the person we become will inevitably be different. Some of us are good, some are kind, some are nice. Some aren't. We do not say men are their own worst enemies, and yet many men attack and criticise and fight and back stab each other all the time. Competing with other men is built into the performance requirements of most forms of masculinity

Most of us are familiar with, and probably believe in, the idea of the Queen Bee. When we see women bosses being bitchy and unsupportive to other women, we take it as a confirmation of our beliefs.

A report by Conrad Liveris, one of Australia's leading employment and workplace experts, "Gender Equality at Work in 2018" showed that the belief in the Queen Bee is a myth. In his report he states "… *when women hold management roles, they tangibly support other women. Though only 6.5% of Australian companies have a female board chair, they are more likely to bring more women onto the board and have more women in senior management. I found the same with female Chief Executive Officers, who create pathways to management for other women. The idea that women are their own worst enemies just doesn't stack up."*

Obviously, not all women are benevolent any more than all men are, but the Queen Bee and bitchy boss myth need to be knocked on the head. Sure, there are bitchy, nasty women. Why wouldn't there be? We are not all nice. And neither are all men.

Liveris continues *"Analysing the 500 largest companies in the country [Australia], I also found that when women are in senior leadership roles those businesses are more likely to have proactive diversity and inclusion processes and active mentoring programs."*

Yes, the actions of many women do reinforce Sexism but it is a cruel and self-serving deception to blame women for their own secondary status or invisibility or low income, or rape trauma or broken bones and psychological scars. Society has taught us well from the moment we were born. Each defenceless child is force-fed the "truth" of gender stereotypes and inevitability of gender roles and the less than subtle lower status attached to the female. Most of us have believed the myths.

Some people had mothers or fathers who saw through the myths themselves and helped the growing child to perceive herself as more than the myth pretended. Those girls (and boys) were the lucky ones.

One of our modern-day heroes and a defender of education for girls, Malala, the Pakistani girl who was shot in the head by the Taliban for speaking up on behalf of education for girls, had such a father. He put her name on the family tree – a 300-year-old document that had never mentioned a female. He enrolled her in school and took great pleasure in writing her name on the enrolment form. His own five sisters had never had their names recorded anywhere. They simply did not exist in their own country. Girls have only one virtue and that was obedience. He admitted he taught her to unlearn the lesson of feminine obedience. "I didn't clip her wings," he said.

Sadly, most parents are prisoners of gender roles themselves and continue to pass on the teachings of their culture to their children. However, as women mature and age, many of them begin to question, at least within their own minds, the fairness or the truth of it all. For older women, liberation from the constraints of the feminine stereotype often arrives with divorce or widowhood. Alone with no responsibility for partner or children, invisible to the male gaze which prefers the young and nubile, the older woman begins to please herself often for the first time in her life. But a sharing of perceptions among women is needed to bring about societal change, and a groundswell or rebellion or even a sense of unity of purpose is very difficult to achieve for women.

One of the major hindrances for women is that most of them do not perceive themselves and other women as part of a group. We have seen that their position is unique among subordinate groups because of their intimate relationship with men.

They are closer to some men than they will ever be with other women. This weakens and divides them because they distance themselves from other women and refuse to see the patterns of Sexism within society and the violence and misogyny of some men. Each case is seen as happening to another woman, to individual women who are different from me, women who were in situations I will never be in. Such things do not happen to me or to women I personally know. As members of the subordinate culture, some women find it safer to attack other members of that culture rather than take on the dominant group. It is a survival mechanism forced on women because of their second-class status. Much of what has been written about the effect of colonisation on colonised people explains women's situation, particularly internalised oppression. Women's behaviour is a symptom of their situation. It is the sexist structure of society that is at fault not women, but it is more comprehensible and less overwhelming to see it as the problem of individuals rather than to face the enormity of systemic oppression. Most of us focus on specifics rather than taking on the totality of systems. It probably helps us retain our sanity.

To end this chapter on a cheerful note because I'm guessing you're needing it, stop right now and go and listen to Bebe Buell singing "By a Woman." Make sure you watch the video of her on YouTube.

13

Does it Really Matter?
(LET ME COUNT THE WAYS.)

Because I am a woman, I must make unusual efforts to succeed. If I fail, no one will say, "She doesn't have what it takes"; They will say, "Women don't have what it takes;

Clare Boothe Luce

A gender-equal society would be one where the word 'gender' does not exist: where everyone can be themselves.

Gloria Steinem

MY GRANDDAUGHTER WAS six years old when she informed me that only boys could be heroes because all the superheroes were male. I thought about that. If you think all the focus on the male as the default human with all the admirable characteristics, is pretty harmless, let's check that out.

First up, boys can look around and see role models in almost every area of real life. Not so little girls. And, as my granddaughter observed, no superheroes were female.

When I was growing up, we did have Wonder Woman, Mary Marvel, Super Girl and Sheena, Queen of the Jungle. The only one still around is Wonder Woman, and she's been hard to find until very recently. When I told my daughter what my grand-daughter had said, she went out to buy a Wonder Woman book for the little girl. She had to search in three bookstores before she found one. After some considerable pressure from feminists, a Wonder Woman movie was created and screened in 2017. She now does appear on bookshelves and movies. And a smattering of new female heroes has arrived. Compared to the number of male superheroes, a "smattering" pretty much sums it up.

All those toys for boys, and toys for girls, people assure us are catering to what children naturally want. As we have seen, the problem is, this makes many assumptions about what girls and boys might like to play with, or be interested in. It makes the damaging assumption that all girls are the same and all boys are the same, and the two groups are very different from each other.

Even if this were true, the biggest problem with this, is that differences between the sexes are not valued equally. They are generally used to "prove" one group is superior to the other. There are ways of using difference that intentionally, or some-times unintentionally, imply status or superiority and inferiority. Think of Jews, black people, other people of colour, older people, gay, lesbian, bisexual, and transgender people. And the largest marginalised group of all, women and girls.

We've established that most males and females are raised to be different. Is that a problem? What's the harm in all of this gender stereotyping, conforming and gender role expectations? And if it is harmful, who or what suffers?

Even contemplating the answer to that question, could make any perceptive person dizzy and overwhelmed. Where to begin? When looked into in detail, the situation of women around the globe is overwhelming. From the trivial to the horrific, women's lives are ruled by Sexism, misogyny, subjugation and control.

Where does it start?

It actually starts with you and me, and him and her. On the home front! Personal pressures, expectations, male/ female relationships, family relationships, media, even clothing, posture and language.

Performing to gender stereotype, or "doing gender", puts pressure on both sexes. In the case of males, "doing masculinity" involves such behaviours as being independent, strong, and competitive, all of which sound good, but they must also deny anxieties and insecurities, and the suppression of almost any emotion other than anger or triumph. Male peer pressure requires a relentless presentation of "masculinity" or risk ridicule, ostracization or even violence. Having a job, particularly a blue-collar job that allows a man to take pride in his masculinity is part of the performance for men of lower income status. Their jobs are the very ones that are fast disappearing. The male breadwinner role is becoming more difficult to maintain. Mental health issues, suicide and male family violence have been linked to the pressures of failed expectations of masculinity. Go back and check out The Man Box statistics we saw in Chapter 9: Boys Will Be Boys.

We have already looked at some of the effects of "doing femininity" in relation to participation in the workforce. There is also the induced lack of confidence, diffidence, dependence, and acceptance of the *status quo* which limit women's self-belief and agency. Agency refers to their capacity to act in the world to change their circumstances and environment.

Clothing: Something as simple as appropriate feminine clothing has its effect. In Western culture, women's clothing, particularly formal clothing, is designed to show a woman's shape. This often means there are no pockets. Trivial you might think. What do women do without pockets? They carry handbags containing phones, money, and papers that could identify them. Bags are easily separated from their owners during a disaster. This means that women killed in fires or natural disasters are often difficult to identify. In addition, two-thirds of the people killed in natural disasters are women. The reason? Because their clothing does not allow them the freedom to run or swim. In an earthquake, flood, or tsunami, traditional clothing in many countries subject to these disasters, prevents women from running or, in the case of water, drags them under whether or not they can swim.

Mental Health: Gender stereotyping and gender roles also take their toll on mental health. Frustration, a lack of self-worth, a sense of uselessness, wasted potential - all contribute to unhappiness, and depression. In both sexes and all genders, a sense of powerlessness can lead to debilitating depression and, in too many cases, particularly among males, it can lead to suicide.

Being different is a problem when it is used to separate the sexes so that they come to believe they are polar opposites. It is also a problem when the differences are exaggerated, carefully taught or downright untrue. As if that were not enough, these "differences" are then used to judge and evaluate every one of us.

Believing that men and women are VERY different is a major problem. It stereotypes women and girls, men and boys, and people of different genders or sexual orientations. Problems with rigid gender roles and gender stereotyping are far-reaching. They include:

- Both women and men's development as full human beings is constrained and limited. A staggering amount of human potential is wasted, undeveloped or unused in both males and females.
- Women and others who are not male and/or do not conform to appropriate masculine behaviour and sexual orientation are discriminated against, objectified, ignored, rendered powerless, abused, and worse.
- Many women and girls develop a sense of dependence, lack of confidence and diffidence which greatly limits their own development and any possible contribution to human progress and development.
- Men and boys develop a sense of entitlement and privilege that can lead to harassment, abuse and violence towards women and girls, and other groups considered lesser beings.
- Men and boys' masculinity is deeply fragile. Any threat to their perception of themselves as "masculine" can result in anger, abuse, aggression, murder, self-harm, and suicide.
- The development of whole societies Is limited academically, emotionally, and economically.
- All of these issues are exacerbated when mixed with the intersectionality of race, religion, social class, disability and sexuality. Within every marginalised or disadvantaged group, the burden of, and attitudes to, stereotypical femininity delivers a double whammy.

A good and successful girl or woman doesn't need to be intelligent, inventive, clever, or funny. She doesn't need to earn a lot of money or discover a cure for cancer. She needs to:

- look pretty
- be sweet

- never be loud or opinionated
- smile
- put other people's needs ahead of her own
- and care for others' emotional and physical comfort
- And when she's got all that sorted, she needs to get a man and have some babies. A single woman is bad enough but not having kids pretty much makes her a waste of space.

There is tremendous harm for both sexes and all genders in this stereotypical way of organising people. Gender stereotypes are used to value heterosexual males of all skin colours, ethnicities, and religions, above all other categories of humans within their group. This leads to a sense of entitlement and superiority on the part of men, and harassment, denigration, abuse, rape, and violence against women. This also includes the murder of women and girls as if they were a disposable item to be tossed in the gutter when finished with.

Seeing people as groups rather than individuals, leads to objectifying them and dehumanising them. Once you dehumanise people, lack of empathy on your part allows them to be brutalised. This was the technique used by the Nazis. It enabled them to commit atrocities against Jews and other groups. Dehumanising propaganda is commonly used against the enemy in times of war. Dehumanising propaganda against marginalised groups including women, is used, subtly and not so subtly, all of the time.

The difficulty for achieving any change or progress is the fact that we see our society and our way of doing things, as "normal" and "part of human nature". This is particularly so with gender roles and attitudes to women.

Even more powerful is the fact that it is enforced and confirmed in the privacy and sanctity of most of our homes. Through childhood to marriage, we learn our gendered place in the home and, by extension, our place in the world. Even if our home did not enforce gender roles, the rest of the world puts us right on track for a gendered destiny as soon as we enter kindergarten.

A recent six-year global study of gender expectations found that, by the age of ten, children around the world believe their culture's gender stereotypes. The researchers found a surprising but depressing uniformity across all cultures. Both boys and girls by the age of ten believe that girls are weak and vulnerable while boys are strong and independent.

Societies hand men much more power, status, and privilege relative to women.

Understandably, many men resist change or even the possibility of change. No wonder, since it is they who benefit most from the way things are. It's like asking politicians to vote for a pay cut for themselves. It takes a very aware man to recognise and admit the privilege he enjoys as a male, and to see the injustices and abuse that women face. And a very fair-minded man to try to do anything about it. Fortunately, they do exist. Throughout history and in our own time, some men have worked to improve the status of women. We need many more of them. Not only do men have the influence in the current set up, but their gender identity is fast choking them and becoming damaging to all of us. Toxic forms of masculinity are damaging to everyone and seem to be increasing. "Domestic" violence, road rage, violent assaults, radicalisation, mass murders show us that many men, disturbingly particularly young men are seeking more violent ways of expressing their frustrations and confirmation of their masculinity.

We have a habit of attempting to explain these things at an individual level even to the point of exonerating men. We'll explain it away with proclamations of "She must have asked for it", "He was a good bloke, a great family man, active in the community", "He'd been under a lot of stress lately", "He just lost it!". Of course, these explanations are not offered if the perpetrator is a member of a marginalised group such as an indigenous man or a Muslim in a Christian country. But they are almost invariably used if the perpetrator is white, middle class and heterosexual.

Religion, science, and public attitudes underpin pretty much every aspect of our lives. They are the lenses through which society teaches us to see and interpret the world around us. Our interpretations dictate our attitudes to the world and to ourselves. They are the invisible bars of the cage that holds us "in our place". Not just women, but men too. Although as Gloria Steinem rightly pointed out, men's prison is at least carpeted.

We are surrounded by disadvantage, discrimination, and unconscious bias against women. Our societies suffer from inefficiency and waste of human talent. In every country including yours and mine, women are undervalued and underpaid. Women are harassed, abused, beaten, raped and murdered. If it's not happening to us or someone we know, most of us bury our heads in the sand and ignore it. Particularly if we have loving fathers and husbands, and wonderful sons.

Women are told they do the most important work on earth – raising children. Not to mince words, this is patronising piffle and a brilliant example of gaslighting. If people really believed this, as I've said earlier, women's work in the home would be of high status and highly paid since that is how we express value in Western society and, very likely, men would be doing it.

Women are told their work is important because they are raising the next generation. Half of the next generation are girls who are then told their role is to raise the next generation. It seems the only ones benefiting from all this raising are the men and boys.

So, while the women are raising the next generation, the men can pretty much do and be everything else. While social class is a factor in the amount of freedom and opportunity a male has, all men have far greater freedom, opportunity, and more privileges than most women.

The vitally important role performed by women, housewives at home caring for their children and providing all the domestic services that a man needs to keep him sustained and comfortable and bringing home the bacon, this vital work is hardly valued at all. As we've seen, it isn't even included in the calculation of a nation's Gross National Product, even though it's likely that without this performance of work, there would be very little other GDP possible. To add insult to injury, a study of contemporary stereotypes mentioned in the previous chapter, showed that "housewives" were seen to be in the lower half of all social groups in status, below blue-collar workers, and women in general, and well below men in general. They were considered of similar incompetence to the elderly and disabled.

It's also true that women's role as carer and chief cook and bottle washer, does influence or even force some of them to take on casual or part-time work, or work that is not as demanding, responsible, or higher paid. These pragmatic decisions by women are often used to show that women's lower pay and lower promotion levels are due to their own choices and not to discrimination against them. However, research data shows that such practical choices account for only about a third of the difference in men's and women's wages and promotion and career choices.

For example, the Australian Government's Workplace Gender Equality Agency noted that:

The gender pay gap is influenced by a number of factors, including:

- conscious and unconscious discrimination and bias in hiring and pay decisions,
- women and men working in different industries and different jobs, with female-dominated industries and jobs attracting lower wages,
- lack of workplace flexibility to accommodate caring and other responsibilities, especially in senior roles,
- high rates of part-time work for women to accommodate caring and other responsibilities,
- women's greater time out of the workforce for caring responsibilities impacting career progression and opportunities,
- women's disproportionate share of unpaid caring and domestic work.

It's a cruel joke to taunt women with the saying, "You can't have it all!" No one says that to a man. He traditionally has access to the back-up services of a woman that make it possible for him to come pretty close – in his profession, his social life, his sport and recreation, his toys (cars, bikes, boats). She will take care of the house and the kids and his sick father, if he wants to play golf, or meet up with a few mates for a drink or a poker game or take an extra course of study to ensure his promotion.

The fact is some women, perhaps even many, might take on employed roles with more responsibility and pay, they might apply for promotion or further their own education, if they were not bound to be the unpaid carers of the world. Many women want that role. Others do not. Some would like it to be shared with their partner. And some men would like that too. A man should have the same choice as a woman when it comes to being a full-time parent. The point is, it should be a choice for both men and women, something they decide together.

Sure, there are some male/female relationships where the man pulls his weight and shares the homemaking and the child-raising and the social calendar, medical appointments, and supports his partner's career or education. People see it as highly praiseworthy or highly odd – certainly not "normal".

It is also fair to say at this point that it is humanly possible for men to share the caring and cooking and cleaning particularly if women were paid at the same rate as men for the same work in employment. The usual argument used, if any discussion arises as to who should stay home with the children, is that the man usually earns more. This is so because of the gender pay gap, but also because most men tend to marry down and women marry up. This means that men usually choose to marry a woman who is younger than they are, less educated and, conse-quently, earning less. Women do the opposite. This pay gap between the sexes, makes it appear quite reasonable and prac-tical for the man to continue in his job while she looks after the family. Add to this the stigma for a man being supported by his wife, and it's no contest.

Some men do share the domestic role, some even take on the role of househusband while their wives go to work. Attitudes and organisations, however, do not universally support this progress, even where enabling it is required by the law. Employers are not all supportive of giving men leave or flexible hours to fit in with home responsibilities, and colleagues are often less than sympathetic. It's just not "manly". The man is still seen as "helping" his partner even though it is their house and their children's care that he is participating in. Family and friends still refer to the man as "babysitting" when he looks after his own children while his wife/partner does something else. People still fall about with admiration if a man cooks a meal, and they are quick to tell his wife how lucky she is.

Men often assume they are "helping" equally but when observed and analysed, it is rarely as much of a share as they think it is. Even the words "helping" and "babysitting" his own children, indicate an attitude of mind that says, "It's really her job and I am helping her out".

Judged Differently

Conforming to gender stereotypes teaches many girls and women to be modest, quiet, diffident. These are characteristics that do not help in salary negotiation or promotion to more responsible and better paying jobs. Women who step outside the performance of "femininity", are seen as unlikable and less likely to be employed. A confident, articulate, assertive man capable of putting forward his talents and achievements is perceived as promotion material. A woman exhibiting the same characteristics is seen as pushy, immodest, and unlikable, and not desirable as a colleague let alone being promoted.

Research using an identical job application but with a male name on half of the copies, and a female name on the other half, produces positive reactions for the male, while the female is perceived to be hard, cold, unlikable, unemployable. Women applying for promotion are confronted by a double bias – behaviour expected of a leader and behaviour expected of a woman.

As Alice said to the Red Queen, *Where I come from, when we run very fast, we get somewhere. Here we have to run very fast to stay in one spot.*

And yet so many women deny or seem blind to the systemic imbalance of power and opportunity between the sexes. As we saw in the previous chapter, this is the work of internalised oppression. Much of what is attributed to or expected of each sex, is maintained to be "natural" and therefore accepted as inevitable. Cunning piece of gaslighting because if you don't know you're in a cage, you never try to escape.

As a result of gender roles turning into gender stereotypes, women are disadvantaged in many ways, and the favouring of males leads to dominance and superiority being built into the male psyche. The outcome of this imbalance of power and lack of respect is Sexism. The result can be the selection of mediocre men over more talented women. Women have known for a long time they have to be twice as good as a man to get half the recognition or promotion. It's so obvious but accepted, that it's joked about. This means that countries, companies, and organisations rarely choose from the total pool of talent available and, consequently, may miss the best person for the job. Economies of nations, policies of governments, and the health of individuals, are affected.

At a personal level, Sexism leads to abuse, violence, rape and murder, and the terrorising of women and children in their own homes.

We grow up separating boys and girls and men and women and learning how very different the sexes are. Men say "Just what do women want? I don't understand them." And women say: "He doesn't listen. And he never talks to me."

The most important relationship for our survival as a species, male and female, becomes a journey of misunderstanding and misinformation. At times, it becomes one of manipulation and exploitation on both sides. For the more vulnerable or damaged among us, it also can lead to violence and death.

There are still too many men who do not respect women and consider them good for only one thing. So many women spend hours focussing on their appearance, body shape and size. All done to attract and please men – and impress other women.

Stereotypes harm academic pursuits and career choices. They increase the use of self-defeating behaviours. Trying to conform to the stereotype increases stress and anxiety.

Even the porn industry is moulding the sexual attitudes, beliefs and expectations of men and boys. For many, it has become their main source of sex education. Women's sexual needs and pleasure are rarely part of porn. The location, if not the existence, of the clitoris appears to be unknown to many men. As the old joke goes: A man's idea of foreplay, "Are you awake, dear?"

The male reliance on porn is re-enforcing stereotypes of male dominance and female submission and destroying concepts of intimate, respectful, egalitarian relationships between men and women.

The World's Oldest Prejudice

Writer and commentator, Jack Holland, wrote a book entitled *Misogyny, the World's Oldest Prejudice*. In it, he detailed what has been done to women for more than ten thousand years, simply because they are women. Women have been the largest group oppressed for the longest time. It continues in all societies today in various degrees of severity, sometimes openly and sometimes subtly. It often goes unrecognised because it is so normalised that many people declare Sexism no longer exists.

Sexism, rooted in the PRIME MYTH of difference, not only exists, but it justifies different treatment of the sexes and genders. It justifies different expectations, and different valuing of male and female, as well as feminine and masculine. It justifies different status and different power, different rewards, and different visibility.

It excuses inexcusable masculine behaviour. It blames women and protects men even when they are guilty. It is the myth that limits women's beliefs about their own potential and performance. It condemns men to a limited even dangerous version of masculinity. At the same time, it gives them privilege and power.

This PRIME MYTH is behind the denigration, harassment, violence and horrific deaths of women globally. As the United Nations has expressed it: the greatest abuse of human rights on this planet.

Yes, men and women, males and females are different. That's obvious. The problem is that this fact has been pushed way out of proportion to reality. Differences have been exaggerated or created, taught and reinforced.

Men and women are much more alike than they are different. There are greater differences among men than between men and women. Likewise, there are greater differences among women than there are between women and men.

As mentioned at the beginning of this book, humans are not born with an inbuilt "nature". The commonly used statement, "It's only human nature", is also a myth. Much of our behaviour and attitudes and beliefs are learnt after birth. We may not have the same nature, but we all have the same needs.

Human Needs

An American psychologist, Abraham Maslow, developed a hierarchy of human needs which is very interesting when considered beside the place of women in societies. Maslow found that we all, yes, all humans regardless of sex, gender, or race, have basic needs, but there is a particular order in which we all seek to satisfy those needs. One lot of needs has to be satisfied before we can show much, or even any, interest in the others. Once the first lot of needs is satisfied, we turn our attention to the next in the range. Our needs in order of their importance to us are:

1. Our Bodies – air, water, food, sex, shelter, clothing, sleep.
2. Our Safety – freedom from fear, sickness, injury.
3. Our need for love and a sense of belonging – friendship, family, intimacy, connections with others.
4. Our Self Esteem – confidence, achievements, respect of others, need for individuality.
5. Our need to be ourselves – self-actualisation, self-expression, purpose, creativity, spontaneity, meaning in life, developing our individual potential.

Maslow's work is usually illustrated in a pyramid shape with the needs of our bodies at the base and the need for self-actualisation at the peak.

| *Figure 8: Maslow's Hierarchy of Needs*

The top two human needs of self-esteem and self-actualisation are implicitly, socially and, in many countries, legally denied to women. We have seen in Chapter 8: Stay as Sweet as You Are, how women and girls' self-esteem is deliberately eroded before the age of puberty. This is done to make them "feminine".

Maslow said: *Musicians must make music, artists must paint, poets must write if they are to be ultimately at peace with themselves.* **What human beings can be, they must be.** *They must be true to their own nature. This need we may call self-actualization.*

He is using the word "nature" here in the sense of unique and individual potential. This is different from the slippery concept of "human nature" mentioned earlier.

The place society allocates to women and girls, makes them the carers and the nurturers who, in most societies, are not supposed to strive to become anything else or to serve their own needs, only the needs of others.

In addition, consider the many women who live in relationships with violent men. Worldwide, male violence against women is currently at epidemic proportions. In relation to Maslow's chart, these women don't even get past Level 2: Freedom from fear and injury – in their own homes.

Level 5: Self-actualisation! Most women don't even get close. For women, once they have performed their duty and produced children, thinking about themselves is a luxury. Before that, their self-care is usually directed solely to "looking good" so that they will please and attract men and being "nice" so they will please everyone. And don't forget to smile.

Most women and girls do not spend hours with their friends practising a musical instrument and jamming till they're good enough to form a band. They don't spend hours surfing with mates till they're really good at it. They don't go down to the skate park and practice till they're hot shots. They rarely throw a ball around with friends just for the sheer joy of it. The invaluable times that boys spend informally doing things together that build their skills are not part of most girls' lives.

Next time you see a sports field with boys or young men running, shouting, laughing, and enjoying themselves together in an informal game of football, or a skate park with boys and young men enjoying the thrill of movement and the adrenaline rush of risk, pause to celebrate the fact that not only are they improving their physical skills, but they are also stimulating their intellect. Then ask yourself, "I wonder what all the girls are doing. Where are they?"

Having time to paint or write or develop a scientific theory or become the leader of a political movement you're passionate about, is not considered part of normal feminine activities. To their great credit some women do succeed at self-actualising activities, against all the odds, the discrimination, and the criticism. On a far more practical level, those activities require someone who will cook your meals, wash your clothes, do the shopping, and mind the children if you have them. In other words, you need a wife. Relatively few women have such support.

Years ago, there was a satirical story circulating about Dorothy Wordsworth. She was the sister of the great poet William Wordsworth who wrote the memorable poem *Daffodils*.

The poem begins:

I wandered lonely as a cloud

That floats on high o'er vales and hills,

When all at once I saw a crowd,

A host, of golden daffodils;

William and Dorothy lived together and neither of them married. They were both writers, he was a poet, and she was both a poet and a diarist, but she is better known as Wordsworth's sister. Dorothy appears to have happily served as maid and housekeeper for her brother but, although imaginary, this story does spotlight the hurdles women's caring role can place in the way of any other talent. Here's the story:

One morning as Dorothy took pen and paper and sat down to write a poem, she was interrupted by William's voice upstairs.

"I can't find my socks."

Dorothy called out, "There in the second drawer of your dresser, William." She picked up her pen. "Now, where was I? *I wandered lonely as a ....*"

"I still can't find them," came the voice from upstairs.

"Just a minute. I'm coming," she called back. A few minutes later, she returned and sat down, picked up her pen and began to write. *I wandered lonely as a cloud, That floats...*

"Dorothy, I'm getting hungry. Could I have some soup?"

Dorothy put her pen down and went into the kitchen. She served the soup, cleaned up the kitchen, and returned to her writing desk.

"Dorothy, could you bring my notebook and pen. We could go for a walk in that field with the beautiful daffodils."

Dorothy sighs, picks up his notebook and pen.

"Coming William," she replies.

William Wordsworth was a great poet. This story is not meant to belittle him or his work. It is a playful way of demonstrating the different hurdles facing talented women and men. We have no idea what Dorothy could have achieved if she had the services of a housekeeper.

Virginia Woolf wrote a similar story, about Shakespeare's sister, imagining "what if" Shakespeare had an equally innately talented sister. The hurdles that would face her would include lack of education available to girls, the ability to travel safely to London without being raped or murdered, and freedom to mix with others in taverns and theatres, and the unlikely acceptance of fellow playwrights and producers. This was at a time when women were not permitted to act on the stage (female roles were performed by men). Even being in the audience was not what respectable women did. I suspect any work that the talented Ms Shakespeare might have produced, would never see the light of day.

Women's role in the home and in society has not been conducive to developing potential or even providing the opportunity for creativity.

Author and inspirational speaker, Barbara Winter, maintains that creativity is nourished by:

- A sense of adventure
- Rejection of sexual stereotypes
- Exposure to new experiences such as travel or hobbies

- Healthy habits, including nourishing food, and getting enough sleep and exercise
- Laughter and good spirits
- Challenging yourself by working at the height of your skill and competence.

Interestingly, Maslow also said, "A first rate soup is more creative than a second-rate painting". Sadly, while women the world over might be expressing their creativity by creating first rate soups, it doesn't seem to have raised their status or their income.

14

You, Me and the Whole Damn World
(STILL COUNTING.)

Gender inequality holds back the growth of individuals, the development of countries and the evolution of societies, to the disadvantage of both men and women.

State of World Population Report

Gender equality is more than a goal in itself. It is a precondition for meeting the challenge of reducing poverty, promoting sustainable development, and building good governance.

Kofi Annan

THE CONTINUED APPLICATION of Sexism and misogyny affects more than individual human beings. It's a problem of global proportions, affecting the wellbeing of societies, the progress of humanity, the invention, discovery, or development of healthier, happier ways of life on earth, enriching societies through the development of the talents of all their citizens, growing economies, and protecting the environment.

Societies and individuals have been operating on the tenets of Sexism, patriarchy and male dominance for around ten thousand years. Ten thousand years is a long time to wait for fairness. And yet there are those who say women have made great progress in the last 150 years, or maybe the last 60 years in spite of continuing opposition and backlash. They seem to think women should be impressed and grateful.

Women's progress towards equality is slower than a snail race to the stars.

Figure 9: A Snail Race to the Stars. Women's Equality: 10,000 years and still not achieved -

The rules, beliefs and restrictions of bygone eras and necessities have been kept intact, given force through law and religion and the collusion of science. This ensures that change is slow or in many cases non-existent.

This resistance to change in culture, still ensures that each society and each individual usually only explores a tiny fraction of their horizon of possibilities. Individuals seeking greater knowledge have had to fight, often at great risk to themselves, to convince their societies that there was more to know and do and be, just beyond that horizon. Think of the philosopher and mathematician Hypatia or the astronomer Galileo, the explorer Christopher Columbus or the feminist writer Mary Wollstonecraft. Christian monks pursued Hypatia for being way too clever for a woman and skinned her alive with oyster shells; the Catholic Church threatened to burn Galileo at the stake until he recanted his observation that the earth moved around the sun, Mary Wollstonecraft was labelled a "hyena in petticoats" for suggesting men and women could be equals. The only one to come out reasonably intact was Columbus. He was fortunate to put forward a proposal based on the belief that the world was round and could make his sponsors very rich. In fact, they almost made him a Saint – many years after his death of course. He and Joan of Arc were up for consideration. Joan's case was looking shaky since she was apt to ignore the priests in favour of listening to angels. Then it was discovered that Christopher had fathered an illegitimate child. Christopher was out on his ear, and Joan got the Sainthood.

But, more seriously, we are all still required to live within the horizon of possibilities established by men who lived thousands of years before us. We conform to and believe in the patterns of behaviour, and the myths and rituals they established. We quote texts written by men who lived two to three thousand years ago. They lived in a totally different natural environment from us. They had limited knowledge and technology, and different survival needs. The dead hand of their fears and needs pulls the strings of our beliefs and actions right up to the present.

Most humans have a strong desire to conform in order to be accepted. Belonging to a family or a tribe was essential to survival in the early days of human development. To be rejected or cast out meant death. Conformity was a survival technique. Still is in some parts of the world.

We are all different, but society is not built on the recognition of individual differences. Societies are built on categories and groups and the perception of superiority of one group over another.

But, as time went on, the number of groups we divided each other, and ourselves, into, increased and societies fragmented as a result. Group membership conferred privileges on some, and gross disadvantage on others.

While writing this book, I watched a video demonstrating the nature of privilege. It used the example of a foot race. The starter lined the runners up. There were men and women, people of different skin colours, social class, and cultural backgrounds.

The starter then said, 'I am going to make a few statements. If a statement applies to you, take two steps forward. If it does not apply to you, stay where you are.' He then made statements relating to social circumstances such as parents still married, presence of a father figure when growing up, private education, private tutor, never having to help parents pay bills, never having to worry about your cell phone being shut off, and so on.

People began to move forward two steps at a time if a statement applied to them. What an eye-opener to the inequalities of life in modern America and possibly most Western societies.

The starter then said to the people who had reached way out in front even before the race had started, 'Look behind you.' Some of those behind them were still on the starting line. Some were a few steps ahead but still way behind the front runners. 'You people here at the front have a very good chance of winning this race,' he said. 'In the race of life, you have a very good chance of winning too. And none of it is related to anything you personally have done.'

He paused to let that sink in, then he continued. 'Does that mean the people at the back can't race well? I bet if you all started on the same starting line, some of those people back there would leave you way behind.' He paused for effect then concluded, 'That's privilege.'

I thought about that video and how it equally applies to many forms of privilege and inequality. Does it apply to males and females for example? Let's see.

'Take two steps forward if, when you were a child, family and friends encouraged you to get out and be physically active, adventurous, take a few risks, try things out and cope with problems for yourself.

'Take two steps forward if most of the toys you were given encouraged you to be adventurous, curious, inventive, and active in the wider world.

'Take two steps forward if most of the toys you were given provided you with knowledge of the world or helped you become skilled at maths or science.

'Take two steps forward if you received a higher salary than some of your colleagues because of your sex or gender.

'Take two steps forward if you rarely had to put your career on hold to look after children or sick or elderly relatives.

'Take two steps forward if people took your ideas seriously because of your sex or gender.

'Take two steps forward if you rarely, if ever, had to worry about someone of the opposite sex hurting you or assaulting you sexually.

'Take two steps forward if people think it's natural and admirable for you to take control or give orders.'

The list could go on. These are all privileges that most men, particularly white men, enjoy. However, they hold women back in their lives outside the home, in their earning capacity, in the development of their potential and their enjoyment of life in general. And, for so many women, they leave them in poverty in old age.

Men and women may not come from different planets, but they certainly live in two different atmospheres.

These privileges for males and constraints on females from early childhood lead to and ensure inequality between the sexes. Inequality of status, reward, recognition, expression, learning, influence, and freedom of movement.

It is easy to see that many men would not want to give up their privileges or status even though some of them might protest that they have no such privilege. Remember those who benefit from privilege tend to feel that the coming of equality is oppression rather than a levelling of the playing field. They are likely to react with what author Michael Kimmel calls "aggrieved entitlement".

We now know that the damage to individuals is not all there is to this inefficient way of operating. Sexism and gender stereotyping are the most inefficient ways of running a society, particularly in this day and age. It wastes the talents of both sexes, stifles creativity and is economically wasteful. (Stereotyping of any group ignores their potential and possible contribution to society and, in the case of women, to the entire world.)

So here are a few of the problems at a societal and global level.

As well as holding back billions of women from achieving their full potential, and asserting their right to live full, healthy lives, this has an impact on the global economy.

The UN's ICPD (International Conference on Population and Development) Beyond 2014 Global Report, found that gender inequality is costing the global economy trillions of dollars every year.

According to the International Monetary Fund (IMF), closing the gender gap in the labour market would raise the GDP of the USA by 5 per cent, the UAE by 12 per cent, Japan by 9 per cent, 27 per cent in India, and Egypt by 34 per cent. While money isn't everything, although some may disagree, it is one way of showing that when women gain, whole nation's gain.

Prejudice is not profitable

Investing in women and girls creates measurable economic benefits for families, communities, and nations. The most effective way to accelerate a nation's economic prosperity and productivity by as much as 11 to 12% is to enable women to participate in the workforce and pay them fairly and equally with men.

If Nigerian women had the same opportunities as men, they could drive GDP up by $13.9 billion. Njideka Harry, President and Chief Executive Officer, Youth for Technology Foundation.

Fortune 500 companies with the highest representation of women board directors attained significantly higher financial performance, on average, than those with the lowest representation of women board directors, according to a Catalyst report, *The Bottom Line: Corporate Performance and Women's Representation on Boards*. In addition, the report points out, on average, notably stronger-than-average performance at companies with three or more women board directors. The study, which is the second of Catalyst's Bottom Line reports, looked at three critical financial measures: return on equity, return on sales, and return on invested capital, and compared the performance of companies with the highest representation of women on their boards to those with the lowest representation. In May 2015, Kevin O'Leary of *Shark Tank* noted that, of the 7 companies he invests in, the only ones making money had female CEOs.

According to recent studies women actually run better-performing businesses than men. In addition, one study showed women rate higher than men on 12 out of 16 attributes tested. After analysing 7,280 of their clients' performance evaluations, the researchers found two traits where women outscored men significantly: taking initiative and driving results. In a study of men and women as leaders, women have also been found to be better communicators, better community builders, more patient, better at activating enthusiasm and possess stronger work ethics than men.

Women are generally better investors and handlers of money than men according to the science of neuroeconomics. Michael Lewis, author of *The Big Short*, said that the single thing he would do to prevent another global financial crisis would be to put 50% of women in risk positions in banks. Research has shown that young male testosterone-driven traders become euphoric when winning and take higher and higher risks to the point of delusion. Women are far less affected by this euphoria.

Remember though, all of this is not to say that women, are superior to men. That is as incorrect as the reverse statement. What these results show is that the way we mould the two sexes into gender stereotypical behaviour, is detrimental to society as well as to the individuals themselves. The problem is compounded when we then favour one gender with blind bias, disregarding actual competence or performance. Both sexes could benefit from developing the best of their human potential rather than being hobbled to one half or the other.

Until quite recently – historically speaking - most of the work done by women was menial, low-skilled, and low paid. It was also highly undervalued and had no status. Men would not do women's work because it was considered inferior and beneath them. This is still the case in many societies. In Western societies, when women began to move into some professions, the status of the work went down, and men moved out.

The Wealth of Nations

To return to the ignored or undervalued labour of women, it's estimated that women perform two-thirds of the world's work, most of it underpaid or unpaid. Women's unpaid work supporting, feeding, caring for children, the sick and the elderly, and keeping society running, is worth billions of dollars. However, it does not show up in any economic calculation of a nation's wealth or health. Yet, without women's invisible unpaid work, most of the activities which are included in measures of GDP (Gross Domestic Product), could not occur as effectively as they do, or even at all. It seems women hold up more than half the sky but get no credit for it.

This is also another example of women's invisibility. Since most of the statistics and economics policies have been decided and described by men, and men are often totally unaware of, or disinterested in, what women do, it's really no surprise that women's major contribution to society as a group, goes unremarked and unrecorded. Add the unconscious internalised Sexism of any women who just may be involved in economics, and the invisibility of women's work is pretty much a done deal.

Economist, Marilyn Waring, DNZM (New Zealand Order of Merit – the NZ equivalent of a knighthood), sums it up in the title of one of her books – *Counting for Nothing: What Men Value and What Women are Worth*. She points out the inadequacies of the measure of a nation's progress currently used globally, the GDP. She lays bare the travesty of global economics in its exclusion of one-third (at least) of the world's work, work that is unpaid. This includes the unpaid work of women and men, but by far the most unpaid work is done by women – everywhere. GDP is a grossly inadequate tool to measure the growth and development of any nation. She points out that the loss of lives, land, and buildings in an earthquake in Christchurch is of no consequence to the GDP, but re-building the demolished city adds to the nation's GDP and, from an economist's point of view, is a good thing.

Marilyn Waring tells the story of a woman injured in a tractor accident on her farm. She had to be replaced by a shepherd and a roustabout who were paid, and compensation was provided. She also needed to be replaced in the kitchen as she provided meals for the employees on the farm. Her mother came to help out with that job but was not paid or compensated for, because that's what family members do. Her work had no monetary value.

Here's one that my female readers will "love". According to this way of calculating a nation's value, women giving birth to babies are engaged in a non-productive activity. They are technically economically "at leisure". It's amazing we still call it "labour". Anyone who is performing work but is not paid for it, is considered to be "at leisure" economically. Cow's milk and goat's milk are of economic value. Human breast milk is not.

And yet, unpaid work is the single largest section of a nation's economy. Marilyn Waring poses the question: How can governments make equitable policy decisions for their citizens when half of the labour force is invisible. She proposes that use of time is a better measure of a nation's productivity than market exchange. The GDP is a tool that sees protection of our environment as of no value, while earthquakes and war are great for increasing GDP.

While decision-making is in the hands of one sex disproportionately, the decisions made are going to lack half the population's perspective. Women's opinions are not sought or valued. Women's voices are not heard. Women's ideas are ignored or appropriated without recognition. Women's needs are not a high priority and often remain unrecognised. Most women in leadership roles are not as respected as male leaders and are constantly criticised for appearance rather than action or ideas. And, as mentioned before, women are still paid less than men for the same work – a lot less – and the pay gap in 2014, was the widest it's been since we began keeping records.

Violence against women is a global scourge.

It's been estimated by the United Nations that one in three women has been subjected to male physical violence because of their gender, world-wide.

That's a staggering one billion people. Our minds understandably boggle at the concept of six million Jews being exterminated by the Nazis. Or ten million murdered by Stalin. Figures that rightly provoke horror, outrage, and a desire for justice. But one billion women is not even a figure that most of us can comprehend. The overall lack of horror, outrage, or action demonstrates the power of cultures to instil acceptance of these attitudes and violent actions towards women at a very early age.

Belief in women's subordinate status and men's dominance over them, has culturally embedded men's sense of entitlement to treat women as their property or as objects to do with as they will. The United Nations has declared global violence against women to be the greatest human rights abuse of our time.

These views are the product of gender stereotyping. And yes, it is happening in your country.

Sexism, like Racist, is about power and value. It is about beliefs in superiority and inferiority; it's about oppression, dominance and subordination and all the actions, attitudes, beliefs, prejudices, discrimination, and assumptions that flow from that.

Sexism is built into our culture, our institutions and organisations. Sexism is built into our language and speech patterns, our social interactions, our marriage customs, our child-raising practices, our sports, our entertainment, our humour, our attitudes, our news coverage, our education, our history, our songs and stories and many if not most of our religions. Every one of these areas exaggerates and reinforces gender differences and divisions with males dominant, prominent, competent, and potent. Men are also depicted as in control, active, vocal, and important. Women and girls? Not so much. Often invisible. This is Sexism at work.

Sexism requires difference, and difference is provided by gender stereotypes. **By conforming to stereotype, we are ensuring inequality and all that goes with it.**

The anthropologist Levi Strauss observed that women in all cultures provide the social lubricant that prevents societies from falling apart. And, I might add, they do it all for free.

All this loving and caring, pleasing and accommodating, or perhaps because of it, hasn't helped women one bit. Anthropologists have found that most societies believe and demonstrate that what men do, say, and think and like are considered more important and more valuable than what women do, say, think, or like.

Let's not be blind to the subtle ways in which both sexes assume that what males do is more important than what women do. And let's not be blind to who benefits from most of it. We don't need to look for someone to blame but we do need to recognise it and counteract it.

I do hope that, having come this far with me, you are crying out for solutions. So, what can be done to achieve ways to make life fairer for females and males. Mind you, some males will consider equality of the sexes unfair because it will involve the loss of a privileged position. Respect and reward may need to be earned by both sexes and all genders, in a truly fair and equal world - rather than assumed.

But – first we need to look at one more aspect of what we are dealing with. Our own brains.

15

Myth Busters
(WHO YA GONNA CALL?)

Mars-Venus sex differences appear to be as mythical as the Man in the Moon.

(Journal of the American Psychological Association, 20 October 2005)

Each time a woman stands up for herself, without knowing it possibly, she stands up for all women.

Maya Angelou

Nothing keeps us from changing more than our tendency — our willingness — to remain locked into versions of ourselves, into personae and identities barred in by heavy leaden rods of self-righteousness.

Maria Popova

THE MYTH of almost alien differences between the sexes persists, in spite of the evidence that most of those differences are created by culture. We continue to believe that the unequal way society is organised is "natural". Evidence that men and women are not so very different is largely ignored or repressed. Why?

The answer, my friend, is hiding in your brain. Earlier I referred to the oldest part of our evolving brain as the lizard brain. That part of our brain is still working away in there, today.

As a result, when the lizard brain takes control:

- We believe what we have been taught before the age of seven.
- We fear uncertainty.
- We dislike or even fear change because it leaves us feeling uncertain.
- We conform to our tribe's behaviour patterns so we can belong to a protective group.
- We need to be liked, or respected or even feared but not ignored or ridiculed.
- We cling to our beliefs as a means of certainty.
- We see confirmation of our beliefs all around us but do not notice the contradictions.

We can see that those who gain privilege, power or profit from the situation would want to maintain things the way they are. In modern times, obscene profits are gained from products and services that cater to the insecurities of women who are constantly bombarded with images of the ideal feminine woman. Men are also being targeted more and more by the marketing industry.

In the previous two chapters, we looked at a mind-blowing set of disadvantages and downright perils faced by women globally. What about men? They are constrained by a straitjacket of almost inhuman proportions although, to be honest, many of them seem to enjoy their privileges without acknowledging them as privileges. But what about the men who suffer mentally with a sense of worthlessness, powerlessness, inadequacy when they can't conform? What about the men driven to suicide by these pressures? What about the violence towards women and children resulting from masculine despair, rage, or entitlement? Why or how do we, the majority, let it continue?

Between the lizard brain's myths and the power of profit, what hope of change is there? None, unless enough of us bust the myths. Because, after all, we're rational thinking creatures, aren't we? Well, no, we are not rational creatures first and foremost. Our brains play many tricks on us, tricks that served us well when we first stood up on our hind legs. We make our decisions most of the time based on our emotions and attitudes and justify and rationalise them immediately after. This gives us the illusion of being rational, but it is a sleight of hand. And yet, there is evidence under our noses that the story of Mars and Venus is a myth.

So, who ya gonna call? Mythbusters – that's who. Fortunately for us, the lizard brain is only one part of our thinking organ. There's the more evolved part of our brain that can rise above fear, hate and irrationality. That's the part that we need to call on because that lizard brain has been thoroughly brain washed. We need to understand how that lizard brain is thinking first before we can move on to changing the way we, as whole human beings can think.

First, very few people like change. Second, why would men want to give up their advantages? And third, why would organisations want to give up their profits. People will usually fight harder to avoid losing something they already have, than they will fight for something they do not yet possess. That's the lizard brain at work.

Before the age of seven, we have very few filters and absorb what we are taught like a well-trained sponge. We also have no collection of past experiences that contradict the incoming flood. Among the things we are taught are gender stereotypes, and both men and women have learnt to believe that men are more competent than women – except for the domestic and caring chores. We have been taught this since we were born.

Here are a couple of questions to women readers: Are you inferior to men and boys? Are you less competent, less intelligent, worth less than men? Most of you will probably say, "Of course not!" Which begs the question: Why do most of us accept this nonsense? Partly because all these things have been said about women for a long time. They've been believed for a long time. And most of us probably don't think about it very often because it's not stated out loud, it's just implied in every aspect of our lives. Whole societies, and roles and rewards within societies are built on this belief. It's there, like the air we breathe, so we don't notice it and take for granted that its impact is "normal".

Ask yourself: Are there things you don't do because you think you can't? Do you think you can't do them because you're female? I'll bet there are plenty if you're honest with yourself. I'll grant you there are some things men do that most reasonable women wouldn't want to do anyway, and I don't mean jobs that are dirty. Ask most men to change a nappy/diaper and see who can't stand dirty jobs!

Here's just one simple example I come across often because I tow a caravan on my own, enjoying the beautiful country I live in. I'm not unique in this. There are thousands of women travelling on their own and loving it. I am constantly saddened by the women travelling with their husbands who say to me, "I couldn't do that." Well, there was a time when I couldn't either – until I had a go and practised and learnt.

In fact, all those men towing things, couldn't tow anything till they tried – and practised. The advantage they had though was their belief in themselves. After all, they had plenty of role models. Everywhere you see caravans being towed, it's almost always a man towing it while his wife or female companion sits by his side. The other advantage a man has, is his fear of being seen as incompetent or unmanly if he doesn't tow the damn thing.

The idiocy of this situation is that sometimes out there in the middle of nowhere, men get injured or become sick. Their wives can't tow the caravan and they're stuck. If only she'd learnt. When I ask why they haven't learnt, apart from thinking they can't, they sometimes also tell me, "He won't let me tow the van." How short-sighted is that?! It appears that his ego is more important than their safety. Some men have admitted to me that they like to keep a few things that they can do, and their wives can't. They want her to be dependent on them. Understandably, I guess, because most of us want to be needed. But at what a price. Her learned helplessness in exchange for his ego can put them both in danger. Certainly, even back at home, if the man dies, we see the result of women's dependence when it has to be transferred to a son or son-in-law. Not always a convenient or satisfactory arrangement.

I have used this trivial example of towing a caravan as a vignette of the wider world for women. As we've seen, much of the everyday Sexism women experience is trivial, which is what makes it so hard to combat. It might be comfortable and easier to let him do the things he does, and it keeps the peace, plus women already have enough to do anyway, with the double shift and the two-thirds of the world's workload. But there is a price.

Elsewhere, we have seen how this protection of male ego versus the equality of women harms the progress and economic development of most countries on earth. But, at the micro-level, there is a mental impact of accepting the myth that men can do so many things that women can't. It shapes a woman's self-image and undermines her ability to even try. No one can outperform their self-image. Like those baby elephants we saw in Chapter 1. They are tethered to a peg in the ground when they're young and weak. Unable to free themselves, they grow bigger and stronger, but remain tethered with the same small peg because they don't even try to break free. They believe they can't.

To go to the source of the problem, check out our child-raising patterns. We teach boys to believe that men must always be in control and never be like a woman or girl. Having a woman be more competent or talented or skilful is emasculating. Emotional word "emasculating" but that's how men are taught to think of any failure to "man up" and show a pair of "balls". Being second to a woman is about as "emasculating" as you can get in the eyes of some men. As mentioned previously, most men tend to marry women who are younger, less educated and earning less than they do. That way their masculinity is not threatened. At least, in the home. This ensures that they rarely meet women who would demonstrate any superiority to them in any area they consider important. If they do meet such a woman, she is probably a "ball-breaker".

We judge one another by anatomical distinctions – gender, skin colour, number of limbs. Then assume qualities and talents on that basis. Do you seriously consider that you are no more than the sum total of your body parts? Or that (even more amazing) anyone else who has the same body parts, genitalia, or skin colour is exactly the same as you – the same amount of intelligence or lack of it, the same interests, skills, and competence or lack thereof! This is what sexist, racist, and other forms of stereotyping are telling us. Except if you are a white, heterosexual male. Then, of course, not only are you an individual, you're also superior to all those other body types, skin colours, and gender assignments.

This is all about how we use our brains. Some researchers within the field are themselves often astounded at the way the popular media falls with delight on any suggestion that the brain's activity proves that the structure of societies is the product of genetic activity rather than learned or coerced behaviour.

Supporters of gender stereotyping and the-way-things-are, have seized on the relatively new field of neuroscience and concepts of the "female" and "male" brains. Scientists themselves have admitted that brain imaging is not an accurate way of determining inborn differences between the sexes. Neuroscience reveals that the brain can change itself with remarkable plasticity in response to experiences, including socialisation, punishment, and reward. Since girls and boys are taught to grow in opposite directions, to be feminine or masculine, their brains will obviously adapt to accommodate their different experiences. This would logically explain any differences found in their malleable brains.

Neuroscience supports the fact that our brains are moulded by our experiences rather than being stuck with the brain we are born with. In addition, brains designated "female" are not confined to female bodies. Some men can have "female" brains and some women can have "male" brains. Some people even draw on both, depending on experiences. The male/female labels indicate a brain's way of working, not its "sex" or "gender". The brain is more a process than a thing. Or perhaps more accurately, a set of processes.

Remember, female and male are biological facts. Feminine and masculine genders are social constructs.

An American professor at the University of Wisconsin (Madison), Janet Shibley Hyde, and her colleagues, did a massive analysis of hundreds of other analyses of studies on gender differences. Instead of testing the hypothesis or theory that men and women are very different as most studies do, she tested the theory that men and women are actually more similar to each other than they are different. Combining the results of hundreds of studies, she found that most differences between the sexes are non-existent or very very small. There were a few exceptions. They were, on average:

- men can throw further and faster,
- men masturbate more than women, and
- men have more positive attitudes to casual sex and uncommitted relationships than women.

It could be argued that the last two are cultural and not inborn anyway. So, we are left with speed and distance of throwing. Not much to justify all the centuries of denying women their rightful place as equal human beings.

Remember, this was not just one study. This was a study of many studies of studies of gender difference. Yes, that's right – a study of studies of studies.

Janet Hyde's analysis revealed that numerous studies had shown that gender differences in maths and verbal ability were quite small. Even gender differences in assertiveness and self-esteem are also quite small.

Dr Hyde's study also found that possible gender differences fluctuate with age, sometimes more pronounced and sometimes less so. Given the findings of the evolving science of neuroplasticity which shows that the brain changes itself over time, this would seem inevitable. Also, the tendency for many older women to stop behaving "like a girl", might explain some of this fluctuation.

A report on Dr Hyde's study, published in the Journal of the American Psychological Association, 20 October 2005, summed it up in these words: *Mars-Venus sex differences appear to be as mythical as the Man in the Moon.*

But we are still left with the question: what about all the differences we do see in people – all around us? Their behaviour. Their choices in almost everything. Their interests too. They're all gendered.

Unfortunately, beliefs have a nasty habit of becoming self-fulfilling prophecies. The more we believe something is true, the more likely we are to act in a way that makes it come true. As Henry Ford is credited with saying:

If you think you can, or you think you can't, either way you are right.

If you don't think you can do something, it's quite likely you won't even try. After all, none of us likes to make a fool of ourselves.

But what about those tests where boys do better than girls at Maths?

Studies have uncovered a phenomenon labelled "**stereotype threat**". They have shown that when participants were subtly reminded of their gender or racial background, they tended to behave in more stereotypical ways. For example, the simple act of responding on a questionnaire to a question such as what their gender was, could lead women to perform more poorly on maths tests in accordance with stereotypical expectations. Similarly, black students performed poorly when race was highlighted. The fear of conforming to the stereotype resulted in conforming to the stereotype. Psychologists and educators are, through this innovative research, coming to understand the true nature of one of the barriers to equal educational achievement.

The opposite can occur when gender or race are not involved and stereotype threat does not become a factor. In one study, researchers demonstrated that gender roles and social context strongly determined people's behaviour. For example, after being told that they would not be identified by sex nor wear any identification, participants moved away from "normal" gender stereotypical behaviour when given the chance to be aggressive. The men became less aggressive, and the women became less passive. Each sex moved towards a more common middle ground. In other words, they became more similar.

According to the American Psychological Association, stereotype threat can lower performance academically and in other areas. It can also lead to self-defeating behaviour, lack of effort and "gender appropriate" career choices. For example, some boys will "dumb down" their academic skills because it's nerdy and not masculine to be academically smart. (http://www.apa.org/research/action/stereotype.aspx)

Why we are the way we are, is so much more complex than our genitals. Or our hormones.

It is neither "biological fact" nor "nature" that is driving the secondary status of women and other groups.

In modern times as we have seen, pushing gender differences sells more magazines and other gender specific items. It allows researchers to publish papers and gain scientific recognition. As mentioned earlier, the popular press is more likely to publish an article if it shows differences between the sexes than they are to publish something that minimises differences. They have found it definitely sells more magazines.

The push to believe in, teach and require major differences proving the superiority of the male and the inferiority of the female,
has been a constant force throughout the centuries, particularly
in most religions. It is hard not to conclude that certain male
privileges are being protected whatever the truth or fallacy of
gender differences.

Gender scholar, Michael Kimmel, concludes in his book *The
Gendered Society:* 'gender difference is the product of gender
inequality not the other way round'. Many of the characteristics
of speech and posture and behaviour of women can also be seen
in colonised or subordinated people.

Subtle and not-so-subtle: Men are taught (subtly and not-so-
subtly) to believe they aren't good at communicating, they lack
tact and can't interpret emotions. Women are taught (subliminally) that they can't read maps, aren't good at maths and they
don't make good leaders or bosses. You can even buy tee shirts
for girls that sport the slogan "Allergic to Algebra" or "Too Cute
for Homework". And we need only look at the toys children are
given to recognise assumptions about gender roles.

Counter Examples Ignored: All of this despite the men who
are great poets, authors, orators, and statesmen. All of this
despite the women who are scientists, astronomers, mathemati-
cians, code breakers, artists, chess, and Rubik cube champions.
In the case of the women, you would have to go to some great
lengths to even find their names as, with only a few exceptions,
they are rapidly buried and forgotten as though they never
existed. An excellent example of never letting the facts get in
the way of a good story.

Anonymity: One factor keeping the talent of women hidden has
been their tendency to do things anonymously. As Virginia
Woolf wryly commented: "Anonymous was a woman." Poems,
music, and artworks are unsigned as women hide modestly

behind anonymity. They have been taught not to push themselves forward. I have taught art classes to women who could
not bring themselves to sign their paintings. They felt it was
immodest.

Countering Prejudice: Women, perhaps less conforming to
feminine modesty, also resorted to using male names in order to
have their works published. The three Bronte sisters initially
wrote under the names of Currer, Ellis, and Acton Bell. Mary
Ann Evans is better known as George Eliot, and her work
Middlemarch is considered one of the best novels ever written.
George Sand was the *nom de plume* of Amantine Lucile Aurore
Dupin in France, and Ethel Florence Lindesay Richardson better
known as Henry Handel Richardson is one of Australia's best-
known writers. There are numerous others.

Other women used initials to disguise their sex. They or their
publishers were aware of the prejudice against female writers
particularly in certain genres that were read predominantly by
men or boys. J.K. Rowling of Harry Potter fame is a recent
example.

Assumptions of male initiative: When men and women co-
operate in scientific or academic work, no matter the actual
contribution of each, it is usually assumed that he did the major
part of the work or the idea was his, and she helped him. Or, in
way too many cases, women's creative, inventive, or exploratory
work was taken over and published by a man with no recognition of the fact that it was originally the work of a woman.
Check out astrophysicist Jocelyn Bell Burnell who discovered
pulsars but her two male colleagues got the credit and the Nobel
Prize.   http://www.telegraph.co.uk/news/science/11941453/
Female-physicist-overlooked-for-Nobel-Prize-finally-receives-
recognition-as-Woman-of-the-Year.html

Jocelyn Bell Burnell is only one example. History is full of such cases. Male-centred history is not designed to shatter the myths of masculine superiority.

Even when men themselves do not appropriate the work of women, society tends to believe that brilliant work produced by a woman must actually be the work of her father, husband, brother, or colleague. We saw this in Chapter 2 with John Stuart Mill's work on *The Subjection of Women*. His declaration that most of the ideas were his wife's, met with disbelief and rejection.

It's surprising that any women get to do amazing things given the obstacles put in their way.

The fact is there are as many differences in intellect, strength, emotion, compassion, courage, caring, daring, talking, and any other characteristic, among men as there are between men and women. And similarly, as many variations among women.

16

My Mind is Made Up
(BUT GOOD NEWS - YOU CAN CHANGE!)

The most potent weapon of the oppressor is the mind of the oppressed.

Steve Biko

Stereotypes could be straitjacketing our flexible, plastic brains. So, yes, challenging them does matter.

Gina Rippon

THE GERMAN PHILOSOPHER AND PSYCHOLOGIST, Erich Fromm wrote profoundly of the art of living and loving, being and having. He addressed the issues facing human beings at the height of Western society's twentieth century prioritizing of products over people, and consumption over creativity.

He wrote of our quest for meaning in life, and the nature of our purpose for living. There is no room here to do justice to his line of thought, but he concluded that each of us pursues a different one of many possible goals, with the end belief that it will make us happy. In order to do that, he drew attention to the fact that we need to be free. This involves two types of human liberation, external or political liberation, and internal liberation. We have, he said, devoted our efforts exclusively to liberation from external forces: the lower classes from feudalism, peoples in Africa and Asia from imperialism and, more recently, the working class from capitalism. Elsewhere, I have referred to this as internalised oppression. Although Fromm does not mention the women's struggle for liberation, it is equally true that that most efforts in that sphere have been applied to external forces: gaining the vote, changing laws regarding property, property rights of married women, rape within marriage, equal pay, representation in parliament. Totally necessary, but only part of the problem.

Fromm addressed this issue of focus on external or political liberation with the words:

This is the case in Western democracy, where political liberation hides the fact of dependency in many disguises... We can be slaves even without being put in chains. The outer chains have simply been put inside of us. The desires and thoughts that the suggestion apparatus of society fills us with, chain us more thoroughly than outer chains. This is so because we can at least be aware of outer chains but be unaware of inner chains, carrying them with the illusion that we are free. We can try to overthrow the outer chains, but how can we rid ourselves of chains of whose existence we are unaware?

Earlier in this book, we looked at the many ways in which those internal chains of gender beliefs are placed within us from the moment we are born. The way we are dressed, the way we are spoken to, the toys we are given, the role models we see around us, the books we read and the films and TV that we watch, the expressions we use, our child-raising practices. The separation of male and female humans into gendered beings performing to pattern, is relentless and all around us. As we have seen, before the age of seven, we have no filters and accept all that we take in. Why then don't we see what is happening to us once we get past that stage?

It's all to do with our brains.

In the last chapter, we looked at the constraining beliefs the Lizard brain holds on to in order to survive an existence based back in the Stone Age. I flagged the fact that there was hope of change. That hope lies in the plasticity of the brain and the more evolved parts of our brain. The human brain has been evolving, but we are still toting around the Stone Age brain as well as the wonderful newly evolved parts. They are often in conflict and, looking around us, many scholars and scientists have concluded that the Lizard Brain seems to be in control more and more. But even that is too simple an explanation for something as complex and amazing as the human brain.

As well as an older part of the brain, and the newly evolved part of the brain, the brain works with two halves, Right and Left. They are meant to work together. Popular science has been somewhat simplistic and misleading in its pronouncements about the two hemispheres of the brain. The two halves of the brain do not deal exclusively with separate functions. Both hemispheres are designed to deal with everything - like a co-operative team of two. Each deal with the same issue, perception, emotion or thought but in different ways; then they put the overall picture together to come up with comprehension and response.

In his literally mind-blowing book, *The Master and his Emissary,* Iain McGilchrist, psychiatrist, philosopher and polymath, presents theory and observations of the brain's two hemispheres. The book has been named one of the most important books of the twenty-first century by some of its readers. Its scope is awesome, and people trying to make sense of the world around them and within them, will benefit from reading it. My quote below is in no way intended, nor could it, to express the totality of ideas in Iain Gilchrist's amazing book. That is a joy and an enlightenment you will have to experience for yourself. The following quote is only a tiny section of the wrongness of public perceptions of the brain's hemispheres. I refer to it because of its relevance to the incorrect belief in the gendered brain, a potent part of Sexism's tool kit. Iain McGilchrist wrote of this particular misconception:

In reality, both hemispheres are crucially involved in reason, just as they are in language: both hemispheres play their part in creativity. Perhaps the most absurd of these popular misconceptions is that the left hemisphere, hard-nosed and logical, is somehow male, and the right hemisphere, dreamy and sensitive is somehow female.

McGilchrist's warning is that, in Western society, we are drawing more and more on the left side of the brain and stifling the contribution of the right brain. We are not using our brains as they are capable of being used, that is both sides working as a team contributing different ways of processing the same information, with the final response being that of the right hemisphere. The left hemisphere appears to be gradually usurping the right brain's final say. Makes sense when you look around.

What we do know and observe are the ways in which the overall brain operates and is responsible for our beliefs which lead to our actions. However, we've seen in previous chapters that it's not very progressive most of the time. We all have inbuilt mechanisms to keep us believing and seeing proof of the things we were taught. This gives us a sense of security and stability, as well as a feeling of belonging, within our groups and culture. It also makes us very controllable and even predictable.

Let's take a look at some of the ways our brain accomplishes this.

Confirmation Bias

In all of our fears and prejudices, our brains often work very hard to make us feel better about ourselves, secure, comforted, and safe in our beliefs. One of the strongest tools we have for this is Confirmation Bias. This is the name given to our tendency to look for confirmation that what we think we know is correct. We briefly met this shape-shifter in Chapter 11.

Confirmation Bias means we actively look for evidence that proves what we already believe, and we reject or even are blind to evidence that contradicts our beliefs. We give great weight and credence to things that confirm our beliefs and ignore or give little weight to those things that contradict them. We actively seek to confirm our beliefs as we choose to read books and newspapers that verify them. We choose and prefer to mingle with people who share our beliefs. We are unaware of our blindness to contradictory beliefs. None of us is immune to this beastie.

This is one of the brain's major tricks in the Sexism toolkit. We look for evidence of men's superior competence and ignore women who can perform equally well, or else we see such women as an unnatural exception and not at all "normal" – not a "real woman".

This is Confirmation Bias, and it ensures we are confirmed in our beliefs that little girls behave in a certain way and prefer a certain type of toy or book. We do the same for little boys. Then we all feel secure that everything is as it should be. Rock the cradle but not the boat.

As well as subconsciously looking for things to confirm our beliefs and ignoring or failing to notice things that contradict those beliefs, we have blind spots, a kind of social scotoma. We actually do not notice or see contradictions to our beliefs and assumptions when they are right in front of us.

All this confirmation of our beliefs makes it extremely difficult for us to change our minds. We have a built-in tendency to look for, interpret and remember information that confirms the beliefs we already have. if we notice contradictory information at all, it will be interpreted in some other way by giving it less weight or importance or blaming someone or the current circumstances. For example, men are perceived by both men and women to be naturally more talented and competent than women. If a man succeeds at something it confirms our belief in his competence. If a woman succeeds at the same thing, it is generally seen as luck or helpful circumstances or assistance from someone else, or part of a team effort.

Confirmation Bias dictates the way we gather information by forming the questions we ask so that they confirm our beliefs. It also biases that determine what we remember and what we forget. A classic case is the addicted gambler who remembers the wins but not the usually more numerous losses.

Remember the palaeontologists back in Chapter 2. Their modern belief in male dominance led them to look for and find confirmation of male dominance in the Man the Hunter myth of Stone Age People. They failed to notice the evidence that contra-dicted their beliefs.

We all have selective thinking and selective memories. We like to think we hold beliefs for rational, logical, and objective reasons, but our ideas are often the result of paying attention to information that upholds what we already believe and ignoring ideas or information challenging those beliefs. As we have seen, these are often beliefs acquired before we reached the age of seven. A frightening aspect of this is now becoming evident as we enter an age of "fake news" with the technology to spread it almost instantly.

As Winston Churchill put it:

A lie gets halfway round the world before the truth has a chance to get its pants on.

And his world didn't have the technology we have today.

To sum up, Confirmation Bias impacts on:

- how we look for and gather information,
- how we interpret information,
- how or what we remember of the information we do gather.

This is one excellent way in which stereotypes can be maintained in spite of contradictory evidence.

Form versus Function

We also have a habit of maintaining the status quo by focusing on "form" rather than "function". When faced with a problem or a task, we tend to look at the means we have always used to deal with it and, if it's not working well, we tinker or try to improve on the means we have been using all along. That is focussing on form.

We could solve a problem or improve a means of operating by going back to basics and asking, "What were we trying to achieve in the first place?" What was the purpose or function of this process? Divested of preconceived ideas about means or form, we can very likely see several ways of providing the required function, some of which could be an improvement on the way we are currently dealing with a situation.

The following story is a myth, but it illustrates the point of form versus function. In the space race of the 1960s, according to this myth, Country A and Country B realised that ordinary pens would not write in zero gravity. Country A spent their time and millions of dollars trying to invent a pen that would write in space. They focussed on the "form" they were already using and tried to improve it. Country B focussed on the "function" which was to write in zero gravity. They issued their astronauts with pencils.

I repeat, that story which circulated on social media, is not true, but I have used it because it illustrates the point beautifully. We do tend to fixate on the form of the problem rather than the function or goal we are trying to achieve.

We have taken this approach with men and women. When faced with a task we associate with a male, we look for a male rather than "the best person for the job". We choose the male "form" rather than consider the best means of providing the required function.

Sometimes, the best pen for the job is a pencil. Likewise, sometimes the best man for the job is a woman.

When the US army considered putting women in fighting roles on the front line, you could have heard the outcry on Mars. "They won't be strong enough to carry the necessary equipment and that will lead to cutting back on the equipment and that will put everyone in danger. Ergo - you can't put women on the front line." If it really was the equipment that worried these nay-sayers, they could have focussed on the function required. All that needed to be stipulated was that only soldiers capable of carrying the equipment at its current weight, would be permitted on the front line. Then anyone, male or female, who couldn't carry the equipment would not be eligible. Instead, they focussed on the form, male, because they believed men are the only ones capable of fighting. The weight of the equipment was a smokescreen for sexist prejudice. There were probably some other prejudices going on there as well, but the overt argument was about the weight of the equipment. If it had truly been about the weight of the equipment, there would have been no need to mention gender. Weight testing would have filtered out anyone incapable of carrying the load. I suspect the nay-sayers basically did not want women at the front of the fighting for whatever reason, but they successfully had everyone discussing women's lack of strength for quite a while. It's an interesting example of the circuitous route taken by many anti-feminists. Next time someone tells you a woman can't do something, ask them to focus on the function and then ask them to tell you that no woman on earth could do that task.

Gender stereotypes have ensured that we associate roles and skills with gender rather than looking at what we actually want to achieve with those roles or tasks before deciding on how-to-achieve the goal.

A simple example that I hear often. A woman driving alone, gets a flat tyre. The first thing, or maybe the second thing, she says is, "I need a man." Mmmm. Men are helpful and skilled with lots of things, but that's not actually what she needs. She needs a solution. What's her problem? She has a flat tyre on her car, and the tyre needs to be changed. She doesn't have the skill to do it. It's true, many women have never learnt or desired to change a tyre. Others have. What she probably needs to solve the problem is a person with a jack and the skill to change a tyre. I have actually seen a damsel in distress running around looking for a man. She was totally ignoring the capable woman who had pulled up behind her, took out a jack and offered to help. On a number of occasions, I have watched in disbelief and frustration as a woman, or a man ignored another woman's suggestion of a simple solution and sat and waited over an hour for a man to turn up and tell her or him exactly the same thing.

This is a simplistic example of a way of thinking. It operates in most fields and prevents us from solving a problem or achieving a goal through a new or different method. It definitely hampers our thinking in looking for talented people regardless of sex or gender. Instead, we are blinded by the stereotypes.

The Pressure to Conform

Another powerful, perhaps the most powerful influence on our behaviour is our tendency to conform. We conform by changing our behaviour to fit in, to be liked or avoid rejection or punishment. We change our beliefs to those of the majority in order to be correct. We conform in order to fit in. The scary thing is, we can become the very thing we are performing. We grow ardent through kissing. We grow servile through saluting. Fake it till you make it. To say that gender is an act is not to say that everyone is pretending to be masculine or feminine. It is a reminder that we become what we perform if we perform it regularly over a long period of time.

Perils of Perception

Another way we reinforce our beliefs about men and women is to perceive the evidence before our eyes differently in order to fulfil our expectations. For example, the perception that women talk more than men or to put it bluntly, women talk too much, can, through observation, be shown to be incorrect. But both men and women believe it. Sure, we all know women who talk a lot but so do men. You can't get a word in edgeways once these men and women get going. What you are receiving is a monologue not a conversation, and both men and women are guilty of it. I'm sure you've experienced it too.

Researchers found that, in mixed company, when a woman talks one third as much as a man, both men and women perceive her to be talking more than the man, and there is a sense of irritation that she is talking too much.

Try this little experiment. Watch a group of men and women talking. Who is doing the most talking and who is doing the most listening? Don't be fooled by your own misperceptions. Try counting as they speak to get an accurate assessment of time in the limelight. Watch that same group of men and women and figure out who decides the topic of conversation. Mixed groups usually talk about the subjects that men are interested in or knowledgeable about. If the women raise topics of interest to them (not necessarily about cooking or children) but not of interest to most of the men, the men usually drift away, or talk to each other or change the subject.

It's also been found that other perceptions do not correspond to reality. When 20% of a group are female, the men "see" 50 %. When teachers give boys and girls equal attention, boys "see" the girls getting "all" the attention.

Invisibility

History: Another way we avoid seeing contradictions to our beliefs in women's lack of achievement compared to men's, is the phenomenon of women's invisibility. This is a type of social scotoma. Previously, we looked at the ways we have successfully buried many of women's actions and achievements throughout history. We have done this by ignoring them entirely even when they are recorded or attributing their work to a male colleague or relative, or quite simply leaving any mention of them out of the history books. The problem has been compounded by women's efforts to skirt around the bias they faced by using a male pen name or hiding their sex by using only their initials.

Everyday mixed gender gatherings: Women also experience invisibility in everyday situations. In professional meetings, women find themselves putting forward ideas that are rejected, only to have a man put forward the same idea ten minutes later, and it is applauded and accepted by both men and women. At first, she'll think perhaps they misunderstood her, until it happens repeatedly. Or she discusses it with a female colleague who confirms that she too experiences it. Researchers have found it is a definite phenomenon and not women's imagination. It happens all the time.

A *Washington Post* article highlights this problem at the highest level of government.

When President Obama took office, two-thirds of his top aides were men. Women complained of having to elbow their way into important meetings. And when they got in, their voices were sometimes ignored.

So female staffers adopted a meeting strategy they called "amplification": When a woman made a key point, other women would repeat it, giving credit to its author. This forced the men in the room to recognize the contribution — and denied them the chance to claim the idea as their own.

"We just started doing it and made a purpose of doing it. It was an everyday thing," said one former Obama aide who requested anonymity to speak frankly. Obama noticed, she and others said, and began calling more often on women and junior aides. ('White House women want to be in the room where it happens', by Juliet Eilperin)

Genealogy: Women's invisibility is a problem for genealogists. The custom of dropping their family names and using their husbands' can make it difficult to trace them for more than a couple of generations.

In the New Testament of the Christian Bible, the lineage of Jesus is traced in two gospels to indicate Jesus' connection to the royal line of David. Matthew begins with Abraham while Luke kicks off with God and Adam. They both end up with Joseph! I'm not sure why since the Bible also declares that Joseph was not the father of Jesus. But, in Matthew's record there are forty-one begettings (which means generating something, usually a child). Forty-one men. Interestingly, there are also four wives mentioned as having been involved in the process! In Luke's account 3 23 -28, there are 77 begettings and not one of them involves a woman. Not even Mary is actually mentioned. That's a lot of female invisibility. It has stood for more than two thousand years, clearly telling every male in Christendom that his sex is the more important one even in the birth of the next generation. Clearly telling every Christian woman that in spite of nourishing an embryo, carrying it for nine months within her body as it grows into a human baby, then giving birth to it – a painful and often death-defying act of labour – feeding, nursing, carrying, caring, teaching - in spite of all this work, she is pretty much irrelevant.

Language: Invisibility of the female is also built into our language and our symbolism. Although efforts were made with some success in the 1970s and 1980s to use gender-inclusive language, we have slipped back to masculine usage to represent both sexes. We use the word "man" to mean a person, and "Mankind" when we could say "humanity" or "human beings". We are back to referring to Chairman rather than Chairperson. Decades ago, researchers showed that using masculine words brought up the image of a male person to most people. Women just weren't considered. Even animals and insects are personified as "he". "Look at the bird. He's caught a grasshopper." Not a female in sight.

When the letters "man" appear at the end of a word, it is usually an Anglo-Saxon word and it does mean man. It used to mean "human", when there were separate words for male human and female human. These were *wereman* and *wifman*. Over time, males gradually took over the generic term *man* to mean male human, and females were left with the specific label, *wifman, which explains the* irregular pronunciation of the letter "o" in the word "women".

To those nay-sayers who dismissively suggest that if we change it, we should change all words with "man" in them to person, so we would end up with "personagement", "personhandle", "person" the pumps, "personipulate", and that would be ridiculous. Here they reveal their ignorance of the origins of the English language. When "man" appears at the beginning of the word, it is usually a word of Latin "origin and the "man" is from the Latin root for hand. "Manuscript" originally meant written by hand. "Manoeuvre" meant to work by hand. Similarly, with "manipulate", "manicurist" and so on. There are words, usually of more recent origin, that start with "man" that do mean male human. For example, manly, mannikin, and mannish. More recent words such as manpower, first proposed in 1824 as a unit of measurement, are not using Latin as their basis, so they are exceptions.

"Mano a mano" in Spanish, does not mean "man to man" as it is often interpreted. It means "hand to hand", as in combat or competition.

Symbolism: We don't even need to use masculine words to conjure up the image of a male. Our symbolism does it for us. Street symbols and doctors' medical charts all depict the male form to represent the human being. Ethnicities are depicted in male form almost exclusively. Think of a symbolic or iconic image of a Scot, an Aussie, Aborigine, Indian from India, a Native American. Even charts of the evolution of our species depict a row of males, although it's hard to tell with the chimpanzees depicted as our ancestors.

The male is now re-established as the default human in every aspect of our lives. In 2016, we re-visited the absence of meaningful female characters doing anything other than providing a decorative accompaniment to male characters in movies. A very minimal test is occasionally applied to see if female characters have any other purpose in a film or story. The Bechdel-Wallace test checks if a work of fiction features at least two women who talk to each other about something other than a man. Sometimes, the requirement that the two women must be named is included. Movies about women are often dismissed as chick flicks, and many men would not be seen dead at one of these movies.

Trivial, you say?

By now, some readers are probably saying, "This is all so trivial. Get over yourself and suck it up, Princess". Heard that before?

If it's all so trivial, you won't mind changing it then, will you? How about we make everything female for a few thousand years, just to balance it out. Let's see if men are happy to be called women. Or asked to be Chairwoman of the Board.

And by the way, go back and have a look at Ms Gulliver and see what trivial can do when it consists of hundreds of tiny threads holding us down. Or millions of grains of sand burying us. "Trivial" is unbeatable when it is an infinite, unrelenting, ubiquitous bombardment.

For centuries, women have been controlled, marginalised, and kept "in their place". "In their place" – now that brings us back to the division between the sexes that has been maintained for thousands of years. It's the idea of two areas of life, the home, and the outside world. The private sphere and the public sphere. Women's sphere has been defined as the private sphere, the home. Men's sphere is everywhere else, the public sphere. Hardly a fair division.

In some cultures, and societies, life for women is a lot better than it used to be as recently as the 1970s but there is still a long way to go. Laws have changed but for many, attitudes have not. Some of the progressive changes have been reversed or forgotten. Women are now less controlled by laws but still controlled by myths.

As mentioned before, the sad fact is that the exciting and long overdue progress achieved by women in the 1960s and 1970s, actually stalled in the 1990s. Some things such as the gender pay gap are even worse in spite of the legal requirement to pay men and women equally for the same work. In the 1960s and 1970s, we gained awareness of women's absence from text-books, story books, sporting pages, movie heroes, educational presentations, panels of experts, interview panels, and common daily expressions of speech. That awareness is now lost again except for the occasional fluffing of feathers and shuffling on the perches when women's absence from parliamentary front benches or even from parliament in total, is commented on. Even if things improve slightly, the improvement is seen to be much more than it is. Remember how 20% is perceived to be 50% or feels like it when it comes to women and girls.

Women are front and centre in the public's attention if they are victims of sex crimes and are more likely to be talked about than the perpetrator. They also get headlines if they are "bad" moth-ers, strippers, prostitutes, or a celebrity just having a bad hair day or wearing the wrong underwear.

Each time women make gains, there is a tremendous backlash to return to the way things were. For men who have enjoyed the privileges of being male, equality is felt as a loss or even as oppression. This is evident in the outright misogyny (hatred of women) seen in social media when a woman dares to tackle Sexism or speak out about rape or violence against women.

A stream of abuse is frequently directed at women who have the audacity to express an opinion on anything. The words and images used by some men responding in their hundreds, are obscene and sickening. And they usually involve threatening rape with a sharp object or even murder. That so many men are threatened to the point of violent irrational outbursts reveals a vile underbelly of self-perception and entitlement among some males – and an obsessive hatred of women. This boils over into obscene reality with serial killers and rampage murders. The problem is, we see these individual men as criminals and monsters, mad or bad. This allows them to hide in plain sight and provides a smoke screen for the causes of their behaviour. These men are more often the man next door, or your work colleague, or a favourite uncle. We turn away from the fact that this is a pattern of behaviour which has common causes within our society. Instead, we focus only on punishment of the bad/mad man or "blame-or-disbelieve-the-woman and exoner-ate-the-man" reactions instead of attempting to fix the root causes based in the childhood or the mental health of such men.

Yes. #notallmen. Other men, when asked to read the hate-filled messages of misogyny directed at individual women on social media, have been shocked by the violence of the expressions of hate. Some men were moved to tears with the horror of the hatred expressed by their fellow men. It is a problem that requires both men and women to work on solving. How did those misogynists get to be that way? It begins in childhood and the experiences of boys of abuse, toxic masculinity, a sense of entitlement, rigid gender roles and misogyny.

We could do well to learn from the childhood experiences of men who like and respect women, who relate to them with love and friendship and are not threatened or "emasculated" by women who earn more than they do or beat them at chess. They are the men we need as equal partners in holding up the sky. How did they get to be that way? Let's do more of it.

The response #notallmen is not helpful. It is self-righteous denial showing more concern about men's reputation than women's safety. True – not all men harass or harm women, but ALL women are vulnerable to male violence and abuse, and all women are constrained by the fear of it. Women, in growing numbers, are now revealing the everyday harassment, physical touching and putdowns they are subjected to on a daily basis. They are also revealing the violations of their bodies by men in positions of trust or power. For some men to respond with bleats of "not all men" is an obscene lack of empathy and compassion, contributing further to the very putdowns and humiliation women are talking about. There are women who similarly respond with cries of #butnotallmen, and we looked at the roots of that in Chapter #12: Women are their own Worst Enemies.

Author Margaret Atwood commented that "Men are afraid that women will laugh at them. Women are afraid that men will kill them." She has a relevant point.

If you're female, you will already have come up against the efforts of those around you to turn you into an 'acceptable' girl or woman. See Chapter 8: Stay as Sweet as you Are. And in Chapter 9: Boys Will Be Boys, we saw that boys have similarly been moulded into men. Men's health and rates of suicide testify to the effects of repressive masculinity. The Taboo of

Sameness ensures men must never do or be anything like a woman.

Most of that is based on myths and stereotyping. Who benefits from this? It isn't you if you're female or feminine. And it isn't a bed of roses for many men either.

If you've read this far, then I'm sure you'll agree it's time to make the necessary changes. What should we do? How can the gendered society be rendered obsolete and replaceable? What follows are suggestions and observations I have culled from many experts in a wide range of human studies and experience. They are only a selection and require a book or several books in their own right to do justice to them. The bibliography at the back of this book will give you a guide to further information.

Now, let's dive in and examine some achievable strategies.

17

Tell me Where I Will Die, and I Won't Go There.
(INVERT. ALWAYS INVERT.)

Invert, always invert: Turn a situation or problem upside down. Look at it backward. What happens if all our plans go wrong? Where don't we want to go, and how do you get there? Instead of looking for success, make a list of how to fail instead - through sloth, envy, resentment, self-pity, entitlement, all the mental habits of self-defeat. Avoid these qualities and you will succeed. Tell me where I'm going to die, that is, so I don't go there.

Charlie Munger

You never change anything by fighting the existing reality. To change something build a new model that makes the existing model obsolete.

Buckminster Fuller

IF WE AGREE that the current gendered society is doing more harm than good, we might feel that we need to change or improve components of the system. But this would be to ignore the fact that our current social arrangements are working extremely well. That's right. They are very successful.

Very fit for their purpose. They do exactly what they were designed for.

If you wanted to design a society that ensured continuation of the species, the maintenance of heterosexuality, the dominance of heterosexual males, the subordination and co-operation of females, and the protection of property and inheritance, you could hardly come up with a better system than we currently have. If privilege, wealth and status for some, was a by-product of your design, all the better – for the winners. If destruction of lives, waste of potential, and gross inequality resulted, that's the price, and the winners are willing to let it happen, as long as they are in control.

How would you design such a society?

You'd need to control the females. Without their compliance there would be no offspring, or no guarantee of paternity hence no confidence in passing on property to offspring. There would be no guarantee of a serving class providing sex, offspring, food, comfort, home fires burning, ego massage and admiration. You'd need to convince males and females that they were so different they complemented and attracted each other naturally. We looked at the beginnings of this type of social arrangement in Chapter 2. You would also need to demonise homosexual males.

You might initially have to force the females to comply, and that could be tedious. You need a way of making them self-regulate and even enjoy complying. Remember the baby elephants, get 'em young and train them the way you want them. Teach them their role, make a fuss of them when they perform, punish, or ostracize them when they do not. The human brain will help you by ensuring that they believe they are what you tell them before the age of seven. Continually reinforce that they are weaker in body and mind than males. Keep them away from education. Make it close to impossible for them to live in society without a man to provide for them or protect them. This can be done by ridiculing those without a husband, by preventing them from earning and keeping money or property. Don't give them time to think too much, so you'll have to keep them busy. Two-thirds of the world's work should do it. Keep them focussed on small things so they don't get around to thinking about the whys and wherefores. Keep them busy paying attention to their appearance! Grooming! Pleasing others! Caring and sharing! Now we're on a roll. Make sure they teach their daughters and monitor other women. Just to ensure they realise how much they need you, let's throw in an element of fear. Enter the Predator. He's the harasser, the stalker, the wife beater, the rapist. Now, women will need a Protector from the Predator. You're it. And they'll even be grateful. Job done. Sit back and enjoy the ride.

Yes, tongue in cheek perhaps, glib even, but not too far from the resultant societies we've ended up with for several thousand years.

The type of societies we have will not improve by tinkering or tweaking. Think of function and form. The current form was designed for a specific function. Control by men. It also ensures the subordination of other groups stereotyped by race, ethnicity, social class, religion, gender, sexual orientation, and ability.

What can we do? We need to design a society that is actually able to free people to be themselves, to develop their full poten-tial, to be more caring and sharing, and less self-centred. We need to eliminate stereotypes and the attached prejudices.

There is a mental model, a problem-solving technique recom-mended by Charlie Munger. Mr Munger applied it to investment and money-making strategies, but it's useful for most planning and problem-solving. It is so counter-intuitive, you'll probably laugh and turn away, but hang in there. It's powerful stuff.

Charlie Munger is the lesser-known business partner of Warren Buffett. They are two of the most successful investors in the world. Both Warren Buffet and Bill Gates consider Charlie Munger the smartest man they know.

Charlie Munger's process for solving problems involves a reversal of the usual way we go about solving problems and planning processes to achieve goals. I believe it is a useful tool to help us through the current unjust structure and processes of societies and, in particular, relevant to this book, the sexist nature of those processes, structures and cultures.

Charlie Munger's Inversion Method was inspired by the German mathematician Carl Jacobi. The principle behind it is: Invert, always invert.

Instead of addressing a problem or a goal and working to change it for the better or planning on achieving the goal, the idea is to actually look at what you would need to do to ensure failure.

I did mention it was counter-intuitive.

For example, if you wanted to ensure you did a workout at the gym regularly, what could happen that would ensure you failed to achieve that goal? List the possibilities. They could include not setting the alarm, staying up late drinking the night before, not having your gym clothes and gear ready, not having a set workout program. So now you know what to avoid doing. You could then devise a program based on the opposite or avoidance of those things.

Another example: If you wanted a happy life, what could you do to ensure misery? Now avoid those things.

Apparently, avoiding stupidity is easier than seeking brilliance. And it works. Inversion often forces us to uncover hidden beliefs about a problem because we are approaching it from an entirely different perspective. Try it out on a simple situation you want to improve. Ask yourself what could happen or what could you do, to ensure failure. Then avoid doing those things or do the opposite to them. Any would-be writers reading this could come up with a few ways to fail to finish a writing project, I'm sure. Invert, and you have your path to success.

It is the dead opposite to the way most of us try to solve problems or achieve goals. Don't knock it till you've tried it.

To paraphrase Charlie Munger: Just tell me where I will die, and I won't go there.

Let's try it on the personal and societal problems we have been looking at in this book, mainly those caused by Sexism and misogyny. Let's start with a broad-brush approach so we don't get bogged down in detail. We can get to the detail later.

What's our goal? Let's say we want to build:

1. a society that allows everybody to be themselves, to fulfill their potential and contribute to family and society in a way that made use of their talents and passions;
2. a society that raises our children to be human beings first, respecting other human beings by developing compassion and empathy, rather than competition and contempt;
3. a society that responds to and accepted people as individuals in ways relevant to their skills, knowledge, and behaviour regardless of their appearance, sex, gender, ethnicity, or any other characteristic irrelevant to the task;
4. gives all people freedom, opportunity, status, power,

reward, and visibility, based solely on their individual merit.

Let's invert. What would we have to do to ensure the failure of our goal?

We'd have to:

1. continue assigning and teaching gender stereotypes and other prejudices to young children;
2. continue teaching boys that their characteristics and behaviours were superior to feminine characteristics, and consequently provide them with a sense of entitlement;
3. continue brainwashing boys so that they become less sensitive in order to demonstrate strength, and at the malignant end of the spectrum become violent and controlling;
4. continue teaching girls to be people-pleasers whose role is to focus on their appearance, get a man, have children, and provide paid and unpaid service to family and society, and don't be too smart, too loud, or too bossy;
5. ensure there is fear of rejection for non-compliance and danger or harm to women and men if they do not stick to the script.

No need for me to continue. You've probably recognised that for us to fail at our goal of a just society for people regardless of sex or gender, we just need to continue what we're doing now. It's been a proven success for ten thousand years. Totally fit for purpose.

If we apply Charlie Munger's process and invert, always invert, we realise that our plan of action must be to avoid doing those things.

We need Fromm's concept of external and internal liberation. Painting stripes on a leopard does not make it a tiger, either to the outside world, or to the leopard itself. As necessary as it is to change laws, or provide opportunities, changing laws and offering alternatives have created neither a just society free of prejudice and exploitation, nor dissolved internal invisible chains. While the numbers are small, enough men and women have taken up the opportunities to give the appearance that the system is working. It has even led to complaints that it's gone too far. The backlash is well and truly under way.

Changing laws and providing opportunities are necessary but not sufficient. We also need to remove the internal subconscious chains that control or constrain our behaviour and our beliefs. We know what they are. They are the very things we have shone a spotlight on throughout this book.

As I write this, there is much talk of taking the opportunity not to revert to the way things were before the 2020 Covid 19 pandemic. There will be hurdles. Not least of all the fact that we have been fed "fake news" about males and females for millennia. Fake news is not new. Today the all-encompassing scope of our news media makes it even easier to spread.

Writing on research on this topic of "fake news", Rachel Visontay at the University of New South Wales, explained the phenomenon in *The Sydney Morning Herald* on 4 July 2017. She wrote:

There is no simple cure once we are exposed (to misinformation) because the effects cannot be fully overcome by just promoting fact. Hanging on to mistaken beliefs or fiction occurs not just when people don't want to change their minds – our brains are actually bad at updating information even when we're trying to. Using the terminology of some researchers, misinformation is "sticky".

What can we do about this "stickiness" when it comes to the myths/fake news of gender stereotyping or any stereotyping for that matter?

We need to make a conscious effort to see the evidence. To those who might ask "Why should we bother?" I would say: Please go through this book and keep an open mind. Particularly re-read Chapter 13: Does it Really Matter? (Let Me Count the Ways.) If you still don't care, by all means just walk away.

If you've come this far with me, you'll have come a long way down the path of a perception of Sexism and misogyny. Let's just pause and look back for a few moments. So far, we have seen many things that we often don't question. Let's also look at why that might be.

Most of us appear to want to believe in gender differences, and it generally appeals to the male ego. It also gives some women a comforting sense of "being taken care of" – although for many women, in reality, that is a myth. The number of women who need protection from the men who are expected to protect them, is a major social issue around the world. It's euphemistically called 'domestic violence'. In Australia, police deal with 5,000 matters of domestic violence on average every week. That's one every two minutes. Apart from the fear, pain, and death they cause to women and children, these abusive and violent husbands, partners, fathers, and "lovers" are costing the community millions of taxpayers' money, money that could be far better spent on services such as health, childcare and education.

In addition, for women the concept of being taken care of with a male breadwinner is also no longer the case. Jobs men gravitate to have been disappearing faster than female-attracting jobs. For women, their jobs are frequently part-time or casual, which suited when their role was mainly child -raiser and homemaker. These days, a man is more likely to lose his job than his wife is – at least in the lower echelons of the paid workforce, those families who are already economically struggling. For women, the transition from "helping out with pin money" to major breadwinner is now a common experience, either as single parents or with a male partner. The mental toll on men in this situation is exacerbated by their apparent "failure" to live up to the masculine stereotype. For such a man, violence towards his partner may result. Or he may kill himself. She, on the other hand, may be physically exhausted by the burden of work as well as fearful and anxious in the face of his attitudes. And yet the gender stereotype juggernaut rolls on crushing spirits and lives with no apparent remedy from governments or official organisations on the horizon.

Natural desires for a mate and children, cleverly entwined with romance and a concept of inevitability of role, do a great job of continuing the species and protecting the male ego.

Women like many other female animals, seem less concerned with proving themselves mightier than the male. Those who seek males as mates, seem mostly to want love, respect, and friendship. Not a continuing Battle of the Sexes, a battle for control. Guys, so far, the majority of women want you, love you and would like you to be a decent human being. Kind, gentle, funny, and caring. Get out of that macho armour and give it a go. The whole planet will thank you. And for those men who are already decent human beings, please help your brothers. Women can't do it alone. Nor should they.

In Western societies, women's oppression and male dominance are seen to be so "natural" that most of us cannot contemplate any other way of living.

There are women and men fighting for women's equality but not enough of them. Too many people, particularly women themselves simply refuse to see the problem. Why wouldn't they? They have been taught to believe in the *status quo,* the-way-things-are, since they were born.

With each success for women, there is an inevitable backlash. It is sometimes strident, sometimes subtle. Inequalities, prejudices, patronisation, sexist assumptions, injustices, harassment and violence against women continue. Privileges are threatened, and the privileged are fighting back. We know that our minds will work harder to prevent loss than they will to achieve success. Cleverly, opponents to change have convinced many women that Feminism is the enemy to be ignored or resisted. Sadly, many believe them. A state of mind known as false consciousness; if you do not know you are imprisoned, you will not attempt to escape.

Subtle, subterranean, subliminal Sexism is all around us enveloping and affecting women's (and men's) lives every day. And yet, many people still consider Feminism unnecessary and old fashioned. Of course, women have equality now, they say. Many men and women will scoff at the mention of "Sexism", even becoming angry or derogatory at the very idea.

Galileo declared that the earth moved around the sun when the conventional belief was that the sun and stars all moved around the earth. He would have burnt at the stake had he not backed down and said he was wrong. **When it comes to a conflict between an entrenched point of view and actual evidence, the entrenched point of view will win most of the time.**

Let's not sacrifice our daughters and sons to maintaining these gender myths any longer. There is so much more at stake.

18

Be the Change

Today you are You,

That is truer than true.

There is no one alive

Who is Youer than You.

Dr Seuss

A woman's strength should not be in her role, whatever she chooses it to be, but in the power to choose that role. It is amazing to me that I even have to make this point, as I see it as the very foundation of our conversation."

Brandon Sanderson, *Words of Radiance*

CHANGE IS POSSIBLE. It can begin at the personal level, in our minds, as well as our homes, our schools, our jobs and our relationships.

If you feel resistance to change within you for whatever reason, look at your life, look at the way things are around you. Now ask yourself: "Is this what I would choose? Would I choose the way things are if they were not already in place?" This is not an easy thing to do. We have all been well trained from infancy, and our Lizard Brain is satisfied.

When I was a child, my neighbours bought a collie pup. They intended to use her for breeding. When they found she could not have pups, they lost interest in her. They tied her to a pole in their backyard. There she stayed for months. She ran around and around the pole at the end of the rope until she had worn a deep rut in the ground. One day, someone who will remain nameless, untied the rope from her collar. She gave herself a shake and began to run and run, round and around the pole, in the rut, in the dirt. She didn't realise she was free. Habit bound her by an invisible rope as strong as the real one.

We are all a bit like that poor animal. We do not realise our freedom, our strength, our value, or our power. For women, throughout the last few thousand years, there have been tremendous forces used to keep them in the well-worn rut of the feminine gender role. Religion, the law, science, and philosophy have all been used to make women's secondary status "natural" and to ensure they were never given the education or the legal opportunity to change the laws or attitudes that controlled them. The key is gender stereotypes and the pattern we are expected to fit into. Continuation is guaranteed if we conform and if we teach our children to conform also.

There have been women throughout history, and men who have helped them, who have fought against the subordination of women. But culture and conformity are powerful forces. What hope does a baby or small child have to become aware of freedom when everything around her or him, screams *Behave like this or else*. Or else? Be unloved, rejected, mocked, labelled insane and locked away, beaten, killed. It's a tough call to buck against the pattern.

What can we do to change this subtle and not so subtle control of our lives?

You'll notice there is some overlap and repetition throughout this book. This is not meant to bore you senseless, but to remind you. *Repetition is one of the ways we remember things*. More important, is how you are feeling at the time. It's likely that the first time you read something, you may feel it doesn't relate to you or your circumstances, or you might not feel brave enough to do anything about it, or you might just plain disagree with it. By the time you come across it again further on in the book, you may have changed your circumstances or your mind, or you may have had an "aha" moment and be totally ready to give it a go.

What's Next?

For now, a good place to start is with you.

Beginner's Mind

At the beginning of life, we all start with a Beginner's Mind. We see things for the very first time and ask "Why?" As time goes on, we see the same things over and over. We stop noticing them as they fade into the pattern of "normal" life. We stop asking why and accept that this is the way things are.

Getting our Beginner's Mind back is a major way of seeing through and detecting the myths that are used to shape you into a woman from Venus, a creature quite alien in many ways from your original self. This will open up infinite possibilities. You've only got one go at this life as far as we know, so you might as well make the most of it. If your beliefs tell you there is something more after this life, another place or another life, you still know that you're not here to run on the spot. Get moving. As they say, you don't want to die with your music still inside you. You were born with many talents - use them. As the great Dr Seuss said: *Why try to fit in when you were born to stand out?*

- Stop talking and start asking.
- Don't feel compelled to contribute to the conversation. Just observe.
- Don't look for opportunities to agree or disagree.
- Let go of common sense. Albert Einstein summed it up when he said: *Common sense is the collection of prejudices acquired by age eighteen.*
- Let go of being an expert. Experts are often the last people to see a new creative possibility in what they already know.
- Get rid of fear of failure. If you don't try something, you won't fail, but you won't win either, and you'll never know if you could have succeeded.
- Experience the moment fully. Slow down, concentrate on one thing at time.
- Take one step at a time. Get some small successes under your belt before you tackle everything in sight.

These ideas are from Zen Buddhism. If you keep an open mind, you might like to find out more about Beginner's Mind. It could be the single most useful thing you've done for a while.

Try to look at things as if for the very first time and ask, 'Why is it so?' If someone, anyone, even yourself, tells you that you can't do something, always ask 'Why not?' If you keep asking why or why not, the myths will show up for what they truly are. Ways to keep you "in your place". And here's the thing: The more things you do, the more things you will be able to do, and the more you will actually do.

For some of you, attempting to change yourself and your life can arouse hostility in others. Even in those who protest that they love you. Hostility from those who didn't like you to begin with is less of a surprise, but probably no easier to deal with.

It is particularly difficult for women. Most of us have been brought up to need to be liked. It's a requirement of femininity. We are often afraid to speak or act in ways that will make even strangers dislike us let alone people we know and care about. Start small. Support others who believe in gender equality and share your experiences with them. Knowing you are not alone is a tremendous boost. Change your friends if you need to. There will be some of them who are opposed to your changing. If they persist, it's probably time to move on.

You will find some women will defend the myth of great differences between the sexes. They will tell you the myths that appear to show women are superior to men in some ways. They will talk of women being more caring, less selfish, polite, nurturing, and gentle. Take a deep breath and look around. I'll bet you can recall women and girls who are cruel, self-centred, hurtful, rude, and rough. Just as there are some men like that. There are also men out there who are caring, thoughtful, great with kids, polite and gentle. Society does its best to knock that out of most of them, but there they are.

Besides, if we women are so superior, shouldn't we be using our wonderful characteristics to make the world a better place. No, wait, those characteristics are purpose built to prevent us from doing just that. Like hobbles, they allow us to move around, nibble at life and feel normal, but most of us don't get very far, and we certainly aren't taking down any stallions with our super-powers. Instead, running of the world is mostly in the hands of men who worship personal power. They are often chest-thumping scaremongers, rulers who these days believe productivity and profit are more important than people. There have been some awful female rulers as well. And why wouldn't there be? There are good and bad in both sexes. Why would we expect women to be better than men, saintlier? After all we've done everything possible to prevent them getting into positions of power so it's more than a bit hypocritical to turn around and say we expected them to be better.

Keep your antenna up. Whenever you hear, see or experience anything that portrays the differences between the sexes (except the biological ones), you are in the presence of the Prime Myth. The Myth that rules us all. It's all about the massive, stereo-typed differences between masculine and feminine. You'll see it in assumptions, attitudes, and expectations. You'll hear it in different criticisms of women and men. You'll hear it in the different language we use to describe men and women, girls, and boys, and you'll hear it in our humour. In fact, once you pay attention, you'll find it everywhere.

An easy way to see if something is unfair and/or based on sexist prejudice is to reverse the sexes involved. For example, a simple and obvious one is if you find yourself criticising a woman in public office for her appearance, her clothes or her assertiveness, ask yourself if you would say the same about a man. If a woman gets everybody organised and takes the lead in a task, would you support her if someone declared she was too bossy? How would a man have to behave to be considered too bossy?

Remember, there is nothing wrong with difference. It makes life more interesting. If we were all allowed to be our Selves, we would all be different. But the problem lies in believing and saying that all women are very different from all men and then building a stereotype to say that all women are the same. And the final twist of the sexist blade is to then judge all females as "less competent" than all males. This is a nasty use of difference. It becomes even nastier when you realise that most of the differences have been exaggerated or completely made up.

There is a great deal wrong with creating differences between two groups and then using those differences to evaluate and judge people. It is unjust to give power to any group over another group, to favour one group over the other. It is unfair and constricting to organise society and its institutions, rewards, opportunities, and recognition on the basis of largely false beliefs, prejudices, and stereotypes. This includes not only women but people from different social classes or castes, different ethnic groups, or different skin colours.

It is grossly inefficient to prevent the members of any group from developing their full potential, wasting talent and even genius.

It is obscene to reduce members of any group to the status of objects. It is obscene to harass, denigrate, abuse, or violate people on the basis of differences in sex and gender, or any other perceived group characteristic.

The most constraining, constricting, life-sucking belief is the lack of a sense of your own worth and no appreciation of your unique Self.

In the 1970s, during the height of the Women's Liberation Movement, groups of women met regularly and shared their experiences of being women. This was called Consciousness Raising. It certainly opened our eyes and brought to light the unconscious beliefs we had about ourselves. We learned that, while we might individually be unique, our experiences were not. All of us had learnt about our limitations as women and been told our place in the grand scheme of things. It wasn't particularly about our parents although they featured prominently. It was also our schools, our religion, the books, the movies, history, law, rules and the way men and boys treated us. Even the language, its words and usage of words, proclaimed our secondary status. Most of us had accepted it all and rarely questioned it because "that's just the way things are". The good old, untouchable, unchangeable *status quo*.

It's been observed that **most people would rather give up their freedom than their customs.** This psychological tendency is a powerful clamp on our behaviour and beliefs. Customs and culture give us a sense of security and belonging to our family, our group or our tribe or nation. Uncertainty is frightening, even intolerable. Customs, rituals, and patterns of behaviour do away with uncertainty because they are predictable. It takes awareness and courage to break free. No wonder women's liberation is so difficult to achieve.

To break free, we must want to be free. To want to be free, we must know that we are not. To know that we are not free, we must know what freedom looks like and realise what keeps us from it.

Accepting "the way things are" is not unique to women, and it has held most humans "in their place" since we became human. Teaching children to conform to their culture is the greatest form of social control because it is internalised and therefore invisible and subconscious. Plus reinforcing it through religion, law and social custom makes it a sin or a crime or a social affront to go against it. All punishable in various ways.

Remember you are unique. You arrived with talents and skills and interests in a combination that has never been seen on the planet before. Ever.

What have you always wanted to do? Start today.

Remember: *Minds are like parachutes; they work best when open.* (Lord Thomas Dewar)

If you have the will to be open-minded, start looking for people, stories, articles that contradict your views of gender stereotypes. Below are some suggested ways to break free of your own stereotypical behaviour to open up a much broader way of being yourself. If you're willing to try, don't expect it to be easy.

Know Yourself

- Identify your own skills, talents, interests, and strengths and take pride in them.
- If something outside the typically feminine skills interests you, go for it. There will be people – men and women – who will cheer you on. Ignore the critics.
- Treat yourself and others with respect and act as if you expect it in return.
- Treat men as equals, neither superior nor inferior.
- Stop accepting that women should be responsible for doing two-thirds of the world's work.
- Stop trying to please everyone.
- Learn to say "no".
- Express your needs and feelings. Don't expect others to know what you want.
- Be aware of your own reactions to other women. Do you react negatively to a woman if she appears confident, takes charge, or makes a request without saying "please" or smiling. Do you automatically think she's bossy, bitchy, up herself? Would you judge a man like that? If not, you're probably experiencing unconscious gender

bias. In the interests of women everywhere, STOP. Or should I say, "Please stop"?

Personal behaviour

It isn't fair, but every woman personally represents all women, and her behaviour reinforce stereotypes which harm all women.

A classic case is driving a car. When a man drives badly or causes problems for other drivers, he's labelled a bloody idiot. When a woman does the same, she is scornfully dismissed as a bloody woman driver. The man's behaviour is individual and his personal problem. The woman's is part of her whole group. She is seen to be confirming the stereotype of all women.

Here are some suggestions for women to break the stereotypes.

Body: Don't become a slave to fashion and cosmetics. Find a style that suits you and is comfortable for your lifestyle.

Mind: Remember that Beginner's Mind? This is a good place to use it. When you see or meet someone for the first time, stop and realise that you really know nothing about them. You see sex, gender, race, age, and clothes. You really know nothing about this individual. Those assumptions that pop into your head because of the way our brains like categories, are limiting your life and other people's lives. Find out about THIS person. Talk to them. Ask them things about their likes, interests, skills and experiences.

Men talking to, or at, women could learn a great deal from this exercise. Many women are much more than most men ever dream of. Although I love learning and have had a passion for thinking and studying across a wide range of subjects from Art to Zoology, all my life, I have rarely met a man who thinks he could learn anything from me. It's a rare man who asks me for information on a topic. They assume I wouldn't know. They usually prefer to tell me things without bothering to find out if I know as much or more than they do on the subject. Sometimes, if I tell a man something, he appears not to hear it because he then goes on to tell me exactly the same thing I have just told him. Most men assume they know more than women. I have already mentioned earlier that research shows that, around the globe, men believe they are more intelligent than women.

Make a point of learning something new regularly. If it seems difficult, at least persist. You'll find that if you keep pushing your limits, things that once seemed difficult or obscure appear understandable and easier when you look back at them. The knowledge or skill you gain could be useful in your life as well as making you a much more interesting person and conversationalist. I have found that the more you know about something, the more you appreciate the wonder of it.

Take an interest in something that's not typically associated with "feminine". Try it out. You might like it. You might even be good at it. You'll be surprised that most people will actually admire you if you give something a go. Yes, you'll also meet the knockers who want to push you back into conforming to your stereotypical role of feminine gender. Consider them a challenge and do it, for yourself and for all of us.

Take a course of study in something different just for the hell of it.

Being aware of Confirmation Bias and stereotyping is not easy. It requires us to deliberately look for contradictions to what we believe, to actively seek out information that is contrary to our beliefs about men and women (or any group). Since this is an unusual way for us to behave or think, it may be that most people are doomed to be close-minded and biased. Don't let that be you.

Life: Resist conforming to stereotypes yourself.

Compliment and encourage women and girls for their achievements and talents. Focus on praising positive actions and talents, rather than only appearance or dress.

Avoid gossip and derogatory comments about anyone but particularly about other women because that is so very stereotypical. Besides, the rest of the world is probably on to it already.

Avoid behaviour that really is "bitchy" or "catty". Of course, people will label some things bitchy if a woman does or says them whereas they would go unremarked or even praised if a man did them. That is not what I mean here. If you find yourself gossiping or denigrating or putting someone down, STOP. Better to say nothing than to increase the amount of venom already in the world.

Support and protect other women. Don't believe the stereotype that we are all in competition with one another (see Chapter 12: Women are their own Worst Enemies). Make friends with more women. Avoid the sad, mean-spirited women and men who try to pull you down.

Spend time doing things on your own. You'll enjoy them in a different way. Sharing is good but spending time alone can provide some really awesome experiences. Trust me and try it. If your circumstances allow, do these alone occasionally: go for a walk, eat in a restaurant, go to a movie, go on a holiday – alone.

Language patterns and conversation

- By all means apologise if you have done or said something you realise was hurtful or inappropriate but stop automatically apologising as part of a speech pattern. Feminine speech patterns are designed to make us appear diffident, unsure, non-aggressive.
- Here's a word you could do without. "Just". As in "I just think that ....". "I just feel ....". Leave it out.
- Here's a good one to use when you don't know something. "Yet." Instead of "I don't know," try "I don't know yet". You could even add, "But I'll find out". Or another possible response, say, "I'm not familiar with that." You sound much more capable and in control.
- And get rid of that word "thingy." It might sound cute, but it actually makes you sound childish and ignorant. If you don't know the word for something, find out.
- Speech and words are powerful. Please don't assume this is trivial. Read some of George Orwell's works if you doubt this.
- Don't laugh at or tell jokes about women or sub-sets of women if they rely on stereotypes to be funny. Wives, mothers-in-law, "nagging" women, women drivers and blondes are still the butt of stereotypical jokes. This is worth remembering for all groups who are denigrated, not just women, groups such as indigenous people, people from other countries, non-white people, people with disabilities, older people.
- Get rid of the girlish giggle or the laugh at the end of expressing your opinion. We use this technique unconsciously to assure our listeners that we are not really pushy or full of ourselves, and we certainly don't pose a threat to any man present. That sort of girlish behaviour just takes away from our dignity and authority.
- When you're asked, "Where's your sense of humour?"

come back with a light response such as "Waiting to hear something funny".

- Don't make assumptions, don't share gossip or trivia or negative tales about others, don't take things personally and always do your best. These are the four recommendations offered by Don Miguel Ruiz in his book, *The Four Agreements*. Well worth reading. It's not specifically about women but it would change the world if we all acted on it.
- Persistence and practice make all the difference. Boys and men usually persist till they learn or succeed. They do not have the luxury of looking helpless and calling on another man to help or do it for them. So, as the old saying goes, if at first you don't succeed, try, try, try again. Persistence pays off, and it also gives you a tremendous feeling of satisfaction and triumph when you succeed.

At Work

- Identify your strengths and skills and take pride in them.
- Apply for promotion. even if you think you're not 100% ready for the job. Men do it all the time. And very frequently get the job over more qualified, particularly women.
- Negotiate your salary. Don't gratefully accept the first offer.
- Support other women. Don't let them be laughed at or denigrated or gossiped about.
- Think before you say something negative about another woman. Are you judging her achievements and ideas, or homing in on her appearance and manner?
- If another woman is interrupted or ignored as research

shows women often are, request that she be heard. A simple "I'd like to hear what Dora thinks" can provide support. This can apply to anyone, male or female, who is interrupted, ignored or talked over. Support them. Mind you, you'll have to make sure you're heard.

- At work, support female bosses, and mentor and encourage female employees.

Dealing with disbelievers

You will, no doubt, come across many people who simply don't believe that Sexism exists, or believe that women have equality or Feminism has gone too far. They may even tell you they are sick and tired of hearing feminists bang on about inequality. Having read this book, I hope you have a few things you could say in response. But here's a little something to use as a start. Tell them this:

If you're sick and tired of feminists going on about Sexism and women's rights, here's a sure-fire way to shut them up. Stop telling your sons or any other man or boy, they must never ever do anything like a girl. Teach them to respect women as fellow humans, no better or worse than men. Start paying women the same as men instead of the current two-thirds to three-quarters. Judge women on their talents and achievements instead of on their appearance. Stop using women's bodies to decorate or advertise everything and anything. Women are not objects. Ensure women are meaningfully involved in decision-making at every level. Stop the pandemic of men's violence against women and girls in our homes, our streets, and across the planet. That will keep the feminists quiet. Guaranteed!!

What's next?

Those are just a few personal practical tips for being the change you'd like to see in the world. They are a start, and not all of them will suit you or your circumstances. Just begin with one or two and try them out. Make them a habit.

As for the world around you, try Charlie Munger's inversion technique. We have seen that the best way to ensure inequality between the sexes and genders is to continue doing the things we currently do. If we continue to create the feminine and masculine stereotypes, to teach them to our children, to conform to them ourselves, we will never attain fairness or equality; we will never end the bias against females; and we will never stop the violence against women.

Invert, always invert. Tell me where I will die, and I will avoid going there.

Go back through this book and have another look at the description of things we do to ourselves and each other. Then avoid doing them. Or do the opposite.

19

Over to you

WE ARE NEARLY at the end of our journey together. I'm counting on you. Unborn children are counting on you. The topics in this book are written to raise awareness, to bust myths and seek reality where possible.

These days we talk about "fake news", but it is not a modern phenomenon. It has been with us since the Cognitive Revolution, 70,000 years ago. Check it out back in Chapter 2. Our brains developed the capacity to imagine things that we hadn't actually experienced or seen or didn't know for a fact that they existed. As far as we know, none of the other animals has this capacity.

As we do with most things, we have used our faculty of imagination for good and for harm. We use it for creativity and for pleasure, for well-being, for inspiration, for understanding, for progress. We have also used it for harm, for control, for power and personal gain.

One of the most powerful pieces of "fake news" our imaginations have ever come up with, is the sexist myth of female/male differences – differences exaggerated or imagined, taught, policed, enforced, and used to give males dominance, power and privilege over females for 10,000 years.

No other subordinated, oppressed, or marginalised group believes the myths and stereotypes about themselves that their oppressors or colonisers have devised. No other group routinely teaches its children to conform and comply with the dominant group's stereotypes of them.

Women, as we have seen, are held "in their place" by forces that apply to no other marginalised or subordinated group. Those forces arise because they have a unique and intimate relationship with members of the dominant group, men who are their fathers, sons, grandfathers, grandsons, brothers, lovers, and friends.

Other marginalised or colonised or subordinated groups are usually physically separated from the dominant group. They are herded into ghettoes, reservations, communities, or designated areas to live. They have often been forbidden to enter the facilities or areas reserved for their "masters".

Women have been marginalised, confined to the home, hidden behind veils, excluded from men's clubs, educational institutions, parliaments, armies, most of the public sphere. But, unlike other groups, they have not been excluded from the intimate lives of the dominant group for one very good reason. So far, only they can nurture and give birth to children.

Women also provide sexual gratification, but men are quite capable of finding substitutes to provide that as they do when removed from women in prisons or isolated areas. But no other way has been found yet to provide men with heirs, preferably male. They need women.

As tribes and kingdoms formed in human society, women had been "given" by men to men of other tribes to increase territorial possession, manpower and ensure peace. It also provided "new blood" within the gene pool. Marriage evolved from the custom of the woman's father giving her to the prospective husband. The words of the traditional Christian wedding ceremony, "Who gives this woman?" still retain this reminder of its origins. The woman's vows also contained the promise to "love, honour and obey" her husband, but have, in recent times, been eliminated in most modern ceremonies.

As we saw in Chapter 2, men took possession and control of women to ensure their paternity of heirs. This occurred at different times in various parts of the world, probably with the end of nomadic life and the beginning of agriculture and domestication of animals. This conversion of women from partner to property was probably brought about in a variety of ways including force, flattery, or a sense of duty reinforced by religion or tribal custom.

The characteristics encouraged in females included traits that were pleasing to men, particularly docility, a childlike innocence, silence, and invisibility unless needed for sex or domestic service. This led to the assumption that women were not fully adults in the way that men were but were somewhere between men and children in development.

Religion was one of the main enforcers of these beliefs, and branches of some religions still teach the right of men to control and rule over their wives. The rest of society still retains some of these attitudes in the femininity stereotype.

Throughout this book, we have seen the harm and the waste of maintaining societies based on the "fake news" of gender stereotypes of both sexes. Both males and females have been duped into believing and behaving in a manner that is far less than their true potential. Individuals, families, societies, nations and their economies, and the planet itself, have suffered as a result. This "fake news" was launched thousands of years ago, and it is more than time it was stripped of its power and thrown out on the rubbish heap of history.

We have seen that the continuation of these inefficient, unfair, and wasteful beliefs about human ability and potential, requires nothing more than "business as usual". All you have to do to ensure its continuation, is to believe in and comply to, the stereotype assigned to you at birth. Then teach it to your children. And judge, ridicule or ostracize children and other adults who do not conform or perform.

But if you would like to contribute to changing the world for the better, to giving your children and grandchildren a fairer opportunity to grow and develop their potential, and to stretch your own wings to realise that you actually can fly, then here's what you need to do.

Start with You. Check out Chapter 18 again. Be the Change. Get started.

Then change the way you teach, talk to, and train your children and grandchildren. Teach them all to be adventurous, curious, brave, caring, helpful, kind, strong, useful. Tell them there is nothing off limits for them to be or learn or do unless it causes harm to themselves or others. Teach both sexes the life skills that are currently assigned to one sex. Teach them to plant and grow things. Teach them to care for and respect animals. Encourage them to be the best that they can be. Never let the words "like a girl" pass your lips not even in praise. We're not aiming to make boys feel inferior either. Let your daughters try to do things. Don't rush to help them. Don't clip their wings with stereotyped expectations. Let all children be themselves regardless of sex, gender, ethnicity, skin colour, physical appearance or any other grouping.

Throughout this book, we have looked at the harmful ways we have constrained and metaphorically clipped the wings of our species to almost a parody of our potential. Go back and re-read them. Then invert, always invert.

To sum up:

- Human characteristics and behaviour are spread across all humans.
- We deliberately foster one set of behaviours in males and another in females.
- Two constellations of behaviours given unequal status, power, and reward – one admired and rewarded for strength and control, the other praised for beauty and service.
- The Taboo of Sameness keeps the sexes divided and constrained. Praised for conformity to gender. Punished for non-conformity.
- Equality is impossible because the characteristics assigned to each gender do not provide equal outcomes.

Each of us needs to spread our wings according to the talents and gifts we have. Developing our potential. Choosing how we dress, comfortably or not. Making no assumptions. Breaking through rigidity of roles and expectations.

While women accept the hobbles of traditional femininity, they will never have equality with men.

While men accept the limitations of traditional masculinity and particularly rigid toxic forms of masculinity, we will never have a safe or peaceful world for men, women or children in our homes, tribes, or nations, and we may even destroy our planet.

Teach your children and grandchildren to develop a full range of positive human skills and interests. Let boys and girls be friends and teach them mutual respect, sharing and caring.

Start small or large. Speak out. Act out. Treat men as equals expecting no more nor less of them than you would a woman. No excuses.

Treat women in the belief that they are as capable, intelligent and, given the chance, as knowledgeable as men, no more nor less. No excuses.

And most of all, women, believe in yourselves. Don't say, "I can't," until you've tried – at least three times. Don't wring your hands in a maidenly manner or bat your eyelashes to get things done by a man. You're doing us all a disservice.

Believe you can or believe you can't, either way you will be right.

Now, it's over to you.

Bibliography

Banyard, Kat, *The Equality Illusion: The Truth about Men and Women Today,* Faber and Faber, 2010

Bates, Laura, *Everyday Sexism,* Simon & Schuster, 2014

Benedict, Ruth, *Patterns of Culture,* Routledge & Keagan-Paul, London, 1935

Berne, Eric, *Games People Play: The Psychology of Human Relationships,* Penguin, 1968

Biddulph, Steve, *Raising Boys in the Twenty-First Century,* Finch Publishing, 2018

Bogue, Anea, *9 Ways we're Screwing up our Girls and how we can Stop,* Dunham Books, 2014

Brownmiller, Susan, *Against our Will,* Simon Schuster, 1975

Duffy, Bobby, *Perils of Perception,* Atlantic Books, 2018

Engels, Frederick, *Marx/Engels Selected Works Vol 3,* Online Version Marx/Engels 2010, Zurich, 1884

Faludi, Susan, *Backlash*, Chatto & Windus, London, 1992

Farrell, Nicholas, "Stand UP, all male feminists", Mail and Guardian, 12/09/14

Fey, Tina, *Bossypants*, Sphere, 2011

Fine, Cordelia, *Delusions of Gender*, W.W. Norton & Co, New York, 1992

Fisher, Helen, *The First Sex*, Random House, *1999*

Frieden, Betty, *The Feminine Mystique*, W.W. Norton and Co., 1963

Greer, Germaine, *The Female Eunuch*, Harper Collins, 1970

Greer, Germaine, *The Obstacle Race: The Fortunes of Women Painters and Their Works*, New York: Farrar Straus Giroux, *1979*

Harari, Yuval Noah, *Sapiens, Random House, 2014*

Holland, Jack, *Misogyny: The World's Oldest Prejudice*, Robinson, London, 2006

Hyde, J, S, "The Gender similarities Hypothesis", *American Psychologist*, Vol, 60, No, 6, 2005

Kindersley, Tanya & Vine, Sarah, *Backwards in High Heels: The Impossible art of Being Female*, Fourth Estate, London, 2009

Korda, Michael, *Male Chauvinism: How it Works at Home and in the Office*, Coronet Books, London, 1974

LaGarde, Christine, The Economic Power of Women's Empowerment", Keynote speech, IMF, Japan, 1914

Leser, David, *Women, Men and the Whole Damn Thing*, Allen and Unwin, 2019

Levi Strauss, Claude, *Structural Anthropology*, Penguin, New York, 1963

Levitt Steven D, & Dubner, Stephen J, *Freakonomics*, Harper, New York, 2009

McGilchrist, Iain, *The Master and His Emissary*, Yale University Press, 2009

McKay, Sarah, *The Woman's Brain Book: The Neuroscience of Health, Hormones and Happiness*, Hachette, 2018

Machiavelli, Nicolo, *The Prince*, originally published in 1532

Manne, Kate, *Down Girl: The Logic of Misogyny*, Oxford University Press, 2018

Manson, Mark, *The Subtle Art of not Giving a F*ck*, HarperOne, 2016

Mead, Margaret, *Male and Female*, Pelican Books, 1950

Miles, Rosalind, *The Women's History of the World*, Paladin, 1989

Miller, Mary Susan. PhD, *No Visible Wounds: Identifying Nonphysical Abuse Of Women By Their Men*, Contemporary Books, 1995

Montagu, Ashley, *The Natural Superiority of Women*, Collier Books, New Revised Edition, London, 1974. First published in 1952

Moran, Caitlin, *How to be a Woman*, Ebury Press, 2012

Morris, Ian, *Why the West Rules – For Now*, Profile Books, London, 2010

Moss, Tara, *Speaking Out*, Harper Collins, 2016

Penny, Laurie, *Unspeakable Things*, Bloomsbury, 2014

Perez, Caroline Criado. *Invisible Women: Exposing Data Bias in a World Designed for Men*. Chatto & Windus, 2020

Radcliffe Richards, Janet, *The Sceptical Feminist*, Penguin, 1980

Ridgeway, Cecilia L., *Framed by Gender*, Oxford University Press, 2011

Rippon, Gina, *The Gendered Brain: The Neuroscience that Shatters the Myth of the Female Brain*, Penguin Books Australia, 2020

Rossi, Alice S, (ed), *The Feminist Papers: From Adams to de Beauvoir*, Bantam, 1973

Rublack, Ulinka, *The Astronomer and the Witch*, Oxford University Press, 2015

Sandberg, Sheryl with Scovell, Nell, *Lean In: Women, Work and the Will to Lead*, Alfred A. Knopf, 2013

Schlain, Leonard, *The Alphabet and the Goddess: Male Words and Female Images*, The Penguin Press, 1998

Slaughter, Anne-Marie, *Unfinished Business: Women, Men, Work, Family*, One World, 2015

Solnit, Rebecca, *Men Explain things to Me, and Other Essays*, Granta Books, London, 2014

Spender, Dale, *Man Made Language*, Routledge & Kegan Paul, 2nd edition, 1985

Steinem, Gloria. *Revolution from Within*, Corgi Books, 1993

Walter, Natasha, *Living Dolls: The Return of Sexism*, Virago, 2010

Waring, Professor Marilyn, *Counting for Nothing: What Men Value and What Women are Worth*, University of Toronto Press, 2nd edition, 1999

Wertheim, Margaret, *Pythagoras' Trousers: God, Physics, and the Gender Wars*, Fourth Estate, London, 1995

Wollstonecraft, Mary, *A Vindication of the Rights of Woman*, Penguin Classics, 1987, First published in 1792

Woolf, Virginia, *A Room of One's Own*, Hogarth Press, 1929

"Women's Empowerment: Measuring the Global Gender Gap", World Economic Forum 2005

Dear reader,

We hope you enjoyed reading *Bustine the Mythos of Mars and Venus*. Please take a moment to leave a review, even if it's a short one. Your opinion is important to us.

Discover more books by Veronica Schwarz at https://www.nextchapter.pub/authors/veronica-shwarz

Want to know when one of our books is free or discounted? Join the newsletter at http://eepurl.com/bqqB3H

Best regards,

Veronica Schwarz and the Next Chapter Team

About the Author

Veronica Schwarz was born in Darwin and spent her childhood on a cattle station, Victoria River Downs. Since then, she has lived in many cities, towns, and other countries. During her career as a teacher, she has taught people from prep to eighty years of age and loved it. She has also worked as a machinist in a trouser factory in Germany, an office clerk in London, a secretary in Canada, a taxi driver in Melbourne, and curriculum developer and policy analyst in the area of equal opportunity for women and girls in the Education Department of Victoria. She is an artist and a web designer as well as passionate traveler within Australia and around the world. determined to give Gulliver a run for his money.

Veronica has been writing for more than fifty years except for the many times that life got in the way. Her first short story was published in *Woman's Day* in 1965. Since that time, she has published several books for teachers and school children, as well as non-fiction articles on travel, history, mythology, language, politics and philosophy, a children's picture book and a self-help manual on learning.

She founded, edited, and published for ten years an alternative magazine for women entitled *The Dawn* after Louisa Lawson's original nineteenth century newspaper for women.

Her last book told the story of Joan of Arc through a serious of imaginary interviews with Joan. The book, entitled *Ride the Wind*.

Choose the Fire, took some fifteen years of research and several trips to France. It is available online. She also continues to write and publish non-fiction articles and short stories.

Her most recently published book, *Down to Earth: Busting the Myths of Mars and Venus,* lifts the lid on the constraints of gender roles and stereotypes and the damage they do to people and the planet. It also offers strategies for changing the lives of women and men, girls, and boys, for the better. Told with anecdotes, and humor, highlighted with illustrations and supported by ten years of research in fields ranging from anthropology to sociology, history to literature, folklore to psychology, medicine and neuroscience, myth and religion – and many years of life experience. This book offers the reader an unforgettable experience and could change your life. Once you see, you can never unsee.

Busting The Myths Of Mars And Venus
ISBN: 978-4-86747-174-6

Published by
Next Chapter
1-60-20 Minami-Otsuka
170-0005 Toshima-Ku, Tokyo
+818035793528

17th October 2021

www.ingramcontent.com/pod-product-compliance
Ingram Content Group UK Ltd.
Pitfield, Milton Keynes, MK11 3LW, UK
UKHW041325241224
3859UKWH00005B/28